Rhea County
Tennessee

COUNTY COURT MINUTES
(COURT OF PLEAS AND QUARTER SESSIONS)

May 1823–November 1828

Transcribed/Abstracted by
Bettye J. Broyles

Rhea County Historical and Genealogical Society

Heritage Books
2024

HERITAGE BOOKS

AN IMPRINT OF HERITAGE BOOKS, INC.

Books, CDs, and more—Worldwide

For our listing of thousands of titles see our website
at
www.HeritageBooks.com

A Facsimile Reprint
Published 2024 by
HERITAGE BOOKS, INC.
Publishing Division
5810 Ruatan Street
Berwyn Heights, MD 20740

Rhea County Historical and Genealogical Society
1992

International Standard Book Number
Paperbound: 978-0-7884-8957-0

FOREWORD

The following minutes were abstracted/transcribed from a xerox copy of the original minute book. The book is also on microfilm (State Archives Roll No. 47) and a typed copy was made by the W.P.A. during the 1930's (also on microfilm).

The 1823 to 1828 minute book is the oldest of the books presently located in the Rhea County Courthouse. Three of the earlier books are among the Barnes Collection at the University of Tennessee Library in Knoxville and will be transcribed as soon as a good xerox copy can be obtained.

The term "abstracted/transcribed" is being used because many of the entries have been copied in their entirety. Although there is some duplication, no entry has been skipped or omitted.

Prior to May 1825, wills, inventories, and estate settlements were recorded in the minute book. These have been copied in their entirety and include the wills of Isaac Rice Sr. (p. 15), John Woodward (p. 27), and George Walker (p. 47). Inventories and estate sales were recorded for the following: Daniel Rawlings (pp. 1,4), William Walker (p. 8), Robert Ferguson (p. 8), William Lewis (p. 17), John Moore (pp. 27,27), William Floyd (pp. 23,26), John Woodward (p. 32), and John Chapman (p. 35). Settlements made on the following estates also were included: Caleb Martin (p. 30), Jeremiah Dunkin (pp. 32,65), John Shafer (p. 50), and William French (p. 57).

After May 1825, the wills, inventories, and settlements were presented to the Court for approval, but were recorded in a special Will Book. These books can be found in the County Court Clerks office in the Courthouse (also on microfilm from State Archives).

Two Revolutionary War pension applications were included in this minute book: Thomas Moore (p. 59) and Joseph Atchley (p. 64); and two applications for the emancipation of slaves: Mary Walker (pp. 24,36) and Rezin Rawlings (p. 97).

The County Court was presided over by Justices of the Peace appointed by the State Legislature and Commissioned by the Governor. The Court heard cases pertaining to assault and battery, affrays, selling "spirituous liquors" without a license, disturbing public worship, gaming, bastardy, etc., many of which were tried by a jury. Jurors also were appointed for the Circuit Court.

The Justices appointed various County officers (Court Clerks, Trustee, Registrar, Sheriff, etc.), administrators on estates, guardians for orphans and minor heirs, road overseers, juries of view to lay off new roads or change existing roads, committees to supervise the building of bridges and the County buildings, and authorized the establishment of ferries across the Tennessee River. Tax rates, rates of ferriage, etc. also were set by the Justices. Paupers and poor persons were cared for through appropriations made by the Justices, providing for their maintainance and burial.

The minutes of the Court of Pleas and Quarter Sessions (County Court) contain hundreds of names of residents in the County. The road orders not only appoint an overseer, but list the hands (men who lived along the short section of road) assigned to help the overseer.

The Court of Pleas and Quarter Sessions met on the first Monday in the months of February, May, August, and November. Most sessions lasted the entire week, although the number of Justices present was reduced to three or four after the first day.

The page numbers at the beginning of paragraphs correspond to those in the minute book. The page numbers in the index beginning on page 153 refer to the page numbers in this publication.

Bettye J. Broyles

(p. 1) "Be it remembered that at a Court of Pleas and Quarter Sessions continued and held for the County of Rhea at the Court House in Washington on the first
Monday and 5th day of May in the year of our Lord 1823 there were present on the
Bench the Worshipful Jonathan Fine, Thomas Cox, John Cozby, John Robertson, Azariah David, Crispien E. Shelton, John Rice, Stephen Winton, Thomas Price, William
Kennedy, Arthur Fulton, and Jesse Thompson a Majority &c." (NOTE— first names
of Justices added by B.J.B.)

 Woodson Francis to Orlando Bradley. Bill of Sale for sundry articles
dated 14th March 1823. (Woodson Francis, Sheriff)

  John Bailey appointed overseer of road in place of Samuel Holland.
  William Seymore appointed overseer of road in place of John Walker Jr.
  Zachariah Harwood appointed overseer of road in place of Jesse Reese.
  Joshua Tindle appointed overseer of road in place of David Day.
  Washington Morgan appointed overseer of road in place of John Jack.
  Thomas Harper appointed overseer of road in place of Henry Hackworth.
  Edmund Howerton appointed overseer of road in place of Charles Woodward.
  William Cumpton appointed overseer in place of John Woodward.
  William Zeigler appointed overseer of road in place of James Blackley.

(p. 2) Henry Airhart appointed overseer of road in place of Samuel Howard.
 John Benson overseer of road from Morgans Shop on the turnpike road to
the 4 mile post on Blythes Ferry Road; Crispein E. Shelton to make out a list of
the hands to work on said road.

 Samuel McDaniel resigned as a Justice of the Peace.

 John Rice appointed to take a list of Taxable property and polls in
Captain Browns Company.

 Joseph Martin to Francis Land. Deed of Conveyance for 40 acres; acknowledged by Grantor.

 Samuel Holland to Abraham Miller. Deed of Conveyance for 80 acres; acknowledged by Grantor.

 State VS Joseph Ford (No. 1237). Defendant says he is guilty as charged
and puts himself upon the grace and mercy of the Court; fined 50¢ "and to be in
custody untill the fine and costs are paid whereupon Hugh Cunningham comes into
Court and confesses Judgment Jointly with the defendant for fine and costs."

(p. 3) "Inventory of Books Bequeathed by Daniel Rawlings Decd to Rezin Rawlings
Children as per Will which See: 5 Vol Scotts Bible, 1 Vol Butterworths Concor-
dence, 5 Vol of the life of Washington, 1 Vol life of Genl Jackson, 1 Vol of
Paleeys Evidence, 1 Vol Olive Branch, 5 Vol Willisons Works, 1 Vol Clerks Homer,
1 Vol American Nepos, 2 Vol Woodfols Junis, 1 Vol Haywoods Revised Law, 3 Vol
Tom Jones, 4 Vol Burns Work, 1 Vol Esays to do Good, 1 Vol Dialogue of Devils,
1 Vol Humes life of Washington, 1 Vol Herveys Meditations, 1 Vol C. Julii
Ceasaris, 1 Vol Biblical Nominclatur, 1 Vol Perryes Dictionary, 1 Vol Testament,
1 Vol Goldsmiths Esays, 1 Vol Vicar of Wakefield, 1 Vol Easops Fables, 1 Vol
Dyches S. Book, 1 Vol Chalmers Descourses, 1 Vol Domestic Coockery, 1 Vol Scott
on Baptism, 1 Vol Atless, 1 Vol Miltons Paradise Lost, And also one Negro Man
named Polydore Bequeathed in the last Will and Testament of Daniel Rawlings
Deceased which see. One Secretary and Book Case In my hands in Trust at all
times for the fourth coming thereof to the legal claimant as per said will.
This 5th day of May 1823. Then Received all and every of the before inventoried
property which I acknowledge myself my heirs Executors or administrators at any
time and at all times to be responsible for the rightful and legal Claimants
under said will and the laws of the land given under my hand and seal in Washington this day and date written above."   Rezin Rawlings (Seal)
Test— James Berry

2

The foregoing inventory was returned by John Locke and Rezin Rawlings, Exrs. of last Will and Testament of Daniel Rawlings. Exrs. permitted to return a Supplemental Inventory.

On application of John Rice, he is permitted to keep a house of ordinary having entered into bond as the law directs.

(p. 4)   John Gray appointed overseer of that part of the Valley Road leading from Cain Ables to the Hamilton County line; "to have an Eaqual number of hands with William Bice the overseer of that part of said road that lyes from Cain Ables to Mrs. Lauderdales."

William Bice overseer of that part of the Valley Road lying between Cain Ables and Mrs. Lauderdales.

Thomas Woodward allowed $12.00 "as full compensation for his taking into his Care and Maintaining a poor boy by the name of Kimme Longwest untill the next Sessions of this Court Out of the poor money in the hands of the trustee of This County not otherwise appropriated."

Report of Jury of View appointed at November Session 1822 was returned; "leaving the Calhoun road one mile above Samuel McDaniels thence leading to Athens as far as the County line be established."

Allen Holland overseer of above road; to have all the hands from the forks of said road on the side of the Calhoun road so far as to include John Martin and Robert Kelsey.

Shepherd Brazleton appointed Constable in Capt. Brazletons Company.

(p. 5)   Richard Taylor to John Roddy. Deed of Conveyance for 640 acres; proven by John Lea and Thomas Cox; certified for registration.

Jesse Witt, John Morgan, John Benson, Robert Hood, George Manes, Samuel Holland, and William Howard appointed Jury of View "to amend and alter that part of the road leading through John Jacks plantation so as to give more General conveniance."

John Miller, David S. Hudson, Joseph Shalteen, George W. Riggle, and John Wasson appointed Jury of View to lay off and mark out a road leading from the Turnpike road on Waldons Ridge beginning at Jacob Becks thence by Waltons Ferry the nearest way to Athens in McMinn County.

Alexander Caldwell produced a Wolf Scalp "sworn says the Wolf was over four months old and was killed within the bounds of this County . . . ordered . . . that a certificate issue according to the statutes in such cases made and provided."

Ordered "that a former order wherein Henry Collins & John Locke was appointed commissioners to settle with John Rice administrator of all and singular the goods & chattles rights and credits of the estate of Adam Miller Decd stand revived as made at this present Term."

Ordered that James Snelson keep up the road from his ferry to intersect the turnpike road at Dyers old place.

(p. 6)   Elijah Evans overseer of that part of the road from Snelsons Ferry to intersect Waltons Road on the south side of the River; Jonathan Fine to divide the hands.

Mary Rawlings, Widow and relic of Daniel Rawlings, allowed the full amount of the price of all the books containing the records belonging to the Court of Pleas and Quarter Sessions of this County at Cost and cariage. John Rice and William S. Leuty appointed to examine and report the amount of said books. Clerk is authorized to and required to make out a Voucher for the amount to Mary Rawlings.

Robert Elder, William C. Wilson, and David Ragland appointed Inspectors of the election to be held at William Prices on the 1st Thursday and Friday of

August next to elect a Governor, a member of Congress, &c.

(p. 7)   George W. Riggle, Jesse Thompson, and George Gillespie appointed Inspectors of presinct Election to be held at James McCanses to elect a Governor &c.
Jacob Brown, James McDonal, and Robert Locke appointed Inspectors for the election to be held at the Court House in Washington to elect a Governor &c.
Eliza Piper bound to James McCanse for 11 years "from this date in which time the Said James McCanse is to give her Eighteen months Schooling, and to find her in good and sufficient meat drink lodging and clothing, And at the expiration of her said time of Eleven years is to give her two good suits of Home spun cloths and 1 sute out of the Store, one Spinning Wheel, cotton, and one pair Cotton Cards."
Abigale Ferguson and Mathew Hubbert are permitted to administer on estate of Robert Ferguson, dec'd; entered into bond for $2000 with James Ferguson and John Ferguson, their securities.
Henry Wallace, Samuel Logan, and Henry Collins appointed Commissioners to lay off a years provision &c for the widow and children of Robert Ferguson.

(p. 8)   Elizabeth Walker permitted to administer on estate of William Walker, dec'd; bond for $100 with John Rice, her security.
Court adjourned until tomorrow morning 9 Oclock

Justices on bench (6th May)— Rice, McDonald, Walker, Thompson, and Kennedy.
John Collins to John Sapp. Deed of Conveyance for 40 acres; proven by William Randolph, one of the witnesses, "who says he saw John Collins sign seal and acknowledge the same for the purposes therein named and William Johnston being duly sworn in open Court says that John Johnson his son the other subscriber is not in this State and that he believes the signature of John Johnson to be written by himself." Deed certified for registration.
Benjamin Rice VS Joseph Mee. From the affidavit of the Defendant, this cause is continued until the next term of this Court.

(p. 9)   Grand Jury "impanneled sworn and charged to enquire for the body of this County: 1 William Smith foreman, 2 Thomas McKedy, 3 Peter Majors, 4 Samuel Logan, 5 William Zeigler, 6 Drury Sykes, 7 Wilson Putman, 3 Thornton Creed, 9 Joseph Williams, 10 John Lisenby, 11 Moses Ferguson, 12 John Smith, and Anderson Smith."
John Miller a Constable sworn to attend the Grand Jury.
Joseph Love to Thomas J. Campbell. Bill of Sale dated 1st March 1823 for a Negro man named Joe; proven by James Berry and Joseph McDaniel.
Allen Kennedy and Miller Francis appointed Trustees of Tennessee Academy.
Allen Kennedy VS James C. Mitchell (No. 1238). Debt. "Came the plaintiff by attorney and the defendant having been arrested and not appearing to make defence altho solemnly cauled so to do but Made default. Whereupon on Motion of said plaintiff by Thomas J. Campbell his attorney, It is considered by the Court that the plaintiff recover against the defendant his debt . . . amounting to Fifty Dollars debt, Together with Six dollars Sixteen cents damages and all his Costs . . ."
Mary Cranmore VS George Gothard. ". . . from the affidavit of the defendant a rule is granted him to cause the plaintiff Security for the prosecution of this suit to appear at the next term."

(p. 10)   Bartholomew Gwin & Susannah Gwin to William Huff. "A deed bearing date the 5th day of May 1823 for lands lying in Cocke County, Tennessee was this day

4

duly acknowledged . . . by the grantors . . . and on the private examination of said Susannah Gwin by the Court Separate to and appart from her husband and on it appearing that said deed was Executed by her without Coertion Fear or Compultion of her said husband the Same was Ordered to be certified to Cocke County For Registration."

John C. Calhoun, assignee VS Robert Gamble (No. 1239). Appeal. "Came the plaintiff by attorney and the defendant not appearing to defend his Suit alltho solommly Cauled but made default." Plaintiff to recover against the defendant his debt in his Warrant and also his costs.

Thomas Kelly VS John Condley (No. 1240). Plaintiff dismisses his suit and defendant assumes the costs.

John Locke, Clerk of the Circuit Court, "having certified to the Court the costs in the cause The State against Jordan Gibson. . . ordered . . . that the Clerk of this Court certify the same to the County Trustee . . ."

(p. 11) Rezin Rawlings and John Locke, Exrs. of last Will and Testament of Daniel Rawlings dec'd, returned a Supplemental Inventory of personal property belonging to Said Estate: "Inventory of the personal property . . . that is to pass into the hands of Mary Rawlings widow and relick of the said Daniel Rawlings deceased for and during a Specified term and also during the natural lifetime of Said Mary as per Will which see— One Negro Man named Joseph, one Negro Woman named Hannah, one Negro Boy named Primas, one Negro girl named Julyann, one Negro boy named Stephen, one Negro boy named Herbert, one Negro girl named Nancy about two months old, all sons and daughters of the aforesaid Hannah— 6 head of Horses, 13 head of Cattle, 6 head of Sheep, 74 head of hogs, 1 Waggon and her gearin, 3 barsheer ploughs, 3 bul tounge plows, 4 weeding howes, 2 Mattocks, 2 Sprouting howes, 1 pair of Streachers & trees, 1 Spade, 1 fifth chain, 3 pair of drawing chains, 2 pair of hames, 3 clevises, 1 pair double trees & hangings, 6 swingle trees, 1 Sythe & cradle, 2 reap hooks, 1 mowing sythe, 4 faling axes, 1 foot adz, 1 handsaw, 1 drawing knife, 1 side board, 1 beaureugh, 6 tables, 1 candlestand, 1 looking glass, 13 winsor chairs, 14 ditto S.B. chairs, 5 beadsteads, 5 beads & furniture, 4 pair dog irons, 2 shovels, 2 pair tongs, 1 pot rack, 1 fire poker, 1 large kettle, 3 small pots, 4 ovens, 2 pair hooks, 1 cast wash bowl, 2 coffee pots, 1 Tea kettle, 1 frying pan, 1 Stew pot, 1 flesh fork, 1 grid iron, 1 pair of Woffel Irons, 1 skillet, 1 tin boiler, 1 Chanie press, 8 goblets, 12 wine glasses, 2 large decanters & stands, 13 glass tumblers, 1 small cubberd, 6 silver spoons, 1 large ditto, 11 silver tea spoons, 1 glass buisquit diah, 42 delf plates, 5 bowles, 5 pitchers, 2 dishes, 2 sugar bowls, 1 coster, 3 waiters, 4 sets of cups & saucers, 4 candle sticks brass, 2 pair snuffers, 1 carving knife, 1 pair Steelyards, 1 half Bushell, 2 big wheels, 1 check reel, 1 washing tub, 1 churn, 1 pail, 2 piggons, 2 trunks, 1 floor brush, 1 bread basket, 1 riding whip, 1 riding bridle, 1 hammer, 1 rifle gun, 1 powder flask, 3 ink stands, 2 augers, 1 pair compases, 2 small chissels, 2 small files, 1 wooden square, 6 tin cups, 1 tin buckett, 1 pewter dish, 1 pump, 1 well bucket, 1 tin strainer, 2 chamber pots, 1 brass kettle, 1 snuffer tray.

(p. 12) Mary Rawlings acknowledged receipt of the above items.

Elizabeth Kirksey VS William Buster. On motion of the defendant, commissions are awarded him to take the Depositions of Elizabeth Cannon, Maleny Cannon, Wasington Acre and Polly Acre of Roane County. Depositions are to be read as evidence on the trial of the above cause.

State VS Allen Hilburn. Petit Larceny. William Smith, the Defendants appearance Bail, surrenders the defendant in open Court. The defendant acknowledged himself to owe to the State the sum of $500 to be levied on his goods and chattles, etc. and "that the said Allen Hilburn make his personal appearance from day to day at the present Term of this Court and not depart the Court without leave.

Also came James Massey and John Hilburn and acknowledged themselves indebted to the State in the Sum of two hundred and fifty Dollars each . . . to be void on condition that Allen Hilburn for whom they undertake shall make his personal appearance from day to day at the present Term . . ."

(p. 13) Justices on bench (7th May)— John Rice, Jesse Thompson, James McDonald, and Daniel Walker. (NOTE— first names added by B.J.B.)
        State VS Isham Parker (No. 1241). Affray. "Came Thomas J. Campbell Solicitor General in behalf of the State and the defendant in proper person who having heard the Bill of Indictment read for Plea says he cannot gainsay the charge therein exhibited against him and puts himself upon the grace and mercy of the Court." Fined 50¢ and costs; Pulaski Poe security for payment.

(p. 14) State VS Jacob Garrison (No. 1242). Affray. Thomas J. Campbell, Solicitor General; defendant says he cannot gainsay the charge; fined 50¢ and costs. Charles Mitchell security for payment.
        State VS Thomas Swan (No. 1243). Affray. T.J. Campbell, Solicitor General; defendant says he cannot gainsay the charge; fined 50¢ and costs. John B. Swan security for payment.
        State VS John Walker (No. 1244). Assault and Battery. T.J. Campbell, Solicitor General; defendant says he cannot gainsay the charge; fined 50¢ and costs. Michael W. Buster security for payment.
        State VS Allen Hilbourn (No. 1245). Grand Jury returned a Bill of Indictment endorsed not a true bill by the foreman, William Smith. Defendant to go hence and the County to pay costs.

(p. 15) State VS John Walker (No. 1246). Assault and Battery. T.J. Campbell, Solicitor General; defendant says he cannot gainsay the charge; fined 50¢ and costs. Michael W. Buster security for payment.
        State VS James Rogers (No. 1247). Sci fa. T.J. Campbell, Solicitor General; ordered that the forfeiture incurred by the defendant in this behalf as the appearance Bail of Hugh Hackney be set aside upon payment of all the costs. "Whereupon came the Deft and Aron Hackney together [with] George Gillespie the security of the Deft and assumes the payment of the costs aforesaid and agrees that execution may issue therefor."
        State VS Aron Hackney (No. 1248). Sci fa. Ordered that the forfeiture incurred by the Defendant in this behalf as the appearance Bail of Hugh Hackney be set aside upon payment of costs; James Rogers security of defendant.

(p. 16) State VS Hugh Hackney (No. 1249). Sci fa. On motion of James Rogers and Aaron Hackney, securities for the defendant, ordered that the forfeiture be set aside upon payment of all costs. Rogers and Hackney assume costs.
        State VS Thomas Hamilton (No. 1250). Affray. T.J. Campbell, Solicitor General; defendant says he is not guilty; heard by Jury (William Lewis, Charles Ryon, William Wann, Isiah Brown, Charles Goolsby, Michael Stoner, Thomas Thompson, Andrew Evans, Pulaski Poe, Jacob Brown, Orlando Bradley, and Jesse Reese) who say the defendant is guilty; fined 50¢ and costs; John Robinson security for payment.
        Miller Francis to Orlando Bradley. Bill of Sale dated 14th March 1823 for a Negro woman named Rhoda; acknowledged by Francis.
        Grand Jury returned a Bill of Indictment against Jacob Garrison for Petit larceny endorsed a true Bill by the foreman, William Smith.

(p. 17) Woodson Francis to Orville Paine. Deed for one undivided sixth part of 309 acres of land; acknowledged by Francis (Sheriff).
        On motion of John Robinson, Register of Rhea County, James Berry was permitted to qualify as his Deputy and took the oath accordingly.

6

State VS Jacob Garrison. Petit Larceny. Jeremiah Haynes and Charles Mitchell indebted to State for $250 each; void on condition that they appear on the first Wednesday after the first Monday of August next to give evidence in a case the State against Jacob Garrison.

Jacob Garrison acknowledges himself indebted to the State in the sum of $500; James Rodgers and Lewis Wilkerson securities in sum of $250 each for the appearance of Garrison.

State VS Thomas James & Joseph Thompson, his security. "On motion of Joseph Thompson by his Attorney to quash an Execution heretofore issued in this cause. . . considered by the Court that the same be quashed so far as it respects the jailors fees amounting to $16.87½ and that John Parker jailor refund the same to the Clerk, the same being considered not legally collected."

(p. 18) Byram Breeding VS Robert Beard (No. 1251). ". . . the Defendant not wishing further to prosecute his Certiorari as agreed upon at the last term of this Court confesses judgment for the sum of thirty dollars debt." Plaintiff to recover from Defendant and Lewis Wilkerson, his security, the debt and $1.80 interest together with the costs.

State VS Charles Woodward (No. 1252). Bastardy. Defendant together with James Kelly and Jackson Howerton, his securities, indebted to State in sum of $500; void on condition "that the Defendant Charles Woodward abide by, satisfy and perform any order or decree which this Court may hereafter render concerning a Bastard child begotten by the said Defendant upon the body of Elizabeth Mitchell, and for which the said Defendant is now bound . . . and the Defendant also confesses judgment for the costs of this prosecution . . ."

State VS Hugh Hackney. Ordered "that the money now in the hands of Henry Collins for which the Defendant was indicted for stealing be delivered over by the said Henry Collins to Jackson Howerton the rightful owner thereof."

(p. 19) Justices on bench (8th May) — Rice, Thompson, and McDonald.
Jurors appointed for next term of this Court:

Alexander Forbes	Samuel Applegate	Charles Mitchell	Daniel Stockton
Pulaski Poe	George W. Riggle	William Hill	Cain Able
John Able	Reubin Jackson	John Farris	John Redman
John Woodward	Samuel Parks	William Woodward	Thomas Goad
Edward Goad	Alexander Caldwell	Thomas Henry	William Johns
Richard Jones	Lewis Morgan	Richard A. McCanless	James Wilson S.T.
Shepheard Brazelton, Constable to attend.			Joshua Tindall

Jurors appointed for next term of Circuit Court:

Jesse Martin	Samuel Looney	Beriah Frazier	William Allexander
Moses Thompson	Jesse Roddy	Edward Gray	John Hughes
Benjamin Marberry	Benjamin Jones	Gideon Ragland	James Wilson Y.C.
John Ferguson W.C.	John Wassen	Henry Collins	John Lewis
Robert Bell	Robert Gamble	Allen Kennedy	John Lea S.T.
Benjamin F. Jones	Patrick Martin	Wilson Kilgore	Samuel Tillery
	Joseph Thompson	William Lea	

David Chilton, Constable to attend Court.

(p. 20) Asa Rowdon VS Micajah Clack (No. 1253). Defendant by his attorney came, but plaintiff made default. Defendant released and to collect costs from plaintiff.

State VS Thomas D. Paine. Defendant acknowledged himself indebted to State for $250; Thomas Kelly and James C. Mitchell, his securities, indebted in sum of $125 each; void if the Defendant makes his appearance in Court at next term.

AUGUST TERM 1823

(p. 21)   Court of Pleas and Quarter Sessions held on the first Monday and 4th day of August 1823. Justices on bench— Daniel Walker, James McDonald, William Kennedy, Crispien E. Shelton, Azariah David, Thomas Cox, Stephen Winton, Frederick Fulkerson, John Rice, William Gamble, Jesse Thompson, John Cozby, and Thomas Price.   (NOTE— first names of Justices added by B.J.B.)

Daniel Rawlings to William Lauderdale. Deed of Conveyance for 114 acres; proven by Benjamin C. Stout, one of the subscribing witnesses; certified for further probate.

John Rice, Allan Kennedy, and James Berry appointed Commissioners to settle with William Locke, Admr. of Thomas K. Locke, dec'd.

David McMillen to John Hudson. Deed of Conveyance for 219½ acres; proven by John H. Henderson and John Pace, two of the subscribing witnesses, who swear they saw Robert Taylor sign his name as subscribing witness; deed certified for registration.

Ordered that the road leading from John Lockes Ferry on Tennessee River to the McMinn County line be discontinued.

William Smith appointed overseer of road in place of Mumford Smith.

Ordered that the road leading from Washington to John Lockes Ferry on Tennessee River be discontinued.

William C. Wilson appointed overseer of road in place of Daniel Stockton, Removed.

(p. 22)   Certificate issued to William H. West for four Wolf scalps.

Certificate issued to William Humberd for two Wolf scalps.

Return J. Meigs and Henry Steele Purris produced their licenses as practicing attorneys.

Ordered that the Indenture given by Sally Shaver to William Lewis, dec'd, at February Session (10th) 1820 be canceled. Jonathan Fine appointed her Guardian.

Ordered that the road leading from McDonald Ferry to intersect the road leading from Washington to Athens be established as follows: Beginning at McDonalds Ferry and running with the old road to James Grigsbys, thence by James Lea, by John Roddy, by Jesse Martin and William Ziglar and thence to intersect with Kellys Ferry Road, and that Samuel Fry be overseer from Grigsbys Fork of Roddy Branch and have all the hands which work under him to cut out said road; John Roddy to be overseer on said road from his Branch to where said road intersects Kellys Road and that he have all William Ziglars hands to cut out said road.

Jesse Poe appointed Administrator on estate of William Lewis, dec'd; James Stewart and Willie Lewis, securities; bond for $1000.

(p. 23)   Bond of Jesse Poe.

(p. 24)   Azariah David to divide the hands between overseers Joshua Tendal and John Bailey. Tendal to have in addition to his former hands: Richard Lawson, two of Coulters hands, all Woodson Francis hands, Robert Parks, Evan Evans, James Vernon, and Solomon Vernon.

Stephen Winton and Daniel Stockton appointed to divide and designate the hands to work under the following overseers: William Wann, Joab Rignay, and Benjamin Maxfield.

Thomas York VS William H. West. "The arbitrators Stephen Winton Esq. and John Redmond to whom was heretofore refered this matter of Controversy between the parties on a rule of Court to make their award the final determination and judgment of the Court this day returned . . . their award as follows: That

8

the Defendant pay the Plaintiff seventeen Dollars in Corn at two shillens per Bushell from the heap this fall and the costs that may have accrued in this cause to be equally divided and paid by each party. . ."

Ordered that an orphan Boy formerly kept by Thomas Woodward be let for the term of one year from this date to Jehew Kerns for the sum of $44.00.

(p. 25) Isaac West appointed overseer of road from Clear Creek to Lewis Collins and to have all the hands on the lands of Robert Ferguson, dec'd, Isaac West, Samuel Logan, Matthew Hubbart, William Johnson, John Wasson, John Condley, and William Kennedy.

James C. Mitchell overseer of road from Clear Creek to William Darwins and to have all the hands where Joseph Killoug, Thomas G. Goad, James Purser, Edward Robbins, George Ransom, and Edward Goad lives, together with all the hands on the land of Henry Walton, Isaac Crow, James C. Mitchell, and William Goad, And all the hands on the lands of all the Woodwards and Henry Collins, John Lewis, and all the Howertons to work on the road under William Compton.

Elizabeth Walker, Admrx. and Relict of William Walker, returned an inventory and account of sale of goods and chattles &c. (all purchased by widow):

One Mare	$ .50	1 Weeding Hoe	$ .31¼
2 Cows and one calf	2.00	1 do do	.07¼
2 Feather beads and furniture	.50	½ Dozen tin cups	.07½
1 Cart	.75	1 Coffee Pot	.38½
2 Ovens	.04	1 Water Pail	.50
½ dozen pewter plates	.06¼	Plank	.50
1 Pr Drawing Chains	.26	5 head of Hogs	.04
1 falling axe	.56¼		$ 5.76
		1 Rifle Gun purchased by John Rice	12.25
			$18.81

(p. 26) Matthew Hubbart, Administrator, and Abigal Ferguson, Administratrix and relict of Robert Ferguson, Dec'd, returned an inventory and account of sales as follows: Specia on hand $217.87¼; Bank Notes $26.75; one Note Eli Ferguson and William Kennedy for $100 applied to payment of land contracted previously by Robert Ferguson Dec'd; a Note on Samuel Long for ₤13.11.6 with a credit of ₤ 2.15.0; An account on Eli Ferguson for $14.12½; Ditto on William Kennedy for $7.00; Ditto on Henry Walton for $2.00.   Stock 1 Sorrell Horse, 1 Black Mare, 1 Bay Mare, 1 Year old Colt given to Martin F. by his father, 1 Cow given to John T. by his father, 1 Brindle Cow and Calf, 2 Red and white sided Cows and 1 Calf, 2 red Cows with white backs, 2 white Steers, 4 Yearlings, 1 waggon and hind geers, feed trough, Cloth and tar bucket, 32 head of Hogs, 12 head of Sheep, Rifle Gun pouch &c, 2 barshare plows, 2 shovel ploughs, 2 gofer ploughs, 1 pr Stretchers and single tree, 2 Iron wedges and some old Iron, 5 falling axes, 1 Mattock and Sang hoe, 4 weeding hoes, 2 hackles, 1 Log chain, 1 pair door Hinges, 3 pair chaines, 2 pair Haimes and Collars, 3 back bands, 5 clevices and twisted links, 5 Bells, 1 Grind Stone, 2 Sickels, 1 Sythe, 2 Plaines, 1 Auger and Chisel, 1 drawing knife, 2 hammers, 1 pair Pincers, 1 Flat Iron, 1 lamp, 1 handsaw, 4 Still tubs, 3 Pots, 3 ovens and lids, 1 Frying Pan, 2 shovels, 1 Pot rack, 1 chain and hook, 2 pair of Pot hooks, 1 Iron Spoon, 1 flesh fork, 1 pair Candle moulds, 2 pair of Shears, 1 pair ounce weights, 1 candle stick, 5 Bridles and Neck Collars, 1 old Side Saddle, 1 Kipp Skin, 2 Sides and 2 pieces of upper leather, some pieces of Soal and Harness Leather, 5 Pails and half Bushel, 1 Mans Saddle, 1 Side Saddle, 1 Jug, and 5 Bottles, a small quantity of Tobacco, 1 Cotton and 2 Flax Wheels, A set of Warping Spools, 2 pair Cotton Cards, 1 Check reel, 1 Riddle, 2 meal sifters, 1 meal Barrel and tray, 3 Meal bags, 10 Chairs, 1 dining Table, 10 Pewter plates, 14 delf plates, 3 Dishes and 2 basins, 2 sets of knives and forks, 1 Dozen spoons, 9 tea cups and saucers, 7 Tin cups, 1 cream pitcher, 1 pitcher and 2 bowls, 2 glass tumblers, 4 Japan Tumblers, 1 su-

gar dish, 1 coffee
(p. 27) Pot, 1 Bread W--?--, 8 Crocks, 2 tin pans, 1 dresser, 1 Clothes Brush,
1 tin trumpet, 1 Coffee Mill, 3 Books, 1 Looking Glass, 5 beds Steads an furniture, 1 pair Saddle bags, 1 pine Chest and Sugar Kan, 1 Small trunk, 10 head of
geese, a kan, a small quantity of Staves, 1 Carving Knife, an account of Sarah
Craig for $3.20, 1 Kag, 1 tin dipper, 1 peper box, 2 Barrels and a keg of vine-
gar, 1 large keg and sum brandy, 1 funnel and a pad lock, 2 old pots, 1 small
meat vessel, 8 old barrels, a razor box and hone, a small quantity of Corn, Ditto
of fodder, 264 lbs of Cotton first quality in the sead, 49 lbs inferior quallity
of Cotton, 6 Bushels Sweet potatoes.

Here follows A List of property Sold to wit— Abegail Ferguson widow
a Sorrell horse & bridle $50; John Ferguson Junr. a black mare $75; Henry Collins
a bay mare & bridle $30; widow A. Ferguson a young red cow $8; Wm Woodward an
old pided Cow $8.25; John Bailey 2 White Steers $24; Archibald Dean a Young
Brindle Steer $6.25; Eli Ferguson a Spotted Steer $4.50; John Condley a Yearling
bull $3.75; ditto a red pided Steer Calf $2.81¼; Saml Holland 2 pided bull calves
$5.25; John Ferguson Junr. a Waggon & hind gears $40; Widow a Saw $1.50; John
Ferguson Junr. 4 hogs first choise $12; ditto 4 ditto second choise $10.25; ditto
4 ditto third choise $7; Isaac Crow 4 ditto fourth choise $4.75; Saml Holland 3
ditto fifth choice $2.56¼; Widow 5 Shoats first choice $3; Henry Collins 4
Shoats second choice $4; Widow one lame Carrow $1.50; ditto Ewe & lamb & bell
$2.25; Henry Collins 10 head of Sheep $22.12½; Widow a Rifle gun and accoutru-
ments $9; Wm Johnson a barshare plough $2.06¼; Wm Woodward a plough, share
Coulter and heel screw $2.18 3/4; Widow a shovel plough 75¢; Eli Ferguson ditto
$1.25; Henry Collins a bultoungue plough & Single tree $1.13 3/4; Widow ditto
ditto $1; John Ferguson junr Stretchers & single tree $4.50; Chas Woodward an
Iron wedge 75¢; John Ferguson Wolf Creek ditto 62½¢; Widow an ax $1; John Conley
ditto $1.68 3/4; John Ferguson Junr ditto $1; Widow a small meat ax 25¢; John
Dunlap ditto 75¢; Widow a Mattock $2.25; Henry Collins a Sang hoe 31½¢; Oliver
Pike a weeding hoe 12½¢; Widow two ditto 50¢; Wm Kennedy a small ditto 50¢; Widow two Hackels 75¢; Widow a log chain 75¢; John Ferguson Senr a pair of door
hinges 75¢; Widow Collar haims and Chaines $3.43 3/4; Henry Collins one pair
haimes and chains $1.93 3/4; John Ferguson junr. drawing chains & back band
$1.81¼; Widow a Clevis and pins 12½¢; Wm Kennedy a Clevis and twisted link 37½¢;
Henry Collins a Clevis 25¢; Wm Johnson a notched Clevis 56½¢; John Ferguson junr.
Ditto 31¼¢; Wm Woodward a bell and Collar 50¢; Edward Robbins a bell $1.00;

(p. 28) Charles Woodward a bell 31¼¢; Widow a bell and Collar $1.00; James A.
Darwin grindstone $2.25; John Condley a Sickle 75¢; Widow ditto 50¢; Wm Howard a
Sythe and sned $1.68 3/4; John Ferguson W. Creek a Smoothing Plain 50¢; Eli Fer-
guson a Jack ditto 75¢; Widow 5 quarter Auger 50¢; Wm Woodward a Chissel 6¼¢;
Micajah Howerton a Drawing Knife 50¢; Widow a Claw hammer 12½¢; Ditto a hammer
and pincers 50¢; Ditto a flat Iron 75¢; Widow a hand saw $1; Ditto a lamp 6¼¢;
Robert Ferguson 2 Still tubs $2; Ditto one ditto $1.56¼; Widow a Small pot &
hooks 50¢; Ditto a wash pot $1; Ditto an oven & lid 50¢; Wm Kennedy an oven $1;
Henry Walton an oven lid 18 3/4¢; John Dunlap a Skillet 6¼¢; Widow a pot rack
$1.12½; Ditto a fire shovel 50¢; Henry (blank) dirt Shovel $1.50; Micajah Hower-
ton a Still tub 62½¢; Wm Johnson a chain hook 31¼¢; Widow an Iron Spoon 25¢; Eli
Ferguson a flesh fork 18 3/4¢; Widow Candle Moulds 12½¢; Ditto a pair of Sheers
50¢; John Ferguson Wolf Creek ditto 12½¢; Eli Ferguson Ounce Steel Yards 31¼¢;
Widow a Candlestick 12½¢; Matthew Hubbert a Bell Collar 50¢; John Ferguson a
Blind bridle $1.50; Widow a Kirb bridle 50¢; Wm Johnson a Side Saddle $2.62½;
Elisha Gough a hide tanned & dressed leather $3.81¼; Eli Ferguson a hide of Tanned
leather $3.62½; Widow a lot of leather upper and soal $4; John Ferguson junr. Side
of harness leather $1.62½; Betsey Ferguson 2 pails 50¢; Wright Smith a pail 20¢;
Widow one ditto 37½¢; Ditto a half Bushel 12½¢; Ditto a pail 25¢; Wm Ferguson a

10

bag with divers Iron &c $1.18 3/4; Charles Paine a Mans Saddle $2.62½; Widow a
Side Saddle $10; Eli Ferguson a Wine bottle 43 3/4; Widow a jug 75¢; ditto a
small bottle 12½¢; James Ferguson a chunk bottle 25¢; Widow a keg of Tobacco
$2.50; Micajah Howerton a flax wheel $2.06¼; Widow Ditto $1; Ditto a Cotton Wheel
$1.75; Ditto a Reed $1; Ditto a Set of Spools 25¢; Ditto a pair Cotton Cards $1;
Ditto a Riddle 25¢; John Ferguson W. Creek Cotton Cards 37½¢; Wright Smith 2 pr
old Cotton Cards 37½¢; Widow 2 Sifters 25¢; Ditto a Meal Carrell and tray 25¢;
Ditto a Meal bag 37½¢; Ditto pr ditto 37½¢; Wm Johnson 2 old bags 32¢;

(p. 29) Widow 6 Chairs $2; Henry Walton 4 ditto 62½¢; Widow a Table $1; Ditto 10
pewter plates $1; Ditto 14 doz plates $1; Ditto a pewter dish 37½¢; Ditto pr ditto
$1; Ditto a delf dish $1.18 3/4; Ditto a pan and basin $1; Ditto pr ditto 37½¢;
Ditto 2 sets knives & forks & some odd $3; Ditto 1 Doz Spoons $1; Ditto 9 Cups &
Saucers 50¢; Ditto 7 tin cups 25¢; Ditto a pitcher 12¼¢; Ditto 2 bowls & a pitcher
50¢; Wright Smith 2 Glass tumblers 37½¢; Widow 4 Japan tumblers 25¢; Ditto a Sugar
Dish 6¼¢; Ditto a Coffee pot 25¢; Ditto a Waiter 25¢; Wm Johnson 2 Crocks 56¼¢;
Widow 5 ditto 50¢; Widow a Small tin pan 6¼¢; Ditto a dressor $1; Ditto a Clothes
brush 12½¢; Matthew Hubbart tin Trumpet 43 3/4¢; Widow a Coffee Mill $1; Ditto a
Bible Testament & hymn Book 50¢; Ditto a Looking Glass 12½¢; Ditto a feather bead
& furniture Sted &c $9; Ditto pr Ditto $14.50; Ditto pr Ditto $14.00; Peter Min-
nick Ditto $30.12½; Widow a Chaff bed and furniture $4; Matthew Hubbart Saddle
bags $4; Widow a pine Chest and Sugar kan $1; Ditto a Small trunk $1; Eli Ferguson
a Razor Box and hone 50¢; Esther Woodward 9 Geese $4.50; Widow a washing Tub 25¢;
Ditto a Churn 50¢; Ditto a dye kann 25¢; Robt Ferguson Stave for a still tub & 2
Barrels 75¢; Charles Payne a Carving knife 37½¢; Widow a kag 25¢; Ditto a tin dip-
per 6¼¢; Ditto a pepper box 6¼¢; John Ferguson junr. Barrell Vinegar $3; William
Johnson a kag of Vinegar $1.25; James A. Darwin an empty barrell $1; Widow a funnel and pad lock 12½¢; Ditto 2 old pots 6¼¢; Eli Ferguson a pickling tub $1; Ditto
3 barrels 50¢; Wm Kennedy Ditto $1; Widow 2 Barrels 25¢; Ditto 200 Bundles fodder
more or less 50¢; Archibald Dean a small quantity of corn $4.31¼; Widow a chunk
bottle 31¼¢; Henry Collins a small black bottle 25¢.
        The following property Sold at private Sale: William Johnson 30 Wt Cotton
1st quality $5; Spils Bea Dyer 36 lb Ditto $6; John Smith 12¼ at 12½¢ pr lb $1.52;
Martin Ferguson 4 Bush. S. potatoes $2; John Miller 2 Bushels ditto $1.00.

(p. 30) Commissioners (Henry Collins, Samuel Logan, Henry Walton) appointed to
lay off years provision for widow and family of Robert Ferguson allowed the following: 180 bushels of corn; 3 Cows, the choise of the Stock for one year; all
the bacon and fat on hand, all the fruit on hand, what salt on hand and one bushel
and a half more, the choice of two hogs out of the Stock, 2 bushels of wheat, 4
Gallons of brandy and ten dollars for necessaries.
        We further consider that the Widow have all the wool on hand (21 lbs), the
picked cotton on hand (66 lbs), and all the flax on hand consisting of a small
quantity of unbroken and a small quantity that is broke to clothe her family with
and one pot, one dutch oven and one frying pan if the Court considers it lawful.
        Jurors summoned to attend at November Session of this Court:

Jonathan Hill	William Austin	John Jones	Abijah Harris
Matthias Wright	Edmund Templeton	William Collins	James Roddy
Edward Stuard	John Riggle	Peter Majors	Jesse Reece Sr.
Jacob Garrison	Jerry Riddle	John Lillard	Kinsey Moore
Spils Bee Dyer	Jacob Beck	John Wasson	John Singleton
Drury Sykes	William Hill	Jonathan Lassetter	Samuel Howard
			Elisha Parker

Peter Peck VS Henry Aldridge & Matthew Bolejack. Petition for Writs of Certiorari and Supercedious presented by Matthew Bolejack by Attorney; allowed upon giving bond and sufficient security.

(p. 31) Ordered that Lewis R. Collins and all the hands subject to work under him, Robert Beard and all the hands subject to work under him, Peter Daniel and all the hands subject to work under him are all to assist in repairing the Bridge across Piney River at the Mountain Vally road until next Court.

Robert Drennon VS Landon Rector. Plaintiff dismisses suit; defendant confesses judgment for all costs.

Elijah Ronalds allowed $45 for keeping Mary Owens 12 months.

William Walker appointed Constable in Capt. Piper's Company; bond with Mumford Smith and James Walton.

John Clack appointed Constable in Capt. Brown's Company; bond with Henry Collins and John Parker.

(p. 32) The bounds of William Seymore, overseer, to begin at Joseph Williams, thence a line to include John Hill and John Robinson, thence a line to the end of the Knob to include James Wilson.

John Hughes leave to record the ear mark of his live stock: a crop and two slits in the right ear, and a swallow fork in the left ear.

Benjamin McKenzie, Henry Walton, James Henry, and Francis Hardin are released from paying the tax only in one case, being placed on the list twice; also that Thomas Hughes, William Lisenby, and Edward Goad be released from paying a tax this year.

Lewis R. Collins appointed overseer in place of Richard G. Waterhouse.

Wright Carter, an orphan boy, is bound to James Stewart for 4 years.

John Ferris, Hiram Gibson, William Wann, Samuel Riddle, George W. Riggle, Samuel Ferguson, and Thomas Godbehere appointed Jury of View to lay out and mark a road the nearest and best way from the foot of Waldens Ridge near Jacob Becks passing the Tennessee River at James Waltons Ferry to intersect the old Federal Road at Adam Coxes.

(p. 33) Charles Ryan, John Lea, Richard McCandless, Beriah Frazier, John Roddy, Jesse Martin, Alexander Forbes, Henry Airhart, Lewis Morgan, Jesse Witt, Jacob Reynolds, and John Singleton appointed Jury of View to lay off and mark a road from Morgans Turnpike at the foot of Waldens Ridge to cross Tennessee River at Fraziers Ferry and intersect the road leading from McDonalds and Kellys Ferries.

Elijah W. Collins appointed Constable in Capt. Jackson's Company; bond with Henry Collins and Woodson Francis.

On application of John Owens, he is to keep James McKeel until next term of this Court without any payment.

George W. Riggle released from serving as Juror at this Term.

Ordered that the road leading from William Prices be allowed as follows: one half a mile along Thomas Prices Ferry Road thence 300 yards to Farmers Road that he halls his oare along thence along that road to John Stewart to John Brazeltons old road.

(p. 34) Justices on bench (5th August)— Gillespie, Fulkerson, and David.

Richard Jones exempted from further attendance as a Juror at this Term.

Grand Jury empannelled: 1 John Able (foreman), 2 Alexander Forbes, 3 John Ferres, 4 John Redmond, 5 Lewis Morgan, 6 Thomas Henry, 7 Daniel Stockton, 8 William Woodward; 9 Richard A. McCandless, 10 Alexander Caldwell, 11 Cain Able, 12 Reuben Jackson, and 13 Edward Goad.

Remaining of the original Venire: Pulaski Poe, William Johns, Thomas Goad, William Hill, and Samuel Applegate.

John Miller, a Constable, sworn to attend the Grand Jury.

Matthew Stephenson VS William Floyd. Came the defendant by attorney; plaintiff made default; defendant to recover his costs from plaintiff.

Robert C. Gorden VS John Bennit. Came Defendant by Attorney; plaintiff made default; defendant released and recover his costs from plaintiff.

Same VS Same (No. 1257). By consent of the parties by their attorneys and with the assent of the Court the above non pros is set aside upon the plaintiff paying the costs of the judgment and this order; also agreed that each party have leave to take Commissions to take the Depositions of what witnesses they may please. Cause is continued until next Court.

(p. 35) George Gothard VS Mary Cranmore. The parties submit all matters in dispute between them in this suit to the final determination of Abraham Howard and William Smith and if they cannot agree they are to choose an unpire whose award is to be the judgment of this Court. The arbitration of the cause is to be held at the house of Abraham Howard on the First Saturday of September next and report to next term of this Court.

William L. Bradley VS Thomas Hudleston (No. 1258). Plaintiff by attorney dismisses suit; defendant confesses judgment for the costs.

(p. 36) Hiram Worley VS James Coulter (No. 1259). Came the plaintiff by attorney and the defendant having withdrawn his plea to the plaintiffs declaration, judgment is entered against him for $404.50 debt and $48.67 damages and costs.

Philip Cox VS John Rice (No. 1260). Came plaintiff by attorney and defendant failing to file his plea to the plaintiffs declaration, judgment is entered against him for $210 debt, deducting the sum of $81.51½ leaving the balance due $178.48½ together with the further sum of $7.76 damages; also to recover costs.

(p. 37) John Locke VS John Rice & James C. Mitchell (No. 1261). Came the plaintiff by his attorney and the defendants having withdrawn their plea to the plaintiffs declaration, judgment is entered against the defendants for $166.25 debt and $30.75 damages; also to pay costs.

John Locke VS John Rice & John Barnett (No. 1262). Defendant failed to file any plea to the plaintiffs declaration; judgment for $337 debt and $28.13 damages; also the costs.

(p. 38) Thomas Jack VS John Rice (No. 1263). Defendant failed to file any plea; judgment for $120.00 debt with a credit of $33.39¼, leaving a balance of $86.60 3/4 and the further sum of $5.91 damages, plus costs.

(p. 39) David Campbell VS Miller Francis & William Smith (No. 1264). Defendants having withdrawn their defence to the plaintiffs declaration, judgment is entered against them for $1725.00 debt deducting $817.83 credits, leaving a balance of $907.17 and $528.47 damages; plus costs.

Grand Jury returned the following presentments: State VS William York for an assault; State VS John Gassage for an affray; State VS James Stewart and William Piper for an affray; State VS Siles York for an assault.

(p. 40) State VS William Piper (No. 1265). Presentment. Came Thomas J. Campbell who prosecutes for the State; defendant says he is guilty of the Trespass assault and battery as charged; fined $1.00. John Redmond security for payment.

State VS James Stewart (No. 1266). Presentment. Defendant says he is guilty of the Trespass assault and battery as charged; fined $1.00. Joseph McDaniel security for payment.

John Lillard VS William L. Bradley (No. 1267). Attachment. On motion of John Lillard by his attorney James C. Mitchell and it appearing to the satisfaction

of the Court that a writ of Fi. Fa. was issued by John Rice Esqr. in favor of Lillard for $51.59. Woodson Francis, Sheriff, reported that no goods or chattels of
the defendant could be found in the County and "that he had levied it upon a House
and lot in the town of Washington known in the plan of said Town by lot No. 27."
Court ordered that the house and lot be sold to satisfy judgment and costs.

(p. 41) Benjamin Erwin VS William Kennedy (No. 1268). Upon affidavit of defendant
this cause is continued until next Term upon his paying the costs of this Term.

      Justices on bench (6th August) — Gillespie, Fulkerson, and David.
      State VS Thomas D. Paine (No. 1269). Defendant says he is guilty as
charged; fined $1.00 and costs. William Johns security for payment.
      Matthew Stephenson &c VS William Floyd. The non pros entered on yester-
day is set aside and the cause continued until next Court.

(p. 42) William Blyth VS James Darwin (No. 1270). Defendant made default;
plaintiff to recover from defendant $388 debt (less credit) leaving balance of
$258, plus $28.53 damages and costs.
      State VS John Henderson (No. 1271). Came William Lewis who was security
for the appearance of the defendant and surrendered him in open Court in discharge
of himself. Defendant submits to the mercy of the Court; fined $1.00 plus costs.

(p. 43) State VS Jacob Garrison (No. 1272). Nolle prosequi entered in this case.
      State VS Silas York. John Redmon acknowledges himself indebted to State
for $250; void if he appears at next term to give evidence in this cause.
      State VS William York. John Redmon &c (same as above).

(p. 44) State VS John Gossage. John Ferris indebted to State for $250; void
if he appears at next term to give evidence in this cause.
      Townley Riggs VS Joseph McDaniel (No. 1273). Appeal. Came plaintiff by
attorney; defendant failed to prosecute his appeal; judgment against the defendant for $20.00 debt and 48¢ damages plus costs.

(p. 45) On the affidavit of Wm Gamble who made oath that at August Sessions 1821
of this Court he drew his Ticket as a juror for 5 days and that he has since lost
the same. Ordered that a duplicate certificate issue for him.

NOVEMBER TERM 1823

(p. 46) Justices on bench (3rd November) — Thomas Price, Frederick Fulkerson,
Arthur Fulton, William Kennedy, James McDonald, Crispien E. Shelton, Stephen
Winton, Daniel Walker, Thomas Cox, and John Rice (NOTE — first names added by B.J.B.)
      Elihu D. Armstrong appointed overseer of road in place of Wright Smith,
resigned.
      Theophelus Smith appointed overseer of road in place of William Wann,
resigned; hands to be divided as follows: all the hands formerly belonging to
William Wann south of the Morganton Road and west of the Federal Road be assigned
to Joab Rigney as far down as to include Henry Runnels and those north and east
of the Morganton Road formerly belonging to Joab Rigney to belong to Theophelus
Smith.
      Charles Mitchell overseer of road in place of Samuel B. Swan.
      Elisha Sharp overseer of road in place of Benjamin Maxfield.
      Shepherd Braselton resigned as Constable.
      Walter Edwards, William Johnson, James Snelson, Cumberland Rector, James
Bailey, Isaac Baker, and Thomas McCarty appointed Jury of View to lay out and

14

mark a road from Snelsons Ferry to Col. George Gillespies House.
      Calvin Robinson overseer of road in place of William Miller.
      Abner Morgan overseer of road in place of Robert Beard.

(p. 47) George W. Riggle appointed Constable in Capt. Riggles Company; bond with Wright Smith and William Miller.
      Certificate issued to Isaac Rush for one Wolf scalp.
      William Walker resigned as Constable.
      John Parker permitted to keep a house of Ordinary.
      Ordered that the road as reported be established: from the foot of Waldens Ridge near Jacob Becks passing the Tennessee River to James Waltons Ferry to intersect the old Federal Road at Adam Coles; John Miller appointed overseer; to have Henry Richards, Williamson Tod, Curtis Richards, John Berton, Squire Burton, John Richmond, David Hutson, William Beerman, Nathan Harwood, Samuel Cunningham, Thomas Rorick, William Iredale, and Henry Maynard, who is to work from the River bank to Adam Coles.
      Elijah Runnels allowed $45 for keeping a poor person, Mary Owens, for 12 months ending in August last.
      William Smith, overseer of road from Yellow Creek to Piney River, is allowed the following hands: Anderson Smith, Jasper Romines, Mumford Smith, William Smith, George W. Riggle, John Riggle, Thomas Anderson, Landon Rector, Samuel Hillburn, John Hillburn, Allen Hillburn, David Thomas, William Merriman, William Walker, and Hatten Walker.
      Order made by Court at last term is revived (road from Morgans Turnpike at foot of Waldens Ridge to cross the Tennessee River at Fraziers Ferry &c).
      Order made by last Court revived (for William Zeigler, overseer, and his hands to help cut out the road from John Roddy Branch to intersect Kelly Ferry Road.

(p. 48) Ordered that each person employed by the Sheriff as a guard for the purpose of guarding John Prince and Joal McCarry while in the jail of Rhea County be allowed 25¢ each for each night they stood guard.
      Peter Peck VS Henry Aldridge & Matthew Bolejack (Nos. 1274 & 1275). Came Allen Henderson, Agent for the Plaintiff, and dismisses his suit; defendants confess judgment for one half of the costs each.
      State VS James Callison. It appearing to the satisfaction of the Court that an execution for the cost that accrued in this prosecution issued against James Callison and his securities which said execution has been returned no property to be found and that nothing could be made thereon, It is therefore ordered that the County pay the cost of the said prosecution. John Rice allowed $6.50 for supper and breakfast furnished the Sheriff and jury in the said case.
      Ordered that Woodson Francis, Sheriff, be allowed a credit with the Treasurer of East Tennessee and the Trustee of Rhea County the following sums which he could not collect: Jacob Brown $1.37½; Robert H. Davis 62½¢; Solomon Hardin 62½¢; Jacob Miller 22¢; Robert Taylor $1.35¼; Jacob Wassum $5.93 3/4; Edward Goad 62½¢; James Henry 62½¢; Francis Hardin 62½¢; William Lisenby 62½¢; Robert Love $2.00; David McGee 62½¢; George Gothard 62½¢; Edward Cox 62½¢; William H. Duglas 62½¢; James Gough 62½¢; Thomas Hughes 62½¢; John Henderson 62½¢; Charles Ryon 62½¢; James Wilson $10.00; John Chambers 62½¢; William C. Wilson $4.37½.
      Thomas J. Campbell, Solicitor of the 11th Solicitorial District, allowed $50.00 for his exofficio services for 1823.

(p. 49) Woodson Francis, Sheriff, allowed $50.00 for exofficio services.
      James Berry, Clerk of this Court, allowed $40.00 for exofficio services and $25.00 for making out the tax lists for 1823.
      Jane Martin to Jesse Martin. Power of Attorney. Mrs. Jane Martin after having been privately examined Separate and apart from her husband whether she made

and signed the same freely and of her own accord without any coertion or restraint from her husband, Jesse Martin or any other person whatsoever by Thomas Price, Thomas Cox, and Chrispian E. Shelton esquires, Commissioners appointed by the Court.

Jacob Wormack & Mary Wormack to George Davidson. Deed of Conveyance for 100 acres in Lunenburg, Virginia; Mary examined separately by Thomas Price, Crispian E. Shelton, and Thomas Cox. Ordered to be certified for registration in State of Virginia.

(p. 50) State VS William Willmoth. William Miller brought into open Court the body of William Willmoth and surrendered him in discharge of himself as bail and he is ordered into custody of the Sheriff. Whereupon John Clack acknowledges himself indebted to the State for $250 to be void if William Willmoth makes his appearance on Wednesday of this Term.

Roswell Hall to John Parker. Deed of Conveyance for Lot No. 20 in Town of Washington; proven by oath of James C. Mitchell; ordered to be certified for further probate.

Justices on bench (4th November)— Rice, Walker, Cox, Winton, Fulkerson, Fulton, Cozby, and Shelton.

John Mee resigned as Constable.

Henry Henry appointed Constable in Capt. Brown's Company; bond with John Locke, his security.

The last Will and Testament of Isaac Rice Senr. was proven by oaths of Charles Matlock, Henry Matlock, and John Rice, the subscribing witnesses, who say that they saw Isaac Rice Senr. the deceased sign seal publish and declare the said Instrument of Writing to be his last Will and Testament, that they believe he was of perfect sence and memory at the time of publishing the same and that they subscribed their names thereto as witnesses in his presence and in the presence of each other, and it was ordered to be recorded and is as follows:

(p. 51) "In the name of God Amen. I Isaac Rice senr. of the County of Roan and State of Tennessee Being of sound mind and memory do make ordain and publish this to be my last Will and Testament in name and form following, Viz: First, I give and bequeath six hundred and fifty dollars in current money to be equally divided between Isaac Rice son of my brother Moses Rice, Mary Rice wife of said Moses Rice, Elizabeth Cain sister to my wife, Abraham Pence and John Dover Junr. I give and bequeath unto Elizabeth Thompson Wife of James Thompson two Cows and Calves or the value thereof, I give and bequeath unto James Rice son of my brother Benjamin Rice, one Bead and furniture all the ballance of my estate give and bequeath unto Isaac Rice son of my brother John Rice and Joseph Mee to be equally divided between them. And I do hereby appoint Isaac Rice & Joseph Mee to be eucutors [sic] of this my last Will and Testament and I do hereby revoke all former Wills by me made. In witness whereof I have hereunto set my hand and seal this 5th day of May 1818.   Isaac   his X mark   Rice Senr   (Seal)
Witnesses: Charles Matlock, Henry Matlock, John Rice.

Joseph Mee, named as Executor in Will, appeared in Court and took oath of executors; bond with Henry Matlock and Charles Matlock, his securities, for $3000.

Jonathan Evens VS Orville. Paine (No. 1276). Appeal. Plaintiff by his attorney is unwilling further to prosecute his said suit and dismisses suit.

(p. 52) Benjamin Rice VS Isaac Rice (No. 1277). Contested Will. Came the parties by their attornies and plaintiff being unwilling further to contest the Legality of the last Will and testament of Isaac Rice Senr. deceased and to oppose the probate of the same agrees to dismiss the issue made in this Cause and confesses himself fully satisfied for any claim he had upon said estate as heir to the said Isaac Rice deceased. Whereupon Joseph Mee comes and confesses himself liable for the cost.   Considered by the Court that the plaintiff recover of Mee his cost about the prosecution of this contest expended.

Upon the motion of Thomas J. Campbell, Attorney General, and it appearing to the satisfaction of the Court from testimony of George Gillespie and Joseph McCall that John Craig, an aged and infirm man and a Citizen of Rhea County, being possessed of property is not of sound mind and memory. Ordered that James Snelson and William Johnson of Tennessee River be appointed acting Guardians of the said John Craig during his mental infirmity, and that they give Bond and security.

Woodson Francis, Sheriff, returned "a list or Venire facias of good and lawful men, Citizens of said County designated and appointed by the Justices of this Court at their last Session of Said Court as Jurors to serve at this Session" (see list on page 10), of which the following were elected a Grand Jury: William (p. 53) Hill, John Wasson, Samuel Howard, Matthias Wright, John Jones, Jonathan Laseter, Drury Sykes, John Riggle, Elisha Parker, James Roddy, John Lillard, Peter Majors, and Abijah Harris. John Wasson appointed foreman and David Shelton a Constable to attend the Grand Jury.

There remained of the original Venire: Jesse Reece Senr., Jacob Garrison, Jeremiah Riddle, Edward Stewart, and John Singleton.

Andrew Evens VS Lewis Wilkerson (No. 1278). Plaintiff being unwilling to further prosecute, dismisses the suit; defendant acknowledges himself for costs.

Lewis Wilkerson VS Andrew Evens (No. 1279). Certiorari. Plaintiff being unwilling further to prosecute his suit dismisses same; Defendant to recover costs.

(p. 54) Jacob Beck and Jesse Reece Sr. released from further attendance as jurors.

Grand Jury returned a Bill of Indictment against William Wilmoth.

State VS William Wilmoth (No. 1280). Indictment for Assault and Battery. Defendant says he cannot gainsay the charge; fined 50¢ and costs. John Clack security for payment.

Isaac Benson VS Jehu Geren (No. 1281). Original Attachment. Writ of Fi Fa issued by Abraham Howard, J.P., in favor of Isaac Benson for the sum of $24.37½ debt and $1.25 damages; Sheriff Woodson Francis levied same on a lot in the town of Washington (No. 37).

(p. 55) David Ragsdale VS Mary Cranmore (No. 1282). Plaintiff being unwilling further to prosecute, the suit is dismissed.

Court "proceeded to the Election of a Trustee for the County of Rhea for the next succeeding two years. William Kennedy esquire and Col. William Johnson on nomination and upon Collecting and Counting out the Ballots William Johnson had five and William Kennedy four votes. Thereupon William Johnson was pronounced duly Elected Trustee for the County of Rhea . . . And the said William Johnson gave bond with Henry Collins, James Wilson and Isaac Brazelton Senr. his securities as required by law. Whereupon the necessary oaths were taken by him as required by law."

Roswell Hall to John Parker. Deed of Conveyance for Lot No. 20 in Town of Washington; proven by James C. Peper, one of the subscribing witnesses (proven by James C. Mitchell at yesterdays session); ordered to be registered.

(p. 56) Grand Jury returned presentments: State against Benjamin Benson and William H. Douglas for an affray; State against David Ragsdale for an Assault and Battery.

Ordered that a road of the 3rd Class be established commencing at or near to the residence of Clayton Stockton passing by Joseph Thompsons Mill on Sauwee [sic] Creek to intersect the road leading to Athens (McMinn County) at the House of John Jennings and that Joseph Thompson be appointed overseer, and have the following hands to work under him: John Jennings, John Helms, Moses Wyatt, and Nicholas Fhrailey [Fraley].

Robert Parks, Evan Evans, Isaac Holland, Jesse Day, Abraham Miller, Samuel Holland, and James Coulter a Jury of View to turn and lay out a road commencing at

Evan Evans on the Valley Road and running through Orville Paines land.

Richard G. Waterhouse to Luke Lea. Power of Attorney was acknowledged by Waterhouse; ordered to be certified.

Isaac Baker appointed Constable in Capt. Pipers Company; bond with Col. George Gillespie, his security.

(p. 57) Justices on bench (5th November)— Gillespie, Fulton, and Walker.

Woodson Francis, Sheriff, to Charles McFarland. Deed of Conveyance for 50 acres of land; certified for registration.

John McClanahan and Elenor McClanahan, his wife to John Stewart. Power of Attorney dated 18th October 1823. Elenor examined separately by William Kennedy, John Hope, and Henry S. Purris. Certified for registration in Jefferson County, Tennessee.

State VS John Humphreys (No. 1283). Defendant by his attorney James C. Mitchell says he cannot gainsay the charge and that he is guilty of an affray; fined $1.00 and costs; Thomas J. Campbell acknowledges judgment for costs.

(p. 58) Robert C. Gorden, assignee VS John Bennett (Nos. 1284 & 1285). Plaintiff being unwilling further to prosecute his suit, dismisses the same; Matthew English his Agent confesses judgment for half the costs; defendant to pay half the costs.

State VS William York (No. 1286). Assault and Battery. Defendant says he cannot gainsay the charge; fined $1.00.

State VS Josiah York (No. 1287). Assault and battery. Defendant says he is not guilty; case heard by jury (John Ferguson, John Bennett, Gabrial Godby, Jonas Wassum, John Lavender, John McClendon, Eli Reas, Edward Stewart, Joseph Thompson, Jacob Garrison, Jeremiah Riddle, and John Singleton) who find the defendant guilty as charged; fined $1.00; Isaac Baker security for payment.

(p. 59) State VS David Ragsdale (No. 1288). Assault and Battery. Defendant says he cannot gainsay the charges, that he is guilty as charged; fined 6½¢ and costs; Joshua Tindle security for payment.

State VS John Gossage & John Laney. Came John Farris and acknowledged himself indebted to the State for $250 in each of these suits; void on condition that he appear at next term of this Court and give evidence.

All causes not tried at this Term are ordered to be continued until next Court.

(p. 60) State VS Susannah Prince (No. 1289). Peace Warrant. Thomas J. Campbell, Prosecutor in behalf of the State; James Coulter not further requiring sutus of the peace of the Defendant. Defendant "go hence without day upon the payment of the cost acrued upon said Prosecution." George Prince security for payment.

State VS William McDonald (No. 1290). Defendant made default; appears that two writs of Sci Fi had issued (one from May Session and one from August Session) requiring the Defendant to shew cause if any he had why a conditional forfeiture for the sum of $5.00 entered against him at the February Session should not be made absolute. State to recover from defendant the said forfeiture.

Robert Locke and Samuel McDaniel appointed to lay off to Margaret Lewis, widow of William Lewis Jr., dec'd, a years provision out of the stock, crop and provisions on hand of the estate.

(p. 61) Jesse Poe, Admr. on estate of William Lewis Jr., dec'd, returned partial inventory of said estate and has leave to make report complete at next Session. A Schedule of the effects of William Lewis Junr, Dec'd, Sept. 25th 1823 and account of Sales of said estate of Household and kitchen furniture Sold to Margarett Lewis for $35. Margt Lewis Bot 2 Cows & Calves $20. Isaac Lewis 1 do do $10.50, Burley Godsey 1 heifer $6, Wilie Lewis 1 Steer $5.25, ditto 1 do $8.50, ditto 1 do $12, Jas Wilson 3 head hogs $4.62½, Margt 7 head hogs $6, Isaac Fine 3 do do $2.50, Henry Clark 3 do do $7.12½, ditto 3 do do $6.50, Joseph McDaniel 1 Shovel Plough $2, Barefoot Armstrong 1 Barshear do $6, Jesse Poe 1 do do $1.37½, Saml Looney 1 Swingletree & Bridle $1, Soloman Needeffer Curry Comb and Iron wedge 75¢, ditto 1 Clevice 12½¢, Miles B. Davis 1 Mattock $2.25, ditto 1 Bell 75¢, Joseph McDaniel 1 pr Hames and Chanes $3.12½, Wiley Lewis 1 falling axe $2.25, Margaret Lewis 1 hoe & axe 75¢, Do $144.37½. One Note of hand on Miller Francis and Danl D. Armstrong due 14th Jany 1823 for $24.87½ on Jos Harwood & Thos Piper due 14th Jany 1823 $15.65, on Jos Harwood dated Feby 19th 1823 with Ins from date $13, on Saml Craig and S. Brazelton due Jany 17th 1823 $15.05, Sol Neideffer due Dec 3rd 1823 $11.00, Burly Godsey dated March 4th 1822 with ins from date $13.66 2/3, W. Anderson & John Gamble due Dec 1st 1823 $12.62½, Sol. Neideffer & D. Blevins due Decr 1st 1823 $6.25, Geo Greenway & Abrm Miller due Decr 1st 1823 $11.25, Note of hand on Isam Parker & Wm Parker due Decr 1st 1823 $12.62½, John Leuty & Geo Click due Decr 1823 $7.50, John Gamble & Wm Anderson due Decr 1823 $12.50, Jas D. Hanly & Chas Havens due Decr 1823 $12.50, Jas D. Hanly due Decr 1823 $9.00, Henry Newton due Decr 1823 $3.00, Miles Davis due Decr 1823 $5.00, D. Blevins & S. Neideffer due Decr 1823 $10.25, Mark Robinson due 15th Oct 1813 $9.00, Mark Robinson due 15th Oct 1818 $9.00, Thomas Owens due 15th March 1820 $6.85, James Murphree due Nov 1st 1822 20 Bushels corn, Abrm S. Parker due March 1st 1822 $17.00, Wm Parker due 1st March 1822 $7.76, Woodson Francis Rect for Shafer & Henagers Note $86.10, Wm Lewis Senr Recd for D. Stocktons Note for $35 with a credit of $5 $30.00, Recd from Jno Barnett $2.31¼, balance of a note P. Barnett give to Lewis $2.31¼.   Jesse Poe, Admr.

(p. 62) Court proceeded to appoint a jury for next term of this Court:

William Smith	John Hill	Joseph Williams	Benjamin Benson
Samuel Looney	Matthew Allen	Isaac Baker	Walter Edwards
Leonard Britewell	Thomas Little	Robert Walker	Peter Majors
Thomas Thompson	Thomas Fulton	Samuel Fry	Samuel Gamble
Samuel Pharis	Samuel Mantooth	Alexander Brown	Kinsey Moore
Samuel Ferguson	John Ferguson junr.	Thomas G. Goad	Thomas Godbehere

David Shelton, a Constable to attend said Court

Jury appointed for next term of Circuit Court:

William Smith	John Robinson	Robert Bell	Isaac Benson
Robert Gamble	William Howard	William Alexander	George Gillespie
John Cozby	James McDonald	Joseph Love	Jesse Thompson
Frederick Fulkerson	Thomas Price	Samuel McDaniel	Jesse Poe
John Witt	Jonathan Fine	John Bailey	James Preston
Cumberland Rector	Moses Thompson	Moses Ferguson	John Lewis
James Smith, Constable to attend Court			Henry Collins

State VS John Taylor. Assault and Battery. James Kelly security in sum of $250 for appearance of Taylor at next term of this Court.

George Gothart VS Mary Cranmore (No. 1291). Abraham Howard and William Smith, refeeres in this Cause returned their judgment: ". . . having fully considered the testimony we are of opinion that Mary Cranmore owes George Gothart nothing, And that the suit be dismissed at Gothards cost."

FEBRUARY TERM 1824

(p. 63) Court of Pleas and Quarter Sessions met on the first Monday and second day of February 1824. Justices on bench— Frederick Fulkerson, George Gillespie, Jonathan Fine, Arthur Fulton, Jesse Thompson, William Kennedy, Daniel Walker, James McDonald, Thomas Cox, Crispien E. Shelton, and William Gamble. (NOTE— first names added by B.J.B.)

James Berry, Clerk of this Court, produced a receipt for $60.97½ in full for the public Taxes by him collected for the County from 4th February 1823 to

1st October 1823. Signed M. Nelson, Treasurer of East Tennessee.
        William M. Smith resigned as Constable.
        William Smith, Carson Caldwell, William M. Smith, and James A. Darwin
"having been appointed by the Legislature of the State of Tennessee Justices of
the peace for the County of Rhea, their Commissions as such being produced to the
Court, the oath of Office together with the other oaths required by the Statutes
in such cases was in the presence of the Court duly administered to them, and
they were requested to take their seats as members of this Court."
        Audley P. Defriese overseer in place of Bruten Peters, resigned.
        Joseph J. Thrailkill overseer in place of John Bennett, resigned.
        Evan Evans appointed overseer of road in place of John Bailey, resigned;
to have all the hands from a line running across the Valley by the Luminary
Meeting House up the Valley so as to include John [sic] A. Darwin.
        Abraham Cox appointed Constable in Capt. Smith's Company; bond with
Miles Vernon and Samuel McDaniel, his securities.

(p. 64) "In pursuance of an Act of Assembly of the State of Tennessee passed at
Murfreesborough the (blank) day of (blank) 1821. The Court proceeded to a classification on which by ballot it appeared that Arthur Fulton, Frederick Fulkerson, Carson Caldwell, Daniel Walker and John Rice esquires were drawn on the first
class for holding this Court for the trial of causes.
        "That James McDonald, Azariah David, John Cozby, Stephen Winton, and
John Robinson esquires were drawn on the second class.
        "That George Gillespie, Crispeon E. Shelton, Thomas Price, Thomas Cox,
and Jesse Thompson esquires were drawn on the third class.
        "That William Smith, William Gamble, William Kennedy, William M. Smith,
and Jonathan Fine esquires were drawn on the fourth class for said purposes."
        Mary Randolph appointed Administratrix "of all and singular the goods and
Chattles rights and Credits of William Randolph deceased and after taking the oath
prescribed by law Entered into the following bond, to wit: Know all men by these
presents, that we Mary Randolph, Samuel Looney, and John Holland and John T. Meriot are held and firmly bound unto William Carroll Governor and his successors
in office in the sum of four thousand dollars, for the payment of which we bind
ourselves our heirs executors and administrators jointly and severally, firmly
by these present; sealed and dated this second day of February 1824.
        "The condition of the above obligation is such that if the above bound
Mary Randolph Administratrix of all and singular the goods and Chattles, rights
and credits of William Randolph deceased, do make or cause to be made a true and
perfect inventory of all and singular the goods and chattles, rights and credits
of the deceased which have or shall come to the hands knowledge or possession of
the said administratrix or into the hands or possession of any person or persons
for her and the same so made to exhibit or cause to be exhibited to the Court of
the County aforesaid within ninety days from the date of these presents, and the
same goods, chattles and credits of the deceased at the time of his death, which
at any time hereafter shall come into the hands of the said Administratrix or into
the hands or possession of any person him do well and truly administer according
to law and further to make or cause to be made a true and just account of said

(p. 65) administration within two years after the date of these presents, and
all the residue of the said goods chattles and credits which shall be found remaining on the said administratrix account the same being first examined and allowed by the Court of the said County Shall deliver and pay unto such person or
persons respectively to which the sum shall be due according to the true intent
and meaning of the act in that case made and provided and if it shall appear that
any Will or Testament was made by the deceased and the executor or executors
therein named do exhibit the same into Court making request to have the same al-

lowed and approved accordingly, if the said administratrix above bound being thereunto required, do render the said letter of administration (approbation of the said Tentament being first had and made in the said Court) then this obligation to be void otherwise to be in full force and virtue."
[signed] Mary Randolph, Samuel Looney, John Holland, John T. Meriot
Signed Sealed and acknowledged in open Court. James Berry, Clerk

Joseph Mee, · Executor of the last Will and Testament of Isaac Rice Senr., dec'd, returned an Inventory of personal estate: 7 Negroes (1 woman & 6 children), 2 Cows & Calves, 1 Bead & furniture, 1 Small Table, 3 pot vessels, 3 puter [sic] basons & 2 dishes, 5 plates, 1 Cotton Wheel, 1 Mans Saddle, 1 Murren hide, 1 flat iron, 1 tin bucket, 2 Chairs.

William Smith to William Moore. Deed of Conveyance for 94 acres; proven by grantor; certified for registration.

William Smith to Mumford Smith. Deed of Conveyance for 133 acres; proven by grantor; certified for registration.

(p. 66) David Day to Wiley Lewis. Deed of Conveyance for 75 acres; acknowledged by grantor; certified for registration.

Abraham Howard to Allison Howard & Mantion Howard. Deed of Conveyance for 90 acres; acknowledged by grantor; certified for registration.

Abraham Howard to David Day. Deed of Conveyance for 80 acres; acknowledged by grantor; certified for registration.

Daniel Walker, Admr. on estate of Jeremiah Duncan, dec'd, on his application is allowed a commission to Thomas Price and John Robinson esquires impowering them to settle the account of said administration.

John Miller, Admr. on estate of Caleb Martin dec'd, allowed a commission to William Kennedy and Henry Collins esqrs. impowering them to settle the accounts of said administration.

Samuel Fry, overseer, to work said road to McDonalds Ferry; William Boldon overseer of road be exempt from keeping up the road he now works.

Ordered that the road leading from Fraziers Ferry as reported at this session be established from said Ferry to Mrs. Lauderdales and that William Johns be overseer of said road; all hands between said road and Richland Creek to Tennessee River.

(p. 67) Jurors appointed for next Court of Pleas and Quarter Sessions:

Patrick Martin	John Jones	John Benson	William Buyce
Isaac Mahan	William Blackwood	James Jacobs	John Lee
Thomas Eaves	Thomas Godbehere	Edward Goad	Moses Ferguson
Lewis R. Collins	James Montgomery	Bruten Peters	Abraham Miller
John A. Smith	Leonard Brooks	Armsted Breedwell	Roger Reece
James Rogers	Benjamin Marberry	William Gladden	John Smith
	Thomas McCarty	Joseph McCall	

On motion of Rebecca Moore, she is appointed Administratrix of all and singular the goods and chattles rights and credits of John Moore deceased and after taking the oath prescribed by law entered into bond with John Locke, her security, for $300. (NOTE— the bond is essentially the same as the bond signed by Mary Randolph on page 19. B.J.B.)

(p. 68) Rebecca Moore, "administratrix and relect of John Moore, returned into Court an Inventory of the property of said John Moore deceased." Stock. 1 horse beast, 5 head of Cattle, 13 head of Sheep, some stock hogs. Household furniture. 2 beads & furniture, 3 bead·steads, 1 table, 1 Chest, 5 Cheers [sic]. Kitchen furniture. 1 Kettle, 1 pot, 1 oven, 1 skillet, 1 pair pot hooks, 1 pair dogirons, 1 smoothing iron, part of a set of knives & forks, 1 pewter disk, 3 plates Do,

2 sets of delf plates, part of a set of cups & saucers, 3 crocks, 4 Bowels, 1 Churn, 2 pails, 1 bigg wheal, 1 little wheel, 1 pair of Cotton Cards, 1 loom, 4 slays, 2 pair of harness, 1 meat tub. Farming Tools. 1 pair of hames & chains, 1 weeding hoe, 1 falling axe, Some books.

James C. Mitchell appointed overseer of Valley Road from Clear Creek to James A. Darwins.

Elijah Evans appointed overseer of road from Snelsons Ferry to where it intersects Waltons Road and to have all the hands from the mouth of Piney Creek to the mouth of McCarteys Creek.

William Gwin allowed $5.00 for making a jury bench.

(p. 69) Ordered that Tuesday of the present Sessions of this Court be set apart for the further transaction of County business.

William Randolph to Samuel Looney. Bill of Sale for sundry property; proven by oaths of Jane Merriot and Elizabeth Dunn, subscribing witnesses; certified for registration.

On motion of William Smith, Admr. of the estate of William French, dec'd, a Jury of View is awarded him to view examine and asertain what damage a road as viewed marked and laid out from Witts bridge upon Richland Creek to Fraziers Ferry passing thro the plantation of said French, dec'd, where the old lane formerly was will be to said farm and whether the public Interest would be as much subserved by turning said Road around said plantation in such manner as not to interfere with the inclosures thereof as to pay the damages by the County occasioned by said road. Lewis Morgan, Abraham Howard, Jesse Witt, William Howard, Alexander Fobes, Cain Able, and William Alexander appointed Jury of View.

Randolph Gibson released from $2.00 tax assessed on his Stud Horse for 1823; Sheriff to pay the said sum to Gibson; Sheriff released upon the settlement of his accounts and he also is released from the payment of the poll tax of the said Gibson and one half of double Tax of said Gibsons Stud Horse for the year.

(p. 70) Ordered that the Clerk issue Certificates to the Guards who guarded Joel McCrory and John Prince in the Jail.

John Parker, Jailor for said County, allowed $54.75 for keeping John Prince, a prisoner from Hamilton County and that the County of Hamilton pay the same.

John Parker allowed $16.75 for keeping John Surcey and William Howell in the Jail.

John Parker allowed $54.00 for keeping Joel McCrary a prisoner in the Jail.

Woodson Francis, Sheriff, allowed $21.00 for guarding Joel McCrary, a State prisoner, from Rhea County to Hamilton County and returning the same to Rhea County.

(p. 71) Charles McClung & James Cozby to Pleasant M. Miller. Deed of Conveyance proven by oaths of John Able and George Birdwell. John Able swears that he saw Charles McClung and James Cozby sign and acknowledge the same and George Birdwell swears that he saw James Cozby sign and acknowledge the same, whereupon it was ordered to be certified for registration to Hamilton County.

William Kennedy, Carson Caldwell, and Crispeon E. Shelton appointed Commissioners to examine and report to Court the situation of the Paupers for the year 1824.

James Willson having been appointed by the Legislature of the State of Tennessee Surveyor for Rhea County and his commission as such being produced, he took the necessary oaths and entered into bond with William Kennedy, Crispein E. Shelton, Isaac Braselton, William Smith, William Gamble, and George Gillespie, his securities.

Sheriff returned list of insolvent persons listed for Taxes: Joseph Churchmon, Benj. Pacy, William Sullivan, Thomas Bell, George Bennett, Lewis Current, William Carter, George Goles, Sion Price, William Varnel, Archibald Moore, John Hoophey, Robt Kelly, Stephen Lea, Jacob Lea, John Underwood, and John Taylor.

(p. 72) Committee (W. Kennedy, C. Caldwell, C.E. Shelton) to examine the paupers reported that James Purser is an aged infirm and indigent man. He was allowed $35.00 per year and Henry Collins was appointed his Guardian for this year.

Benjamin Jones, James Wilson, and Miles Vernon appointed a Commission to settle with William Johnson, Trustee of the County for his former accounts and "to settle with said Johnson on the terms of equity."

Ordered that the road around Orville Paine land as reported by the Jury of View be established.

William Noblet, Biram Breeding, Moses Thompson, James Swann, William Hornsby, George W. Riggle, and James McCanse a Jury of View to lay out and mark a road from Snelsons Ferry to George Gillespies house.

James Wilson allowed $3.00 for running the line of Rhea County up the mountain side of said County.

(p. 73) Justices on bench (3rd February) — Jonathan Fine, Daniel Walker, C.E. Shelton, George Gillespie, Carson Caldwell, Arthur Fulton, William Kennedy, Thomas Cox, John Rice, John Cozby, and Wm M. Smith. (NOTE— first names added by B.J.B.)

Allen Murphree to William Lewis. Power of Attorney proven by oath of Zachariah Harwood, who says he saw Allen Murphree sign seal and acknowledge the same and that he saw James Dunn, the other Subscribing Witness, sign the same, and that Dunn lives in Alabama. Certified for registration.

William B. Lewis, Attorney in fact for the Executors of William T. Lewis, dec'd, to William S. Leuty. Deed of Conveyance for 2000 acres; proven by James C. Mitchell and James Berry, subscribing witnesses; certified for registration.

Ordered that David Roper have in addition to his former hands, all the hands from Thomas Hunters and Henry Newton (including said Hunter and Newton) down the River to the mouth of Goodfield Creek to work on the road he is now overseer of.

Peter Majors released from further attendance as a juror at this Session.

Woodson Francis, Sheriff, returned a list of Jurors summoned to appear at this Session (see list on page 18) out of which

(p. 74) the following were elected a Grand Jury: John Hill, Samuel Mantooth, Thomas Little, Samuel Pharis, Thomas G. Goad, Alexander Brown, John Ferguson junr., Walter Edwards, Matthew Allen, Samuel Ferguson, Thomas Godbehere, Samuel Looney, and Leonard Bridwell. John Hill appointed foreman and David Shelton a Constable to attend the Grand Jury.

There remained of the original pannal, Benjamin Benson.

State VS Benjamin Benson (No. 1292). Affray. Defendant says he cannot gainsay the charges; fined $1.00 and costs.

Grand Jury returned Presentments, the State against William H. West and Samuel Grigsby.

(p. 75) Justices on bench (4th February) — Rice, Fulkerson, Fulton, Caldwell, and Walker.

James G. Martin to John Thompson. Deed of Conveyance for 200 acres; acknowledged by the Grantor; certified for registration.

James G. Martin to Jesse Thompson. Deed of Conveyance for 700 acres; acknowledged by Grantor; certified for registration.

Burley Godsey to John A. Smith & William Ingle. Bill of Sale for a Sorrell Mare and six head of Sheep; proven by Thomas Cox, subscribing witness; certi-

23

fied for registration.

Robert Locke having been appointed by the Legislature of the State of Tennessee Entry Taker for Rhea County and his commission as such being produced here in Court, He the said Robert Locke took the necessary oaths prescribed by law and entered into bond with Thomas Cox, Richard Haslerig, and John Locke, his securities.

State VS John Gossage (No. 1293). Affray. Defendant says he cannot gainsay the charges; fined 6½¢ and costs; William Gossage security for payment.

Ordered that James Wilson, Surveyor for Rhea County, be directed to run the County line between Rhea and Bledsoe counties from Hamilton County line to Roane County line.

(p. 76) State VS John Taylor (No. 1294). Defendant says he cannot gainsay the charges [not stated]; fined 6½¢ and costs.

The following Justices were appointed to take a list of taxable property and polls for this year:

Carson Caldwell	in Captain Brown's Company
William Smith	in Captain Howard's Company
John Robinson	in Captain Riggle's Company
Jonathan Fine	in Captain McCall's Company
Frederick Fulkerson	in Captain Swan's Company
James A. Darwin	in Captain Lewis' Company
William Gamble	in Captain Jackson's Company
William M. Smith	in Captain Smith's Company
Thomas Price	in Captain Wilson's Company
Stephen Winton	in Captain Mee's Company

Andrew Evans permitted to administer on estate of William Floyd, dec'd; bond with Edward Stokes for $200; Letters of Administration issued.

Spencer Benson Sr. to Robert Cozby. Deed of Conveyance for 35 acres; proven by William Smith and Benjamin Benson, subscribing witnesses; certified for registration.

Andrew Evans, Admr. of William Floyd, returned an inventory of estate taken on 10th November 1823: 7 Shoats $7, 1 Sow $3, 1 Shoat $1, 1 Trunk

(p. 77) 7 Shoats $7, 1 Sow $3, 1 Shoat $1, 1 trunk $3.50, 1 Table $1, 1 Walnut Beadstead $1.50, 1 Poplar Beadstead $1.50; 1 pare of Gears Singletree, 1 Gofer Plough $5.75, 2 Hoes & 2 Augers $1.50; 1 Chesel ax & Mattock $1.50, 1 Oven & 1 pot $3.50, 1 large pot $4.00, 2 pair of pothooks 50¢, queensware $1.50, 4 pewter plates, 1 dish & 2 bassons $5.00, 3 knives & 3 forks 37½¢, 1 Saddle & Bridle $1.50, 1 Blanket $1, 1 bead & furniture $15, 1 wheel & Cards $3, 1 draw knife 50¢, 1 Cheek Reel $1, 1 Sifter $2, 4 Sugar barrels $1.50, 100 feet plank 75¢, 18 bushels of corn $4.50— $72.87½

Allowance made by Lewis Wilkerson and Jesse Reese for the support of the widow for one year. Corn 18 bu $4.50, pork 350 lbs $10.50, 1 milk cow $10.00— $25.00

The following was returned on a separate piece of paper: 1 Cow & Calf $15, 1 Looking Glass $1.25, 1 Side Saddle $3.00, 2 Glass tumblers 50¢, 1 Stock Glass 25¢, 1 Coffee Mill $2.00, 1 Cotton Wheel 62¢, 1 bead tick $2.32, 1 Heipher $7.00, Oats 0.00 — $31.92

Grand Jury returned a Bill of Indictment against William Moore for an Assault endorsed on the back a true Bill by the foreman John Hill.

State VS William Moore (No. 1295). Defendant says he is not guilty; case heard by Jury (Benjamin Benson, Thomas Eaves, John Pharris, Daniel D. Armstrong, Robert Locke, William Locke, George McGhee, William Walker, Orlando Bradley, William Cumpton, James Coulter, and James Kelly) which finds the defen-

24

dant guilty as charged; fined $20.00 and costs. Defendant prays an appear to the next Circuit Court; allowed. James Kelly, security; sum of $250.

(p. 78) Mary Walker to Stephen Kelly, her Slave. Deed of Emancipation proven by oaths of James C. Mitchell and James Berry, subscribing witnesses. "Know all men by these presents that I Mary Walker of the Town of Washington and County of Rhea . . . have by these presents for and in consideration of the many faithful services of my Servant Stephen who is my right and property as a slave for life and for and in further consideration of a bond with security to me given by the said Stephen to me the said Mary to support and maintain me well during my life Sold and conveyed the time of the service of the said Stephen during his natural life to him the said Stephen and do hereby emancipate liberate and free the said Stephen from his present bonds and Slavery to me and from all and every or persons claiming the services of the said Stephen thro, or by me and from my heirs executors and assigns forever and hereby giving and granting to the said Stephen all and singuler the priveleges and immunities that a free man of colour is or can by our laws be entitled to forever. Given under my hand and seal this 4th day of February 1824."   Mary   X her mark   Walker (Seal)
Test: J.C. Mitchell & James Berry.
        State VS William Moore. Came Thomas Cox and acknowledged himself indebted to the State for $250; void if he appears at next term of Circuit Court to give evidence.

(p. 79) Benjamin Erwin Junr. VS William Kennedy (No. 1296). Came the parties by their attornies and a Jury: John Hill, Samuel Mantooth, Thomas Little, Samuel Pharis, Thomas G. Goad, Alexander Brown, Walter Edwards, Matthew Allen, Thomas Godbehere, Samuel Looney, Leonard Bridwell, and John Pharis. Jury says "the defendant did assume and take upon himself in manner and form as the Plaintiff did demand the Cow and Calf mentioned in the Defendants second plea at the residence of the said defendant as in his replification he hath alledged and by means of said assumption and the non payment of the said Cow and Calf upon the demand aforesaid assesses the Plaintiffs damage to the sum of ninety nine dollars." Plaintiff to recover the $99.00 plus costs. Defendant prays an appeal to the next Circuit Court.
        State VS William Moore (No. 1297). Peace Warrant. Came Thomas J. Campbell who prosecutes for the State, "as well as the defendant in his proper person and the prosecutor Beriah Frazier having taken the oath prescribed by law in such case and still desiring surity of the peace from the said Defendant. Therefore it is considered by the Court that the said Defendant be held Securities to keep the peace towards all the good people of the State but more particularly towards the said Beriah Frazier in a recognizance . . ." Defendant entered into bond for $500 along with James Kelly and Alexander Forbes for $250 each; to be void "if the said William Moore keeps the peace . . . for one year and one day from this date."
        Ordered that Arthur Fulton be released from the payment of Tax on two Negroes for 1822; Sheriff allowed a credit accordingly on his settlement with the State Treasurer.

(p. 80) Justices on bench (5th February)— Rice, Caldwell, and Walker.
        All causes not tried at this Term are ordered to be continued until next Court.

MAY TERM 1824

(p. 80) Court of Pleas and Quarter Sessions met on the first Monday and 3rd day of May 1824 at the Court House in the Town of Washington. On the bench— Azariah David, James McDonald, William Smith, William Kennedy, Jonathan Fine, Stephen Winton, Daniel Walker, William M. Smith, Carson Caldwell, John Cozby, Thomas Cox, James A. Darwin, Jesse Thompson, John Rice, and Arthur Fulton. (NOTE— first names added by B.J.B.)

David Shelton appointed overseer of road in place of John Gray; said Shelton shall straighten the road so as to go to the bridge at the corner of Crispien E. Sheltons field.

Mansion Howard appointed overseer of road in place of Henry Airhart.

Woodson Francis to Isaac Braselton. Deed of Conveyance for 100 acres; acknowledged by Grantor; certified for registration.

(p. 81) Thomas Cox to John McDaniel. Deed of Conveyance for 177 acres; acknowledged by Grantor; certified for registration.

James McDaniel, John McIntosh, & Samuel Parks by his attorney in fact James McDaniel to James C. Mitchell & Thomas Kelly. Deed of Conveyance for 640 acres in McMinn County; proven by Thomas Cox, James Berry, Samuel McDaniel, and John Rice, the subscribing witnesses; certified to McMinn County for registration.

David Blevins to James Blevins. Bill of Sale for sundry property; proven by oaths of Thomas Cox and Abraham Cox, subscribing witnesses; certified for registration.

Jonathan Brown to Joseph Babb. Bill of Sale for sundry property; proven by James Swann and Phoebe Green, subscribing witnesses; certified for registration.

Charles McClung to Charles Gamble. Deed of Conveyance for 50 acres; proven by Miller Francis, one of the subscribing witnesses (proven by Asahel Rawlings at a Court in Hamilton County); certified for registration.

(p. 82) John Rodgers appointed overseer of road in place of John Kelly.

Ordered that Samuel Applegate and Thomas Swann, hands working on the road under Charles Mitchell, overseer, be taken from said Mitchell and placed under Peter Daniel overseer of the road.

Ordered that the road called the old Hunters Trace be revived and to start from Crispean E. Sheltons house and run through his lane the way the road now runs until it intersects with the old Hunters Trace at Benjamin Jones' Schoolhouse, then with the old trace until it intersects with the Hamilton County line and that John Jones be appointed overseer of said road; to have all the hands on land of Benjamin Jones and Patrick Martin.

John Lillard appointed overseer of road from fork of road that leads from Kellys Ferry to Calhoun to the McMinn County line; Lillard to have the following hands: Josiah Howser, Isaiah Richardson, John Martin, Caswell Hughes, Robertson Piner, Ambler Grubs, John Fowler, Burwell Brumfield, and William Sea.

James C. Mitchell, overseer, to have all the hands on lands of William Goad, Robert Ferguson Dec'd, George Ransom, Henry Walton, Charles Woodward, and James Smith.

Samuel P. Stewart appointed overseer of road in place of Thomas Harp.

William Wilson, William Givens, and John McClure appointed Justices of the Peace by the State Legislature; presented their commissions and took the oath of office; requested to take their seats as members of this Court.

(p. 83) Ordered that the Jurors be allowed 50¢ a day for this year commencing from the first of February.

County Tax for this year to be as follows: on each 100 acres of land, 50¢; each town lot, 75¢; each White poll, 43 3/4¢; on each Black poll, 87½¢; The Jury Tax shall be as follows: on each 100 acres of land, 12½¢; on each Town lot, 25¢; on each White poll, 6¼¢; on each Black poll, 12½¢. And that the Poor Tax shall be as follows: on each 100 acres of land, 18 3/4¢; on each Town Lot, 25¢; on each White poll, 6¼¢; on each Black poll, 12½¢.

Edward Maloney exempted from paying tax on account of his age and poverty.

John Locke and James Berry, Commissioners appointed heretofore by the Court to settle with the Trustee of Rhea County surrenders in open Court their appointment.

Order made at last Session of this Court appointing John Robinson and Thomas Price as commissioners to settle with Daniel Walker, Exr. of last will and Testament of Jeremiah Duncan Dec'd, be revived.

On application of Mary Randolph, she is appointed Administratrix on estate of John Merriott, Dec'd; entered into bond with security. "It appearing to the satisfaction of the Court that at the last sessions of this Court the entry and bond was taken for her to administer on the estate of William Randolph deceased in place of said John Merriott."

Ordered that all that part of the Federal Road from the County line a half mile beyond William H. West and all the hands north of and including said West is to work under William Matlock and all the hands on said road south of said Wests to the foard of Sewee including Gideon Ragland is to work under Elisha Sharp and that William Matlock is to be overseer of said road.

(p. 84) Andrew Evans, Admr. on estate of William Floyd, returned an account of the sales of said estate held February 7-13th 1824:

1 Bead Stead and cord	to	James Coulter	$ 2.50
1 Reel		Peter Daniel	.65
1 Trunk		Abner Rion	4.12½
1 large Iron pot		do do	3.62½
1 Small do do		Thomas Thompson	2.50
1 pr cotton cards		Andrew Evans	.12½
3 knives & 3 forks		do do	.12½
1 Plow		James Coulter	.75
1 Set of Gears &c		Andrew Evans	2.50
1 Swingletree		Roger Reese	.50
2 Augers & 1 Chissell		Andrew Evans	.75
1 pr pot hooks		do do	.06¼
1 Bead & furniture		Elizabeth Floyd	11.00
1 pr pot hooks		James Coulter	.25
1 oven & lead [sic]		E. Floyd	1.08
1 Small Kettle		William Floyd	.76
Cups & Saucers &c		E. Floyd	.57
1 Pewter dish &c		Andrew Evans	6.25
1 Sadle & Bridle		Peter Daniel	1.00
1 Sadle Blanket		Andrew Evans	.06¼
4 Barrels		James Coulter	.50
100 feet pine plank		Elias Majors	.50
1 Womans Sadle		do do	.50
1 Mattock		James Coulter	1.50
1 Weeding hoe		do do	.12½
1 do do		do do	.18 3/4
1 Looking Glass		Andrew Evans	1.29
1 Coffee Mill		Thomas Thompson	1.00
1 Wooling Wheel		Andrew Evans	4.00

2 Tumblers	James Coulter	.37½
18 Bushels Corn	Elias Majors	4.56
a parcel of Oats	William B. Goron	.26
1 Wire Sifter	Andrew Evans	5.25
1 Churn	John Alexander	.37½
1 do	Peter Daniel	.37½
1 Table	Joseph Evans	2.37½
1 Saw, 5 pigs, & 6 Shoats	Andrew Evans	35.00
		43.63½

I certify the above to be true— J. Gordon   C.S.   Feby 14, 1824

(p. 85) The last Will and Testament of John Woodward of Rhea County was exhibited in open Court and proved by the oaths of John Rice and James C. Mitchell, the two subscribing witnesses, and is as follows:

"In the name of God Amen. I John Woodward of the County of Rhea and State of Tennessee, being weak in body but of sound and perfect mind and memory and considering the uncertainty of this mortal life (Blessed be Almighty God for the same) do make and publish this as my last Will and Testament in a manner and form following (To Wit): First I do recommend my soul to Almighty God who gave it and secondly do nominate and appoint my beloved friend Matthew Hubbert of the County and State aforesaid my lawful Executor to dispose of my worldly effects in manner following (To Wit), To my beloved Wife Susannah Woodward I give and bequeath a certain Cow and heifer with all the kitchen furniture and also one sow and two barrows during her life and no longer. I also give and bequeath to my eldest daughter Elizabeth Woodward one feather bead and furniture; also I give and bequeath to my youngest daughter Teareasaa Woodward one feather bead and furniture. All the remainder of my real and personal property I wish my Executor to sell on twelve months credit and pay all my Just debts and if any thing should be left I want it equally divided between my wife and children hereby revoking all former wills by me made. In witness whereof I hereunto set my hand and seal January 6th day A.D. 1824.   John Woodward   (Seal) Signed sealed published and declared by the above named John Woodward to be his last Will and Testament in the presence of us who have hereunto subscribed our names as witnesses in the presence of the testator. John Rice & Jas C. Mitchell"

Ordered that Isaac Baker be allowed $15.87½ for bringing to the jail of this County Robert Cersey and John Howell.

(p. 86) Mrs. Rebecca Moore, Admrx. and relict of John Moore, dec'd, returned an account of sales of said John Moore's property held on 13th February 1824:

5 head of Cattle	$ 4.00	12 head of Sheep	3.00
3 Sows & pigs, 4 Shoats	3.00	1 Black Mare	.25
2 Beads, 3 Beadsteads &		1 Dresser and furniture	2.00
their furniture	8.00	1 Table, 1 Bread Tray, 1 pr Cards,	
1 Kettle, 1 Pot, 1 Skillet,		1 Smoothing Iron, 1 Chest,	
1 Oven, 1 pr fire Irons,		5 Chairs	1.00
1 pr Pot hooks	3.00	1 Loom, 2 Wheels, 2 pr harness,	
1 Falling ax, 1 hoe	.50	6 Stays, 1 Checkreel, 1 pr	
		hames & Chains	3.00

List of goods sold on 1st May 1824: $ 27.75
1 Bible,Harveys Meditations, Youngs Night Thoughts, some phamplets   1.00
        [signed] Rebecca   X her mark   Moore $ 28.75

Palatiah Chilton, K. Cooper, David Caldwell, Henry Airhart, Samuel Hackett, Audley Defriese, and William Poteat appointed Jury of View to mark and lay off a road the nearest and best way so as not to interfear with any improvements

from Kellys Ferry to intersect the turnpike road at Witts Bridge on Richland Creek.
John Y. Smith produced his licence as a practicing Attorney at Law.

(p. 87)   Jurors appointed for next term of this Court:

Edward Goad	Robert Ferguson	Aron Ferguson	Joshua Green
James (blank)	James Kelly	Ruben Jackson	William Jewell
Edward Gaskin	Joseph Martin	Rezin Rawlings	Orlando Bradley
Byrum Breeding	James McCanse	Farley Brady	John C. Simpson
Thomas McCarter	Allen Gentry	James Nail	Joshua Kelly
	John Arington	John W. Mee	

Jurors appointed for next term of Circuit Court:

James Swann	Matthew Hubbert	Samuel Howard	James Coulter
Jesse Poe	William McDonald	John Able	Samuel Gamble
Caswell Hughes	James Montgomery	Thomas Henry	William Noblet
James Snelson	Absolam Fooshee	Benjamin Bond	John Roddy
John B. Swann	James Rogers	Edward Stewart	John Baker
Adam Cole	Abel Arington	William Hamon	Robert Pharis

Ordered that the road as heretofore marked out from Fraziers Ferry passing French's Mill to Witts Bridge on Richland Creek be discontinued from said French's Mill to said Mill bridge.

Order made at last Session for a Jury of View to lay off and mark a road from Snelsons Ferry to the house of George Gillespie be revived; William Noblet, Biram Breeding, Moses Thompson, James Swann, William Hornsby, George W. Riggle, and James McCanse Jury of View.

Elijah Runnels appointed overseer of road in place of James Moore.

"On application of George W. Churchwell by attorney intimating his intention to apply for a Licence to practice law and the Court being satisfied that he has attained the age of twenty one Years and that he has been a citizen of this County for twelve months and has always demeaned himself as a good and worthy citizen and man of honesty morality and probity, It is therefore ordered that the same be certified."

(p. 88)   Joseph Love, Henry Collins, and William T. Gillenwaters appointed Commissioners to settle with the collector of Tax and County Trustee; Commissioners took oath and entered into bond with James C. Mitchell and Orlando Bradley.

John Kennedy, Thomas Kennedy, William Kennedy & others, heirs of Daniel Kennedy, dec'd, to Valentine Sevier. Deed of Conveyance for one half or moiety of 200 acres of land in Green County, Tennessee, was acknowledged by William Kennedy, Mary Rawlings, Rezin Rawlings, John McClure, and Margaret McClure, wife of John, who was first examined privately and apart from her husband by the Court as the law directs and said Deed was continued for further proof.

John Y. Smith and Henry S. Purris were appointed Commissioners to examine Polly Ann Rawlings, wife of Rezin Rawlings, she being unable to attend Court from ill health, as touching her free will and consent in signing & sealing a deed of conveyance from the heirs of Daniel Kennedy dec'd (she being one of the heirs) to Valentine Sevier in Greene County.

Report of James Wilson, Surveyor: "In pursuance of an order . . . I proceeded to run and designate the lines between Rhea and Bledsoe counties agreeable to an act of assembly passed at Murfreesboro 28th of Sept 1821 which runs as follows: BEGINNING at a white oak corner of Hamilton County standing on the est [sic] end of a knob about half a mile above the gap where Keedys road to Washington comes up the mountain and opposite the head branch of Sale Creek, thence north seventy east crossing a creek of Sequatchey about twenty poles from where it empties down the mountain about one mile from the beginning, thence crossing several branches of Sale Creek to the bridge on the Kiuka Turnpike road, thence north thirty nine east crossing two large creeks and several branches of Richland and some branches of Piney to Looneys turnpike road leaving Julius Sanders house, formerly the house of R. Walker Jr. in Bledsoe County

(p. 89)   thence north twenty nine and a fourth degrees east crossing six creeks and a large number of Branches of Piney, ten creeks and a great number of small branches of Whites Creek leaving the plantation of Wm Butler about half a mile in Rhea, David Knox eighty poles in Bledsoe, McClendens about sixty poles in Rhea, thence on to Burkes turnpike gate late of T. Bounds on the old Cumberland road designated by two blazes fore and aft and two chops under each blaze, side line trees two chops facing the line. Done the 27th of April 1824.   J. Wilson "
        James Wilson allowed $143.50 for his services and expence in running the County line.

(p. 90)   Justices on bench (4th May)— David, Cozby, McDonald, and Robinson.
        Woodson Francis, Sheriff, returned a list of jurors summoned to appear at this Session (see list on page 20), out of whom the following Grand Jury was elected: James Montgomery, Abraham Miller, John Lea, Roger Reece, Edward Goad, Joseph McCall, John Jones, Thomas Godbehere, Leonard Brooks, Thomas Eaves, Isaac Mahan, Armstead Bredwell, and John Smith. James Montgomery appointed foreman and David Shelton, a Constable, was sworn to attend the Grand Jury.
        There remained of the original pannel: Bruten Peters, John A. Smith, James Jacobs, Patrick Martin, and William Gladden.
        Samuel Craig to Susannah Lewis. Bill of Sale for sundry property; acknowledged by the maker; certified for registration.

(p. 91)   William Lowrey & Irby Holt, Admrs of Isaac Rice, dec'd VS Thomas Hopkins (No. 1298). Came the plaintiffs by attorney and the defendant not having made any defence, Judgment is entered against him for $1165.40 debt, deducting the sum of $839 credits on the writing obligatory, leaving a balance of debt of $326.40 and the further sum of $199.80 damages occasioned by the detention thereof. By order of the plaintiffs, execution is stayed for three months.
        James C. Mitchell for Sebourn Jones VS Thomas Hopkins (No. 1299). The defendant not having made any defence, Judgment is entered against him for $817.66 2/3, the debt mentioned in the declaration and the further sum of $67.00 damages, plus costs.
        Andrew Hunter VS Thomas York. Appeal. Came Isaac Baker and acknowledged himself the Defendants security for the prosecution of the appeal in this cause.
        Andrew Hunter VS Thomas York. Edward Stewart acknowledged himself the Plaintiffs security that in case the appeal should go against him that he will pay all costs or he will do it for him.

(p. 92)   Matthew Stephenson VS William Floyd (No. 1300). Plaintiff dismisses his suit; Defendant to recover his costs from plaintiff.
        John B. Swann VS Andrew Evans (No. 1301). Plaintiff by attorney moved the Court for judgment against Defendant for $5.62½ paid by the plaintiff as security for the defendant; Court concurs and orders the defendant to pay the $5.62½ debt plus $1.25 interest.
        Isaac Benson VS Jehu Geren (No. 1302). Richard Haslerig who was summoned as Garnishee by the Sheriff to appear at the present Sessions of this Court to declare on oath what he owed to the said Defendant, appeared and declared "that he did Some time since executed his bond to the defendant, and if he had not assigned the same, he was indebted to the Defendant the sum of thirty Dollars with interest. Whereupon it is adjudged and considered by the Court that the plaintiff recover against the said Garnishee Richard Haselrigg the sum of thirty Dollars for which execution may issue. Yet nevertheless that the judgment shall

not be binding upon the said Richard if the said bond may have been assigned previous to the service of the garnishment upon the said Richard Haselrigg in this suit and that execution stay for that event."

(p. 93) Deed of Conveyance from the heirs of Daniel Kennedy, Dec'd, to Volentine Sevier for one half or moiety of 200 acres of land in Green County was duly acknowledged in open Court by Allen Kennedy one of the heirs.

John Y. Smith and Henry S. Purris reported that they had examined Polly Ann Rawlings, wife of Rezin and one of the heirs of Daniel Kennedy, dec'd. She acknowledged that it was of her own free will and consent and without the coersion of her husband or any other person. The Deed is continued for further probate.

(p. 94) Justices on bench (5th May) — David, McDonald, Robinson, and Cozby.

State VS Samuel Grigsby. Affray. Defendant who was heretofore bound in a recognizance of $200 to appear here and answer a charge of the State for an affray, did not appear "although solomnly called." Considered by the Court that he forfit his recognizance in the sum of $200 and that a Sieri facias issue against him returnable to next session of this Court.

State VS John W. Mee. Security for the appearance of Samuel Grigsby. For his failure to bring into court the body of said Grigsby, Mee to forfeit his recognizance of $100.

State VS William H. West. Affray. Defendant to forfeit his recognizance of $250 for failing to appear in Court when called.

State VS John Burton (No. 1303). Assault and Battery. Defendant says he is guilty as charged; fined 6¼¢ plus costs.

(p. 95) Matthew Hubbard, Exr. of last Will and Testament of John Woodward, took the necessary oath and entered into bond with Woodson Francis and John Robinson, his securities.

Henry Collins and William Kennedy, Commissioners to settle with John Miller, Admr. of Caleb Martin, dec'd, returned the following settlement:

Pr proven Acct from James Ferguson	$	2.50
Do Robert Beard		9.00
Do James C. Mitchell		4.12½
Do Charles Woodward		3.50
Do Robert Ferguson		2.00
Do Jonas Wassum		1.00
Burial expenses		7.75
To 5 days services settling said estate		5.00
To provisions furnished the widow		7.75
To 1 Note of hand pr David Barkley		35.52
To 1 Note to Robert Beard Senr.		13.25
To 1 Note to John Martin		9.75
To Clerks fees		2.00
To Commissioners fees for settling said estate		2.00
Total Amount	$	105.14½
Amount of the estate		164.83½
Due the estate		59.69

Settled by us this 29 April 1824 as Commissioners above mentioned.

Grand Jury returned a Bill of Indictment against James Daniel for an assault and battery; against John Burton for an assault and battery; also a Presentment against John Ball for an affray.

(p. 96) On application of Joseph Harwood and by consent of Mary Chapman, widow
of John Chapman, Dec'd, he is appointed administrator on estate of John Chapman.
Entered into bond with John Robinson, his security.

John Rice, John Robinson, and Daniel Walker appointed to set apart a
years provisions for the widow and family of John Chapman.

AUGUST TERM 1824

(p. 97) Court of Pleas and Quarter Sessions met on first Monday and 2nd day of
August 1824. Justices on bench— John Cozby, Crispian E. Shelton, Arthur Fulton,
John Robinson, Thomas Cox, George Gillespie, Daniel Walker, John Rice, William
Smith, William Kennedy, Carson Caldwell, Jonathan Fine, James A. Darwin, William
M. Smith, William Givens, John McClure, James McDonald, Azariah David, and
Stephen Winton.   (NOTE— first names added by B.J.B.)

Charles McClung & James Cozby, by William Smith, their attorney in fact
to Charles Gamble. Deed of Conveyance for 200 acres in Hamilton County; proven
in part by Robert Cozby; ordered to be certified for further probate to Hamilton
County.

Ordered that the road leading from Fraziers Ferry to Mrs. Lauderdales
be a second class road and in addition to the former hands that work on said road
all the hands on Tennessee River from John McCandless to the Mouth of Richland
Creek including John Moore, Charles Ryon, John Singleton, and John Bolin shall
work on said road.

Woodson Francis allowed $6.00 for keeping a Jury at Adam W. Caldwells
over night and to breakfast next morning.

Woodson Francis allowed $5.00 that he paid to a poor person who was
likely to become an expense to the County.

(p. 98) Wiley Lewis appointed overseer of road in place of Joshua Tindle.
Robert Gamble, Benjamin Bond, James Caisey, Benjamin McKinsey, John
Roddy, and Jesse Marten appointed Jury of View to lay off and mark the road
leading from McDonalds Ferry on Tennessee River to the McMinn County line.

Joseph Love allowed $8.00 for four days settling with the Collector and
Trustee of this County.

Henry Collins allowed $8.00 for four days settling with the Collector
and Trustee of this County; also $3.00 for a bound Book to enter said settlement.

William T. Gillenwaters allowed $10.00 for four days settling with the
Collector and Trustee and one day entering said settlement in a Book.

James Walker appointed overseer of road in place of Peter Daniel.

Rector Preston appointed overseer of road in place of James Smith.

(p. 99) Jesse Thompson & Jane W. Thompson, his wife & others, heirs of Absolam
Looney, Dec'd to John W. Looney. Deed of Conveyance dated 2nd August 1824 for
an undivided 11th part of a tract of land in Madison County, Alabama. Acknowledged by Jesse Thompson and Jane W. Thompson, after having been privately examined separate and apart from her husband; ordered to be certified for further
probate.

George W. Churchwell and Thomas N. Clark produced their Licences as
practicing attornies of law.

Andrew Kincannon appointed Constable in Capt. Miller's Company; bond
with Miles Vernon and Thomas Price.

Samuel F.D. Swan appointed Constable in Captain Swan's Company; bond
with John B. Swan and William T. Gillenwaters.

32

Jehu Kerns allowed $33.00 for keeping Cameral Loyce, a poor boy, for 12 months past, he having undertook at the last August Session to keep him for $44.00, but releases the County of three months pay.

(p. 100) Thomas Price and John Robinson, Commissioners appointed to settle with Daniel Walker, Exec. of last Will and Testament of Jeremiah Dunkin, dec'd, returned the following settlement made by them with the Executor:

To amount of Sales as returned per inventory to Aug Session 1820	$ 1840.34
Additional Inventory Novr Sessions 1820	156.25½
Ditto Feby Sessions 1821	108.35
	$ 2104.94¼

Contra

By Gdn Fines receipt	12.50	By Guardian Fines receipt	40.00
Ditto	55.93 3/4	Ditto	3.50
Ditto	100.00	Ditto	6.20
Ditto	90.85	Ditto	200.00
Ditto	7.24	Ditto	67.09½
Ditto	3.60	Gdn Worleys Receipt	107.53
Ditto	25.00	Ditto	404.50
Ditto	42.07	Ditto	10.00
Ditto	60.00	Ditto	4.00
Ditto	170.00	Ditto	132.14
Ditto	40.51	Ditto	216.72
Ditto	2.00	Col. Johnsons Receipt	1.50
		Sheriff Francis' Receipt	2.00

(p. 101)

Doctor Stouts account	9.00	G.W. Riggles acct	2.50
Esqr. Robinsons Act	3.87½	James Wilsons act	8.00
Clerk Berrys account	.80	Jane Walkers act	8.00
Jasper Romines act	3.33 1/3	William Leutys act	12.06½
Sheriff Johnsons Receipt	4.68 3/4	John Murfree act	1.87½
Ditto	4.68 3/4	William Putmans act	42.90
Sheriff Francis receipt	8.25	Daniel Rect	3.56½
David Leutys account	6.00	Shff Francis rect	21.87½
Shff Johnsons rect	26.93 3/4	John Myers act	12.75
William Noblets account	.50	G. Walkers act	10.00
Shff Francis acct	21.37½	Mary Dunkins rect	10.50
Doctr Wrights Note	11.65		2051.67½
By Joshua Atchleys act	9.66 2/3	Due the estate & unsettled	53.26 3/4
James Wilsons acct as Clk	2.00		$ 2104.94¼

We certify the foregoing is a true statement of our settlement.

Benjamin Putman released from the payment of tax on one White poll for present year.

(p. 102) Matthew Hubbart, Exr. of the last Will and Testament of John Woodward, dec'd, returned an Inventory of said estate:

Tract of land 80 acres more or less; one half of a note of hand on Samuel Craig for $32.00; one half of 100 Gallons of whiskey due from Henry Airhart, 2 horses, 6 head of cattle, 22 head of hogs, 1 shovel plough, 1 gofer plough, 1 pr hames chains & back bands, 1 hoe, 1 axe, 1 drawing knife, 1 Iron wedge & hammer, 2 Clives, 2 feather beads & furniture, 1 Bead stead, 1 Side Saddle, 1 Mans Saddle, 1 table, 11 delf plates, 6 bowls, 11 tea cups & 2 saucers, 7 knives & 6 forks, 1 pot, 1 oven & a skillet & lid, 1 smoothing Iron, Coffee pot & pot hooks, 3 chairs & 2 chair frames, 1 pail & 2 piggens, 1 washing tub, 2 meal barrels, 1 fat kann, 1 Cotton wheel & cards, 1 check reel, 4 crocks, 2 small Jugs, 3 bottles, 1 wine glass, 1 wooden box, 1 bridle, 1 looking glass, 1 sickle, 1 half bushel.

Account of sales of estate of John Woodward as reported by Matthew Hubbart, Exr. of last Will and Testament:

Benjamin Erwin Jun.	a walnut beadstead	.56¼
Ditto	5 chairs	1.56¼
William Johnson	2 Crocks	.68 3/4
Matthew Hubbart	2 Jugs	.18 3/4
Samuel Logan	2 bottles	.75
Widow	a looking glass	.12½
William Gwin	a Smoothing Iron	1.00
James C. Mitchell	an Iron wedge	.50
Matthew Hubbart	an axe	.31¼
Henry Walton	a hoe	.31¼
James C. Mitchell	Haimes and drawing chains	2.75
Benjamin Erwin Jun.	Drawing knife and sickel	.18 3/4
Wm Woodward	a shovel plough and stock	1.50
Ditto	bull tongue plough	.31¼
Charles Woodward	2 Cleveses, a hasp &c	.50
Henry Collins	a hammer	.25
Wm Woodward	a half bushel and churn	.31¼
Widow	a washing tub	.31¼
(p. 103)		12.12½
Benj Erwin Jun.	Cotton wheel & check reel	.87½
Wm Woodward	2 Meal tubs	.25
George Ransum	2 barrows 1st choice	8.00
Orlando Bradley	a Sow & 5 pigs	2.12½
Ditto	a black sow & 5 pigs	1.50
Edmund Bean	a Sow & 5 Shoats	4.50
Matthew Hubbart	a Mans Saddle	2.62½
Widow	a Side Saddle	.50
Benj. Erwin Junr.	a pine table	.56¼
Spilsby Dyer	a Cow & Calf	14.07¼
Wm Lewis	a heifer 2 Years old	6.75
James C. Mitchell	a horse	50.00
John Rice	a pony	31.00
Widow	Cotton Cards	.06¼
William Woodward	tract of land, 80 acres more or less	365.00
		$ 497.94 3/4

John Miller appointed Constable in Capt. Lewis' Company; bond with James A. Darwin and Henry Collins.

Edward Goad produced three Wolf scalps.

Samuel B. Ferguson produced one Wolf scalp.

(p. 104) John Jones & Henry Collins to James Darwin. Deed of Conveyance for 303 acres; proven (as to John Jones signing the same) by oaths of Joseph Rice and Robert Small, the two subscribing witnesses; Henry Collins acknowledged the deed to be his act; certified for registration.

James Coulter to Abraham Howard. Bill of Sale for a Negro Boy named Eseck; acknowledged by Coulter; certified for registration.

Miller Francis to Thomas Cox. Certificate for No. 364 for 160 acres in Hiwassee District; proven by John Locke, subscribing witness; certified for registration.

Thomas Cox to Merideth Cox. Certificate No. 364 for 160 acres in Hiwassee District; acknowledged by Thomas Cox; ordered to be certified.

John Runnels to keep Mary Owens for 12 months for $45.00.

Asahel Johnson released from Tax on one white poll and one black poll.

(p. 105) "An orphan child named Leroy Pope Chapman bound to Micajah Howerton to live with him after the manner of a bound apprentice until he shall attain to the age of 21; at his freedom he is to give him a horse worth $40, a saddle and Bridle worth $20, and a good sute of cloths, besides the cloths he may then have and during his apprenticeship to learn him to read write and cypher to the rule of three and to treat him in a suitable manner for his station."

An orphan boy named George Chapman is bound to John Robinson (same as above except horse worth $50 and Saddle & bridle worth $11).

An orphan boy named James Madison Chapman bound to James A. Darwin (same agreement as with Micajah Howerton).

An orphan boy named George Davis bound to John Thompson until age of 21; to give him one years schooling; at his freedom to give him a horse worth $40 and a good suit of cloths besides the clothing he may then have.

(p. 106) An orphan child named Polly Johnson bound to Abner Witt to live with him after the manner of a bound apprentice until she reaches the age of 13, at which time he is to give her one genteel suit of cloths besides the clothing she may then have and during her apprenticeship to learn her to read and write and to treat her in a suitable manner for her station.

An orphan child named Columbus Johnson is bound to Abner Witt until he attains the age of 21, and "at his freedom to give him one genteel sute of cloths besides the clothing he may then have and one set of bench plains and during his apprenticeship to learn him the art and mastrey of the cabnet making business and lern him to read write and cypher to the rule of three . . ."

Ordered that Edward Guasgins keep Mary David until next session of this Court for which he is to be allowed $10.00.

Ordered that the road from Snelsons Ferry to George Gillespies be established as reported by the Jury of View and that Matthew Allen be overseer of the same and to have John Smith, James Smith, Alexander McCall, Moses Thompson, William Johnson, and George Gillespie as hands to work under him.

Ordered that John Mahan and John Hughes hands now working on the road under Benjamin Mabury work under David Shelton, overseer, and all the hands on John Sullivans land subject to work on the road is to work under said Shelton.

(p. 107) "On application of Alexander McCall by William C. Dunlap his attorney, a Jury of View is awarded him to view examine and acertain what damages a road as viewed and marked out from Snelsons Ferry to George Gillespies house passing thro the plantation of said McCall will be to said farm and that a writ Ad quadammum issue to John Foshee, Absalom Foshee, Elijah Evans, William Johnson, James Snelson, James Preston, Isaac Baker, Samuel Applegate, Landon Rector, Thomas McCarty, William McCarty, and Benjamin McCarty and that they report to the next session of this Court."

Wilson C. Kilgore appointed overseer of road in place of Jehu Kerns,

Jurors summoned to appear at next session of this Court:

Abner Witt	Samuel Howard	John Able	Cumberland Rector
Robert Cooley	John Taff	John Holland	David Caldwell
Samuel R. Hackett	John Bailey	John Chattin	Vaden H. Giles
Isaac West	Semion Jackson	Charles Woodward	William Woodward
John C. Simpson	Jacob Runnels	Joshua Green	Patrick Martin
William Gladden	Moses Paul	James Rogers	James Ferguson
David Shelton, Constable to attend			Jackson Howerton

Palatiah Shelton appointed overseer of road from the Town line to Kelleys Ferry; to have the following hands: John Stokes, George Stokes, John McClure, James Chanly, William Poteat, Kennedy Cooper, Alexander Caldwell, Samuel Hackett, Riley McGee, Richard McCandless, and Jacob Runnels.

"Ordered by the Court that 1000 acres of land the property of the Heirs of Edward Gant which the Tax was paid for in the Year 1823 but not listed, be entered here of record as tho it had been listed the same being reported and paid by John Cozby esquire."

(p. 108) Joseph Harwood, Admr. of estate of John Chapman, dec'd, returned an account of the sales of said estate on 5th June 1824:

Joseph Harwood	19 head of hogs	16.50
Malikiah Harwood	3 hogs	3.50
Mary Chapman	a Cow and Calf	12.00
Ditto	a handsaw	3.18 3/4
Thomas Hamilton	1 Drawling knife	1.06¼
Elihu D. Armstrong	1 auger	.37½
Samuel Minick	1 froe & Iron wedge	.87½
Mary Chapman	1 Chisel	.31¼
Thomas Piper	1 Chisel	.18 3/4
Thomas Preswood	1 round Shave	.37½
James Piper	1 Jointer	.87½
Samuel Minick	1 Chisel	.12½
James Piper	Shoemaker tools	1.25
Mary Chapman	Slay tools	.25
Thomas Preswood	1 Croas	.06¼
Mary Chapman	1 falling axe	2.12
Samuel Minick	1 Saddle & 1 axe	4.00
Mary Chapman	1 Churn	.81¼
William Lewis	3 water pails	1.00
Mary Chapman	1 small pot	1.43 3/4
William Guinn	1 skillet	.75
James Piper	1 oven & hooks	2.87½
Mary Chapman	1 large pot & hooks	4.00
Ditto	1 washing Tub	.25
Samuel Craig	1 fire Shovel	.56½
Robert Robinson	1 pickling tub	.50
Thomas Hamilton	1 Arm chair	.75
William Guinn	1 Chair	.50
Ditto	1 Chair	.25
Samuel Minick	4 Chairs	.31¼
Thomas Preswood	2 Chairs	.75
Samuel Minick	1 Sled	.06¼
Daniel Walker	1 Cotton Wheel	1.00
Robert Robinson	1 Grind Stone	1.00

(p. 109)

Mary Chapman	a bread tray and sive	.25
Thomas Hamilton	1 set geers	2.06¼
William Lewis	1 keg	.75
Mary Chapman	1 lot of Cotton	3.06¼
Samuel Minick	1 plough single tree & Clevis	2.37½
Absolom Barnes	1 plough	.87½
John Clack	1 Book	1.00
Absolom Barnes	1 Bible	.87½
Samuel Minick	1 Bible	.75
Mary Chapman	1 Book	.43 3/4
Thomas Preswood	1 hoe	1.00
Elihu D. Armstrong	1 lot of Deer Skins	2.06¼
Mary Chapman	1 dresser & furniture	2.06¼

Abraham Miller	1 looking glass	1.06¼
William Guinn	2 Smoothing Irons	2.00
Mary Chapman	1 bead & furniture	10.50
Ditto	1 pair of Cotton Cards	.25
William Moore	1 bead & furniture	15.62½
Thomas Hamilton	1 bead & furniture	8.62½
John Clack	1 Small pot	.62½
	Whole Amount	$ 119.57¼

N.B. One note of hand given by Spills Bee Dyer for ten Gallons of Whiskey with a credit on the same for $2.50.   Joseph   his X mark Harwood

Matthew Hubbart, Admr. of estate of Robert Ferguson, dec'd, returned an additional amount of sales of said estate sold 12th June 1824:

Widow, Abigale Ferguson	1 pot oven & frying pan	1.00
Ditto	1 Cow and Calf	3.00
Martin Ferguson	1 Cow and Calf	5.00
Ditto	1 Cow and Calf	9.00
Additional Inventory:		$ 18.00

One Note of hand on John S. Burnet for $65 due 25th Dec 1822 on the estate of Robert Ferguson dec'd.

(p. 110) Ordered that the road from Kellys Ferry to Witts Bridge be established as reported by the Jury of View: "beginning at Witts Bridge, thence down the creek to the corner of his field, thence by A. Davids esqr, thence with Kellys new now marked road on to within one quarter of McClures leaving the marked way on past McClures house, thence crossing the branch at the corner of McClures farm to intersect Kellys marked road about half a mile on the other side of McClures, thence on to Kellys and that Jesse Witt be appointed overseer of said road and to have Henry Airhart, John Witt, Samuel Howard, William S. Merchant, Robert Bolton, Azariah David, Charles Witt, Abner Witt, and James Reece to work under him on said road."

Ordered that the Sheriff pay James Wilson $74.25 for running the County line between Rhea and Bledsoe counties.

On application of James Blakely, he is appointed Guardian for Jane Brannum; bond with Miles Vernon and Joseph McDaniel for $500.

State VS Jordan Gibson. A Nolle proseque was entered in this cause in Circuit Court, and the County to pay costs ($12.13) to the several persons thereunto entitled.

(p. 111) State VS Robert Kelton. A Nolle proseque entered by Circuit Court; costs ($9.14) to be paid by County.

State VS Joel McCrary. A Nolle proseque entered by Circuit Court; costs ($10.28) to be paid by County.

Mary Walker presented a petition for the emancipation of her Slave Stephen Kelly, which is as follows:
"State of Tennessee, Rhea County, August Sessions 1824
"To the worshipful Court of pleas and quarter Sessions now sitting, the petition of Mary Walker an aged and infirm lady of the County aforesaid being possessed in her own right according to the law of the land of a certain mullatto man aged about twenty seven Years by the name of Stephen Kelly and she your petitioner being strongly impressed with the truth that all men are by nature equal and feeling the great evil of slavery as existing in this country and being desirous to contribute as much to the hapiness of her fellow beings as lies in her power, And the said Stephen Kelly having been unto her a faithful servant for a long space of time she feals it her duty to emancipate and forever set free the said Slave, Your petitioner therefore prays your Worships in viewing the

(p. 112)   premises to emancipate and set free the said Slave and as in duty bound
your petitioner will ever pray &c."   Mary Walker   X her mark
Witnesses: Robert Locke, Wright Smith, Robert Small, Audley P. Defriese
          "A majority of the acting Justices being present the Court unanimously
Granted the within petition August 2nd 1824."   J. Fine, Chairman R.C.
          "Upon said petition being granted Mary Walker entered into the following
bond: Know all men by these presents that we Mary Walker, William Smith, John
Parker, Palatiah Chilton, and Joseph McDaniel all of the County of Rhea . . . are
held and firmly bound unto Jonathan Fine, Chairman of the Court of Pleas and Quarter Sessions for the County of Rhea aforesaid in the sum of two thousand dollars
sealed with our seals & signed with our names this 2nd day of August 1824.
          "The condition of the above obligation is such that whereas the above
bound Mary Walker hath this day presented her petition . . . praying that the
said Court would emancipate and set free her Slave Stephen Kelly and the Court
being satisfied with the reasons therein set forth have granted her said petition
and liberated the Said Stephen Kelly.
          "Now if the said Mary, William, John, Palatiah, and Joseph shall indem-
nify and save harmless the County of Rhea from any charge that may accrue against
the said County by he the said Stephen becoming chargable upon said County then
the said bond to be void and of no effect otherwise to be and remain in full
force and virtue . . .

(p. 113)   "Whereupon the said Mary Walker having entered into bond with approved
security in the sum of two thousand dollars conditioned as the law directs. It
is therefore considered by the Court that the said Stephen Kelly be hereby released from his bonds of Slavery and be forever emancipated liberated and set free
and be allowed all the privaleges and immunities of other free people of colour
within this state."

          Justices on bench (3rd August) — Gillespie, Thompson, and Cox.
          John W. Mee released from further attendance as a juror at this session.
          Woodson Francis, Sheriff, returned a list of jurors summoned to appear
at this session (see page 28), out of which a Grand Jury was appointed: Aron
Ferguson, Edward Goad, Robert Ferguson, Joshua Green, James Kelly, Ruben Jackson,
William Jewell, Edward Gaskin, Joseph Martin, John Arrington, Byram Breeding,
Farley Brady, and Thomas McCarty. Aron Ferguson was appointed foreman.

(p. 114)   Thomas Thompson, Précilla Thompson, & other heirs of Absolam Looney,
dec'd to John W. Looney. Deed of Conveyance for an undivided 11th part of a
tract of land in Madison County, Alabama; certified for further probate.
          Elizabeth Kirksey VS William Buster. On the affidavit of the Defendant
by his agent James Wilson, this cause is continued until tomorrow upon the Defendant paying the cost of this day.
          State VS James Daniel (No. 1304). Defendant says he cannot gainsay the
charges; fined 50¢ and costs. John Stewart, security for payment.
          Grand Jury returned Bill of Indictment against Miles Vernon for an
assault and battery.

(p. 115)   State VS John W. Mee (No. 1305). Ordered that the forfiture incurred
by the defendant in this behalf as the appearance bail of Samuel Grigsby be set
aside upon the payment of all costs which have accrued.
          State VS Samuel Grigsby (No. 1306). Ordered that the firfiture incurred
by the defendant in this behalf be set aside upon the payment of all costs that
have accrued.
          State VS Samuel Grigsby. Came John W. Mee, security for the appearance

of the Defendant, and surrendered him in open Court in discharge of himself; whereupon James Daniel became security in sum of $250 for the appearance of the Defendant on Wednesday of this term.

State VS Miles Vernon. Lewis Knight, security for the Defendant in sum of $250 for his appearance in Court on Wednesday of this term.

Grand Jury returned a Presentment against Collier Johnson for an affray.

(p. 116) State VS William Jewell (No. 1307). Defendant says he is guilty as charged; fined 50¢ and costs. William Smith, security for payment.

John W. Mee VS Samuel Grigsby (No. 1308). Plaintiff sues for $8.54, the sum paid by plaintiff as security for defendant.

Ordered that the two Indentures entered into yesterday in behalf of Columbus and Polly Johnson, orphan children, and Abner Witt be suspended until the next Sessions of this Court.

Josiah York VS James & John Massey. Cause heard by jury (James Stewart, William Walker, William McCormack, David Caldwell, John Rue, John Able, Eli Renno, John Singleton, Joseph Thompson, Michael W. Buster, Zachariah Harwood, and William Gwin) which says it cannot agree; new trial is entered and cause continued until next term.

(p. 117) Justices on bench (4th August)— Gillespie, Cox, and Thompson.

State VS Samuel Grigsby (No. 1309). Defendant says he is not guilty; jury (William Locke, Isaac Lewis, Eli Renno, Samuel R. Hackett, Mark Massey, Lewis Knight, Thomas Hamilton, Samuel Minnick, William McCormick, John Bailey, William Hill, and Henry Griffet) finds the Defendant guilty as charged; fined 50¢ and costs. William C. Dunlap security for payment of fine and costs.

State VS William H. West. Defendant says he is not guilty; jury (Edward Goad, Robert Ferguson, Joshua Green, James Kelly, Ruben Jackson, William Jewell, Edward Gaskin, Joseph Martin, John Arington, Byram Breeding, Farley Brady, and Aron Ferguson) says it cannot agree; mistrial entered and cause is continued.

State VS Sashwell McClure. William Hale bond for $250 that he will appear at November Session and give evidence in this case.

(p. 118) State VS Miles Vernon (No. 1310). Defendant says he cannot gainsay the charge; fined 50¢ and costs. John Rice security for payment of fine and costs.

State VS William H. West (No. 1311). Ordered that the forfiture incured by the defendant in this behalf be set aside upon payment of costs. Isaac Baker security for payment.

On application of Woodson Francis, John Lea is permitted to swear in as deputy Sheriff.

Grand Jury returned Bill of Indictment, State against Sashwell McClure for an assault and battery; also a Presentment, State against Cain Able for disturbing public worship.

State VS John Witt (No. 1312). Bastardy. Defendant, together with his securities Crispien E. Shelton and James Kelly, stand indebted to State for $1000; (p. 119) void on condition that John Witt "shall abide by and perform whatsoever order and decree the Court may adjudge upon the said John Witt of and concerning a bastard child by him begotten upon the body of Dorcas Taylor and further to keep the County of Rhea free from expense and liability in about and concerning the maintainance of the said child . . . shall pay the said Dorcas Taylor quarterly the sum of $6.25 for the first year commencing on the 4th day of August 1824, making in the whole the sum of $25.00 . . ."

Elizabeth Kirksey VS William Buster. Cause heard by jury: Aron Ferguson, Edward Goad, Robert Ferguson, Joshua Green, James Kelly, Ruben Jackson, Edward Gaskin, Joseph Martin, John Arrington, Byram Breeding, Farley Brady, and Thomas

McCarty. Jury was respited until tomorrow morning.

(p. 120) Justices on bench (5th August)— Thompson, Cox, and Gillespie.
        Elizabeth Kirksey VS William Buster (No. 1313). Jury says the Defendant is guilty and assesses the plaintiffs damage to $15.00. Defendant prayed an appeal to the next Circuit Court; granted.
        State VS William H. West (No. 1314). Defendant says he cannot gainsay the charges; fined 6¼¢ and costs. Isaac Baker security for payment.

(p. 121) Thomas Laymons VS John Rice (No. 1315). Defendant having withdrawn his plea to the plaintiffs declaration, judgment is entered against him for $130 debt and $11.05 damages plus costs.
        Jonathan Fine, Gdn of heirs of Jeremiah Dunkin, dec'd, VS Joseph Williams, James Berry & John Day (No. 1316). Defendants came not but made default; judgment for $200 debt (less $5.00 credit), leaving a balance of $195 debt and the further sum of $16.85 damages plus costs.
        Jonathan Fine, Gdn. &c VS Joseph Williams, John Locke & Rezin Rawlings, Exrs. of Daniel Rawlings Dec'd, & William Johnson (No. 1317). Defendants made default; judgment for $130.85 debt (less $14.00 credit), leaving a balance of
(p. 122) $116.85 debt and $20.18 3/4 damages plus costs.
        Samuel Bunch VS Miller Francis (No. 1318). Defendant having withdrawn his plea to the plaintiffs declaration, judgment is entered for $109 debt and $38.88 damages plus costs.
        Thomas Murphey VS Allen Kennedy. "Came the parties by their Attornies, and the Defendants Demurrer to the plaintiffs replication, being solemnly argued and fully understood by the Court and because it seems to the Court that the matters and things in the said replication of the plaintiff are good and sufficient in law. It is considered by the Court that the Defendants Demurrer to said replication be overruled and that the plaintiff have judgment against the said Defendant in this behalf, to be enquired of in damages by a jury of the County at the next November Session of this Court."
        Orlando Bradley VS William Smith (No. 1319). On motion of the plaintiff by attorney, leave is granted to amend the original Writ in this cause &c.; cause is continued until next Session.

NOVEMBER TERM 1824

(p. 123) Court of Pleas and Quarter Sessions met on the first Monday and 1st day of November 1824. Justices on bench— John Rice, William Smith, Crispien E. Shelton, James A. Darwin, Thomas Cox, Carson Caldwell, Frederick Fulkerson, Daniel Walker, Jesse Thompson, George Gillespie, John McClure, John Cozby, and Thomas Price.   (NOTE— first names added by B.J.B.)
        John Witt appointed overseer of road in place of Jesse Witt; to have hands that Jesse had and David Shelton and William Walton in addition; to work road leading from Witts Bridge to Kellys Ferry, from said bridge to where said road intersects the road at Mrs. Lauderdales.
        Bolin Fine appointed overseer of road in place of James McCanse.
        William Gray appointed overseer in place of David Shelton.

(p. 124) Lewis Wilkerson appointed overseer in place of Abner Majors.
        Joshua Hill appointed overseer in place of Benjamin Marbury.
        James Stockton appointed overseer in place of William C. Wilson.
        David Shelton to Benjamin F. Jones. Deed of Conveyance for 49½ acres; acknowledged by Grantor; certified for registration.
        James G. Martin, Elihu Barkley, and Roger Barton produced their Licences

as practicing Attorneys at Law; having taken the necessary oaths, they are admitted to practice law in this Court.

James Lillard appointed Justice of the Peace by the State Legislature.

John Rice permitted to administer on estate of David S. Williams; bond with David Ragsdale, his security, for $100.

Wright Smith appointed overseer of road in place of Elihu D. Armstrong.

(p. 125) Adam W. Caldwell permitted to keep a house of Ordinary; bond with John Locke and Isaac Braselton, his securities; Licence is granted him.

George Gordon to Willis H. Chapman. Deed of Conveyance for 160 acres in State of Illinois; acknowledged by Gordon; certified for registration in Ill.

George Gordon to Willis H. Chapman. Deed of Conveyance for 160 acres in Illinois; acknowledged by Gordon; certified for registration in Illinois.

George Gordon to Willis H. Chapman. Deed of Conveyance for 160 acres in Illinois; acknowledged by Gordon; certified for registration.

George Gordon to Willis H. Chapman. Deed of Conveyance for 160 acres in Illinois; acknowledged by Gordon; certified for registration.

George Gordon to Willis H. Chapman. Deed of Conveyance for 160 acres in Illinois; acknowledged by Gordon; certified for registration.

George Gordon to Willis H. Chapman. Deed of Conveyance for 500 acres "of land in the Western district on a creek formerly called Grove creek the waters of Obian River" acknowledged by Gordon; certified for registration.

Ordered that David Ragsdale on his application keep Mary David, a poor woman, for 12 months for which he is to be allowed $40.00.

(p. 126) Ordered that an orphan girl named Delila Ledford aged eight years be bound to James Pharis for 10 years and "at her freedom he is to give her one feather bead (weighing 25 pounds) and furniture, one good suite of cloths out of the Store besides the cloths she may have and to give her a Testament and during her apprenticeship he is to lern her to wright and read in the Bible and Testament and to treat her in a suitable manner for her Station."

Solomon Parker and William Parker released from paying a poll tax, they being over age.

Ordered that the Indentures intered into at the last Sessions of this Court between Jonathan Fine, Chairman of this Court, and Abner Witt binding Polly Johnson and Columbus Johnson to said Witt that the same be revoked.

Isaac Baker, James Blackwell, John Thompson, Absolom Majors, Samuel Baker, John Massey, and John Bennett appointed Jury of View to lay out and mark a road from the Rhea & Roane county line at or near where John Majors now lives passing Absolam Majors house and John Thompson Sr.s so as to intersect the old Federal Road at any place between Stephen Wintons and William Wests.

Thomas Little, Thomas Hunter, Jesse Poe, Robert Locke, Joseph Harwood, John Barnett, and Samuel Looney appointed a Jury of View to lay out and mark a road the nearest and best way from James Taylors to Athens so as to intersect the road leading from Kellys Ferry to said Athens.

David Shelton appointed a Constable in Capt. Howard's Company; bond with Jesse Witt and Crispien E. Shelton.

(p. 127) Thomas J. Campbell, Solicitor of 11th Solicitorial District, allowed $50.00 for exofficio services.

Woodson Francis, Sheriff, allowed $50.00 for exofficio services.

James Berry, Clerk of this Court, allowed $40.00 for exofficio services; also $20.00 for making out Tax lists for 1824.

On application of Richard Cooper, ordered by the Court that Eli Ferguson deliver to the Clerk of this Court the said Coopers Pention Certificate issued by

John C. Calhoun, Secretary of War of the United States of America on or before the second day of this Term and that a copy of this order be served on the said Ferguson.

William Helms, Joshua Atchley, John Murfree, Josiah York, and James Stockton appointed a Jury of View to lay off and mark a road leading from the Morganton Road to Athens, starting either above or below James Wilsons the nearest and best way to the County line.

Samuel Humbert, Isaac Baker, James Massey, James Blackwell, John Redmond, John Massey, and John Baker appointed a Jury of View to examine the route from Col. Prestons to George Gillespies Ferry, thence to intersect the Federal Road at William C. Wilsons and report whether a road would be of public benefit on that route and said Gillespie promises to open said road.

(p. 128)   Ordered that the road from Snelsons Ferry to George Gillespies House as established at the last Sessions be discontinued.

Ordered that the bounds of the hands on the road leading from Fraziers Ferry to Mrs. French's Mill be divided and that William Johns the present overseer have all the hands in the following bounds: beginning at said ferry thence up the River so as to include the hands on Fraziers upper place from thence to include Charles Ryon and Francis Reavely to Mud Creek from thence to the river so as to include the place that John Simpson now lives on thence up the river to said Ferry and to work on said road from the ferry to Mud Creek.

Leonard Britewell appointed overseer of road leading from Fraziers Ferry to Mrs. French's Mill from Mud Creek on said road to said mill; to have all the hands within the following bounds: beginning at and running up Mud Creek so as to include the place where John Bowling now lives thence along said road to where it intersects the Washington Road then down Richland Creek to the river thence up the river to the plantation where John Simpson now lives from thence to the beginning.

On application of William McDonald, ordered that the fine assessed against him at the February Sessions 1823 and the costs accrued thereon be set aside and the County pay the costs out of the fines and forfeitures.

Robert H. Jordon appointed a Constable in Capt. Mee's Company; bond with John Thompson, Joseph Thompson, and Avary Hannah

(p. 129)   The following Justices were appointed to take a list of taxable property and polls for this year:

Crispien E. Shelton	in Captain Howard's Company
Arthur Fulton	in Captain Swann's Company
George Gillespie	in Captain McCall's Company
Daniel Walker	in Captain Riggles' Company
John McClure	in Captain Brown's Company
Thomas Cox	in Captain Smith's Company
William Kennedy	in Captain Lewis' Company
James Lillard	in Captain Miller's Company
Thomas Price	in Captain Wilson's old Company
William Wilson	in Captain Mee's Company
William C. Wilson	in Captain White's Company
William Gamble	in Captain Jackson's Company

Jurors appointed for next term of this Court:

William McDonald	Benjamin Marbury	Elias Majors	James Nail
John Smith	Absolam Majors	Micajah Howerton	Robert Love
Rezin Rawlings	Walter R. Paine	Miles Vernon	Jacob Slover
William Ingle	John Igou	William Sillivan	John Greenwood
Allison Howard	Frances Reavely	William Wann	Calvin Robinson
James McCanse	Joseph Thompson	John Walker	Jeremiah Washam
David Shelton, a Constable to attend Court			Joshua Hill

Jurors appointed for next term of Circuit Court:

Edward Gray	Benjamin Jones	Jacob Garrison	Peter Daniel
Jonathan Fine	George Gillespie	John Lewis	Robert Parks
Carson Caldwell	Joseph Love	John Stewart	Abraham Miller
Robert Gamble	William Baldwin	Robert Cozby	James Stewart
John Cozby	Wright Smith	Richd G. Waterhouse	Thomas Atchley
Mumford Smith	James L. Cobb	John Hudson	

David Shelton to attend said Court.

John Hudson to John H. Henderson. Power of Attorney for the collection of certain money in the Commonwealth of Virginia; acknowledged by John Hudson; ordered to be certified.

(p. 130)   Cain Able VS Spencer Benson (No. 1320). Certiorari. Defendant by attorney confesses judgment for the plaintiffs debt and cost [amount not stated]; Benjamin Benson security for payment of debt and costs.

Justices on bench (2nd November)— Smith, Kennedy, Gamble, Gillespie, and Fine.

Isaac Lewis to William B. Lewis, attorney in fact for Exrs. of William T. Lewis, Dec'd. Deed of Conveyance for 200 acres; proven by William Lewis, one of the subscribing witnesses; certified for further probate.

Thomas Blackburn, Mary Blackburn, & Rezin Rawlings to Rezin Rawlings. Deed of Conveyance for several lots in the Southern Liberties of Town of Washington together with 150 acres; acknowledged by Grantors (Mary having been examined separately); certified for registration.

(p. 131)   Woodson Francis returned a list of Jurors summoned to attend at this Court (see list on page 34), out of whom the following were elected a Grand Jury: Samuel R. Hackett, Vaden H. Giles, Cumberland Rector, Jackson Howerton, Moses Paul, Jacob Runnels, Samuel Howard, James Ferguson, Joshua Green, Charles Woodward, Simeon Jackson, David Caldwell, and William Gladden. Samuel R. Hackett elected foreman and David Shelton a Constable to serve the Grand Jury.

There remained of the original pannel: William Woodward, John C. Simpson, John Able, Robert Cooley, and John Taff.

Moses Thompson VS Jesse Gordon & Kitty Gordon (No. 1321). Plaintiff by attorney dismisses his suit upon the Defendant Jesse Gordon agreeing to pay the costs of the same.

(p. 132)   Moses Thompson VS John Gordon (No. 1322). Plaintiff by attorney dismisses suit upon the defendant agreeing to pay costs of same.

Josiah York VS James Massey & John Massey (Nos. 1323 & 1324). Plaintiff dismisses suit and defendants confess judgment for half the costs.

Azariah David VS John Thompson & John Thompson (No. 1325). Isaac Baker, a Constable, returned a Fieri Facias issued by William C. Wilson, a Justice of the Peace, for $13.68 3/4 upon which is the following endorsement: "No Goods and chattles to be found in my County. I. Baker const. Levied on 200 acres of land on Piney River the place where F. Fulkerson now lives." And upon the motion of the Plaintiff by his Attorney George W. Churchwell; ordered that the land be sold to satisfy the plaintiffs debt.

Grand Jury returned Bills of Indictment: State against Jacob Brown for an assault and battery; State vs James L. Cobbs for an assault and battery.

(p. 133)   James Wilson VS Joseph Thompson (No. 1326). Cause heard by jury: John C. Simpson, John Able, John Taff, William Woodward, Robert Cooley, Anson Dearmon, James Stewart, Joseph Casteel, Edmund Howerton, Micajah Howerton, Orlando

Bradley, and Jacob Brison. Jury says "that they find for the defendant the sum of three dollars and seventeen cents the balance upon the set off of accounts due the said defendant."

State VS James L. Cobbs (No. 1327). Assault and battery. Defendant says he cannot gainsay the charges; fined $5.00 and costs. John Clack and Orville Paine securities for payment of fine and costs.

(p. 134)   Justices on bench (3rd November)— Smith, Fine, and Gamble.

Michael W. Buster to Miller Francis. Deed of Trust dated 4th May 1824; proven by Thomas J. Campbell and James Berry, subscribing witnesses; certified for registration.

William Ramsey to Absolam Gleaves. Deed of Bargain & Sale for 1000 acres; acknowledged by Ramsey; certified for registration.

Orlando Bradley VS William Smith. Came the parties by their attorneys Thomas J. Campbell and William C. Dunlap and the Defendants Demurrer to the plaintiffs declaration being solemnly argued and fully understood; it seems to the Court that the plaintiffs declaration is good and sufficuent in law, it is considered by the Court that the Defendants demurrer be overruled. Plaintiff is entitled to a recovery against the Defendant. Ordered that a jury be summoned at next term to enquire of the plaintiffs damages.

Woodson Francis, Collector of Public Tax, by his deputy William Johnson, returned a Supplemental Tax List for 1823 by which it appears that the said collector is chargable with $21.49¼ to be passed to the Credit of the Treasury of Rhea County.

(p. 135)   Richard Cooper VS Eli Ferguson (No. 1328). Came the Defendant and delivered the plaintiffs Pention certificate; plaintiff by attorney discharges his rule upon the defendant, and Edward Stewart confessed judgment for the cost in this behalf expended.

State VS Jacob Brown (No. 1329). Assault and battery. Defendant says he is guilty as charged; fined $5.00 and costs. John Parker and Henry Henry securities for payment of fine and costs.

Andrew Hunter VS Thomas York (No. 1330). Appeal. Cause heard by jury: William Woodward, Robert Cooley, John Taff, William Hill, Eli Ferguson, Orlando Bradley, John McDonnah, Richard A. McCandless, John Lavender, Robert Love, Daniel D. Armstrong, and John B. Hood. Jury finds for defendant who is to recover from the plaintiff his cost in this behalf. Plaintiff prays an appear to next Circuit Court; appeal is granted.

Grand Jury returned Bill of Indictment: State against William Hill for assault and battery.

(p. 136)   State VS William H. Douglas. Cause is continued until next Session; Samuel Romines security for Douglas' appearance in Court.

State VS Cain Able (No. 1331). Defendant says he is not guilty; jury (Samuel R. Hackett, Vaden H. Giles, Cumberland Rector, Jackson Howerton, Moses Paul, Jacob Runnels, Samuel Howard, James Ferguson, Charles Woodward, Simeon Jackson, William Gladden, and Samuel Craig) finds the defendant not guilty; County to pay costs.

Joseph Williams to William B. Lewis, attorney in fact for Exrs. of William T. Lewis, dec'd. Deed of Conveyance for 308 acres was in part proven by oath of Rezin Rawlings; certified for further probate.

(p. 137)   State VS William Hill. Assault and battery. Defendant says he is not guilty; jury (John C. Simpson, John Able, John McDonnah, John Taff, Robert Cooley, John B. Hood, Daniel D. Armstrong, Richard A. McCandless, Robert Love, John La-

44

vender, Samuel Romines, and Vincen Oden) says it cannot agree. By consent of the parties, the jury is withdrawn and a misstrial entered. John Rice and Samuel Howard, securities for the defendants appearance at next Term of Court.

State VS John Griffen (No. 1332). Thomas J. Campbell, Attorney General, with the assent of the Court, a Nolle prosequi is entered in this cause. Came Aron Griffen and confesses judgment for the costs.

Wright Smith VS Hugh Gavin (No. 1333). Defendant makes default; plaintiff to recover the sum of $55.00 debt and $3.89 damages plus costs.

(p. 138) John McGhee, Matthew W. McGhee, & John L. McCarty VS William McCormick (No. 1334). Came the parties by their Attornies and a jury: Samuel R. Hackett, Vaden H. Giles, Cumberland Rector, Moses Paul, Jacob Runnels, Charles Woodward, Simeon Jackson, Joshua Green, James Ferguson, William Gladden, David Caldwell, and Samuel Howard. Jury says that the Defendant has not paid the debt of $127.22 in the plaintiffs declaration nor any part thereof and they assess the plaintiffs damage to $6.37½.

Robert Brabson for the use of James Thompson VS Michael W. Buster (No. 1335). Jury (same as above) says the Defendant has not paid the debt in the plaintiffs declaration nor any part thereof; plaintiff to recover $133.00 debt and $4.65½ damages plus costs.

(p. 139) William Cannon for use of Brown Morgan & Guthrie VS Michael W. Buster & Thomas Price (No. 1336). Jury (same as above) says that the Defendants have not paid the debt of $134 nor any part of it; damages assessed to $9.38.

John Locke VS John Lavender, Edy Lavender & Betheny Lavender (No. 1337). Came the parties by attorneys and a jury (John C. Simpson, Vincen Oden, Vaden H. Giles, Samuel R. Hackett, Jackson Howerton, Orlando Bradley, Samuel Howard, Joshua Green, Simeon Jackson, Charles Woodward, David Caldwell, and William Gladden). Jury says "that the defendants did assume and take upon themselves in manner and form as the plaintiff against them in his declaration hath complained and they do assess his damage by occation thereof to fifty one dollars and twenty five cents." Plaintiff to recover his damages and costs.

(p. 140) Isaac Lewis to William B. Lewis Atty in fact for heirs of Wm T. Lewis, dec'd. Deed of Conveyance for 200 acres acknowledged by Isaac Lewis; certified for registration.

James Berry VS Isaac White, John White, & A.D. Richardson (No. 1338). Plaintiff dismisses this suit upon the defendants paying the costs of the same.

Justices on bench (4th November)— Smith, Kennedy, and Gamble.

Orville Paine VS John Rice & John Robinson (No. 1339). "The rule heretofore entered in this cause to dismiss the Certiorari and Supercedas by the plaintiffs attorney after having been solemnly argued, it is made absolute, and the judgment of the Justices is affirmed amounting to $39.66 and $1 costs, together with the further sum of $1.23 damages . . ." Defendant by attorney prays an appeal in Writ of Error to the Circuit Court; appeal is allowed.

FEBRUARY TERM 1825

(p. 141) Court of Pleas and Quarter Sessions met on the first Monday and 7th day of February 1825 at the Courthouse in Washington. Justices on bench— James McDonald, John McClure, Carson Caldwell, Jonathan Fine, William Smith, James A. Darwin, George Gillespie, William M. Smith, Thomas Price, James Lillard, William Kennedy, John Cozby, Jesse Thompson, Crispian E. Shelton, William Givens, Thomas Cox, and Frederick Fulkerson.   (NOTE— first names added by B.J.B.)

Abraham Miller appointed overseer of road in place of Evan Evans.

Vaden H. Giles appointed overseer of road in place of Samuel Fry.

George Preston appointed overseer of road in place of Elijah Evans.

James Berry, Clerk of this Court, produced a Receipt for $181.20 3/4 in full of the public Taxes by him collected for this County from the first of October 1823 to first October 1824, signed M. Nelson T.E.T.

(p. 142) Archibald Taylor appointed overseer of road in place of Audley P. Defriese, resigned.

Willis H. Chapman produced Licence as a practicing attorney.

Jesse Martin, Stephen Moore, Robert Elder, Miles Vernon, and John Hackworth appointed a Jury of View to turn the road on the land of Samuel McDaniel.

James Walker appointed overseer of road in place of Peter Daniel, resigned.

Jacob Garrison appointed overseer of road in place of Charles Mitchell, resigned.

John Mahan and John Hughes, hands working on road under Wm Gray, be taken from said Gray and attached to the road and work under Joshua Hill, overseer.

On application of James Cowan, he is permitted to administer on the estate of Polly Lauderdale, dec'd (widow of John Lauderdale); entered into bond for $400 with James G. Williams, his security.

James Houser released from payment of poll tax for 1824 as he was not living in Rhea County in time to be taxed.

(p. 143) Abraham Howard, Crispein E. Shelton, and Robert Bell appointed Commissioners to settle with William Smith and James Cowen, Exrs. of the last Will and Testament of William French, dec'd.

Grief Howerton to Jackson Howerton. Deed of Conveyance for 80 acres; acknowledged by Grantor; certified for registration.

Grief Howerton to Micajah Howerton. Deed of Conveyance for 128 acres; acknowledged by Grantor; certified for registration.

Grief Howerton to Edmund Howerton. Deed of Conveyance for 150 acres; acknowledged by Grantor; certified for registration.

Jesse Martin, William Baldwin, Vaden H. Giles, Matthias Benson, John Chattin, and Robert Bell appointed Jury of View to turn part of the road leading from McDonalds Ferry to the Town of Athens to turn off from Samuel Frys to pass by the Widow Blythes and Jacob Conners and then the nearest and best way to intersect the other road.

Williamson Todd appointed overseer of road in place of John Miller, resigned.

John Rogers appointed overseer of road in place of John Kelly, resigned.

(p. 144) Samuel Price appointed overseer of road in place of Joseph Thrailkill, resigned.

William Moore appointed overseer of road in place of Zachariah Harwood.

Robert Ferguson appointed overseer in place of Lewis R. Collins, resigned.

James Wilson and Randolph Gibson appointed Justices of the Peace by the State Legislature.

Robert Elder, Leonard Brooks, William Tillary, John Ramsey, and Andrew Kincannon appointed Jury of View to examine a road lately cut out from William Tillarys to Leonard Brooks.

Grief Howerton, Jackson Howerton, Edmund Howerton, James Darwin, and Micajah Howerton appointed Jury of View to turn a road on the land of John Lewis.

James Smith appointed Constable in Capt. McCall's Company; bond with George Gillespie and Joseph McCall, his securities.

(p. 145) Allen Kennedy, Richard Haslerig, and David Caldwell appointed Commissioners to settle with Andrew Evans, Admr. on estate of William Floyd, dec'd.

In pursuance of an act of the General Assembly of the State passed at Murfreesborough in 1821, the Court proceeded to a classification on which by ballot it appeared that John Rice, James A. Darwin, Thomas Cox, John Cozby, William Kennedy, Frederick Fulkerson, and Arthur Fulton were drawn on the first class for holding this Court for the trial of causes.

And that James Lillard, Stephen Winton, Randolph Gibson, Crispein E. Shelton, William Smith, William Givens, and Azariah David on the second class.

And that Jesse Thompson, William M. Smith, George Gillespie, Thomas Price, John Robinson, and Daniel Walker on the third class.

And that James Wilson, William C. Wilson, John McClure, James McDonald, Carson Caldwell, and William Gamble on the fourth class for the above purpose.

Ordered that the County Tax for this year shall be: on each 100 acres of land, 25¢; on each white poll, 25¢; on each Town lot, 25¢; on each black poll, 50¢. And that the Jury Tax shall be: on each 100 acres of land, 6¼¢; on each white poll, 6¼¢; on each Town lot, 6¼¢; on each black poll, 12½¢.

And that the Poor Tax shall be: on each 100 acres of land, 6¼¢; on each white poll, 6¼¢; on each Town lot, 6¼¢; and on each black poll, 12½¢.

Woodson Francis, Sheriff, to Jesse Poe. Deed of Conveyance for 1500 acres; acknowledged by Francis; certified for registration.

(p. 146) Ordered that the precinct election heretofore authorized to be held at the house of James McCanse be hereafter held at the house of Moses Thompson, under the rules and regulations prescribed by laws for the precinct elections at the house of said McCanse.

Edward Guaskin allowed $10.00 for keeping Mary David, a poor woman.

Cain Able permitted to keep a house of Ordinary; bond with securities (not named).

Jurors appointed for next term of this Court:

William Howard	John Witt	Jacob Beck	William Carnahan
James Jacobs	Archabald Taylor	William Locke	Roger Reece
Joshua Kelly	David Cooper	Edward Templeton	James Snelson
Biram Breeden	George Marlow	Bartholomew Gwin	Peter Fine
Tavner Mason	Henry Hackworth	Robert Taylor	John Acred
John Mee	William McCarty	Benjamin McCarty	Samuel Gamble

David Shelton, a Constable to attend Court   William Lea

Miles Vernon, Samuel Looney, Samuel Tillary, Thomas Lucas, and David Blevins appointed a Jury of View to lay off and mark a road from Kellys Ferry up Goodfield Creek near Thomas Cox's Mill so as to intersect the road leading from Rosses Ferry a small distance above the house of Samuel Tillary.

Ordered that the road leading through the land of John Lewis as reported by a Jury of View appointed at this session be turned and that the overseer work on said road as turned.

(p. 147) Ordered that the road which has been lately cut out as reported instanter by a Jury of View appointed at this session leading from William Tillerys to Leonard Brooks be established.

Ordered that the road leading through the land of Samuel McDaniel as reported by a Jury of View appointed at this session be turned and that the overseer work on said road as turned.

Ordered that a former order for a road leading from Prices Ferry to the Town of Athens in McMinn County be revived and that John Farmer, Samuel Price, Avary Hannah, Willie Murphy, Jacob Helm, Joseph Thrailkill, Joshua Atchley, and Thomas Atchley be a Jury of View to lay out and mark a road the nearest and best way to the McMinn County line to intersect the McMinn County Road.

Ordered that the road as reported by the Jury of View appointed at the last session leading from James Taylors to Athens be established; from James Taylor's leaving the big ridge to the left up the big hollow to James Lillards past Bredwells Still House to the County line.

Jonathan Fine resigned as Chairman of this Court.

John Rice appointed Chairman of this Court in place of Fine.

Jacob Runnels and all the hands on the land of John McCanless to work under Joseph Love, overseer of the road, and said Love to be overseer of road from where Kellys Road crosses the Washington Road down to the Grassy Branch.

(p. 148) Woodson Francis, Sheriff and Collector of Public Taxes, by his deputy William Johnson, returned a Supplemental Tax list for 1824 by which it appears that the said collector is chargable with $35.57 to be passed to the Treasury of East Tennessee and Treasury of Rhea County.

Ordered that part of Tuesday next be set apart for the Transaction of Public business.

Justices on bench (8th February)— McDonald, McClure, Caldwell, Fine, Smith, Darwin, Gillespie, Given, Price, Kennedy, Cox, Cozby, Fulkerson, Fulton, Rice, Walker, Robinson, Winton, W.C. Wilson, David, Thompson, Lillard, J. Wilson, Gibson, Shelton, and W.M. Smith.

The last Will and Testament of George Walker, dec'd, was produced in open Court. William Smith and Anderson Smith, two of the subscribing witnesses, say that they saw George Walker sign seal publish and declare the said Instrument of writing to be his last Will and Testament and that they believe he was of perfect sense and memory at the time and that they subscribed their names as witnesses thereto in his presence and at his request. Whereupon it was ordered to be recorded and is as follows:

"I George Walker of the State of Tennessee Rhea County being of perfect mind and memory do make this my last Will and Testament in the following manner and form (to wit) first I desire that all my Just debts that may remain after

(p. 149) my death may be paid according to justice and contract, secondly I give and bequeath unto my son William Walker one hundred and fourteen and a half acres of land being the land on which I now live also one rifle gun and a Town lot in Washington Rhea County with this provition that my wife and other children is to have the préviledge of living on and useing said land untill my son Jefferson Walker is ninteen years of age, I also give and bequeath unto my said son William one plow and gears and one bed and furniture, 3rdly I give and bequeath unto my daughter Sally Nelson one negro woman named Franky and negro or melatto child named John to her and her bodyly heirs for ever, 4thly I give and bequeath unto my son David Walker two negro children namely Hambleton and Caroline the children of my negro woman Sarah my said son David is to receve the said negroes when he arives to the age of twenty one years and if he the said David should die without any issue the said negroes or the vallue thereof is to be equally divided bettween my three children namely Jefferson Mary Abagail and Elizabeth Walker, 5thly I give and bequeath unto my three youngest children Jefferson Mary Abigail & Elizabeth Walker the ballance of my slaves namely Peter, Daniel Anderson & Hariett to be eaqueally divided amoungst the three children when the girls are eighteen years of age and Jefferson twenty one years of age, I also desire that my said three youngest children Jefferson Mary A & Elizabeth Walker should have all the increase that may arise from my three negro woman namely Sarah Cassey & Mary and if the increase when equally divided between my three youngest children as above mentioned if each part amount to more than Davids then the ballance is to be equally divided between the four until there portion are made eaqueal, 6thly I also desire that my negro woman Mary be set free on these conditions that she will pay to my executors of my estate the sum of two hundred and fifty dollars the money to be paid any time before my son David becomes of age, 7thly I desire also that my negro woman Cassey be set free on condition that she dose pay to the executors of my estate the some of five hundred dollars any time before my son David become of age and is to

(p. 150) be allowed a credit of one hundred dollars for each child she bears alive during the time allowed her to raise the money. 8thly I also desire that my negro woman Sarah be set free if she pays the sum of four hundred dollars within the time above mentioned or bears four live children, either the money or the children will extricate her from slavery for life. 9thly I desire that my two youngest daughters Mary A and Elizabeth Walker have two beds and furniture that are now in the care of my negro woman Nell, in Washington, also all the cupbord ware and kitchen furniture that remains in her care, I desire that my wife Clarissa Walker take possession of the same at my death in trust for the children untill my son Jefferson is nineteen years of age. 10thly I give and bequeath unto my wife Clarissa Walker all the household and other property which she now claims, also one set of plowing gears. 11thly I give and bequeath unto my daughter July Glover daughter of Jane Carrol one bed and furniture at the death of my mother Mary Walker, also my pleasure carriage and harness, two cows & calves, one hundred acres of land in South Carolina Spartingburgen District including the fork of Sunats Creek, also a debt owing to me by Jonathan Walker of two hundred and fifty dollars money paid by me as his security, also one horse due me from Obediah Watson to be worth ninety dollars, and two town lots in Washington Rhea County. 12thly I also give my negro Fan her freedom for life and the use of Daniel so long as she lives to wate on her. I also desir that all the rest of my property that is not mentioned here, after my death be collected together and sold for cash, giving twelve months credit and the money to be lade out for land to the best advantage, and the land to be equally divided between my two youngest sons David and Jefferson Walker if either of my children which are under age should die before they become of lawful age or have issue in that case I design that the bequest is made unto such children as may die under age, or without issue and my will is that it be equally divided amongst my children named in this will, which then may

(p. 151) be living. Lastle I give and bequesth unto my mother Mary Walker the use of one of my aforesaid negro woman to wate on her during her life time, and the said negro is to have credit for the time they live with my mother and I do hereby nominate and appoint my son William Walker, my friends Daniel Walker Esqr and Thomas Price and Zacheriah Nelson my executors of this my last will and testament. I do hereby notify and confirm the same revoking and disannulling all other former wills and testaments heretofore made by me. In testimony whereof I have signed sealed published and declared this to be my last will and testament this 5th day of October 1824."   George Walker   (Seal)
In presence of us William Smith, Anderson Smith, David   X his mark   Thomas

        John Rice for use of James Wilson VS William Walker & D.D. Armstrong (No. 1340). John Clack, a Constable, returned a Fieri Facias issued by Carson Caldwell, Justice of the Peace, for $62.50; Clack levied on a house and lot No. 49 in town of Washington; Court orders house and lot to be sold to satisfy said plaintiffs debt.
        William Gwin released from payment of Tax on three town lots for 1824.

(p. 152)   John Clack, a Constable, allowed $4.00 for attending on the Court at August Session.

Arthur Fulton to James C. Mitchell. Bill of Sale for a Negro man named Bob; acknowledged by Fulton; certified for registration.

Power of Attorney from James Cowan, Admr. on estate of Polly Lauderdale, dec'd, to James Standifer; acknowledged by Cowan; certified.

Roberts & McCallie VS Jacob Brown (No. 1341). Woodson Francis, Sheriff, returned a Fieri Facias issued by Carson Caldwell, J.P., for $6.75; levied on a lot (No. 41) in Town of Washington.

James Montgomery, Lewis Collins, John McClanahan, Jackson Howerton, and William Locke appointed Jury of View to lay off and mark a road leading from Tennessee River on the land belonging to James Montgomery to the Blue Pond to intersect the road leading from Washington to Henry Collins.

(p. 153)   Deed of Trust from William Gwin to John McClure for the use of John Locke for sundry property; acknowledged by Gwin; certified for registration.

William Ingle overseer of road from James Taylors to the McMinn County line; to have hands in the following bounds: Jesse Poe, Pulaski Poe, Thompson Merriot, Brinkley Strickland, and all the hands above the road formerly from Jesse Poes to the McMinn County line not interfearing with the hands on Braseltons road.

Woodson Frances produced a receipt from the Treasurer of East Tennessee for the County taxes for 1823 and 1824; also a receipt from the Trustee for all taxes due.

The following persons were appointed commissioners for school lands in Hiwassee District: "for section first in range second west of the meridian George Gillespie, Stephen Winton and Isaac Baker. For section second in same range, Gideon Ragland, Elisha Sharp and William C. Wilson. For third section in same range, James Wilson, Samuel Price and William Gwinn. For tenth section in third range in second fractional township, John Farmer, Michael W. Buster and Thomas Price. For same range third Township, William M. Smith, Miles Vernon and Jacob Sloan. Fourth range school section on Highwassee Robert Gamble, John Lea, and John Roddy."

Duke Ward to John Bailey. Transfer of Certificate No. 290 for 160 acres being the NE¼ Section 24 of Fractional township 2, range 3 west of the meridian; proven by Andrew Kincannon; certified.

(p. 154)   Jackson Howerton VS Lewis Wilkerson & Spilsby Dyer (No. 1342). Plaintiff dismisses suit; Lewis Wilkerson confesses judgment for costs.

Miles Vernon appointed guardian of James Hill, Rebecca Hill, Malvina Hill, and William Hill, infant children of David Hill, dec'd; bond with Thomas Price and Jacob Slover for $1000.

Abraham Howard appointed a Commissioner in place of Henry Collins, resigned, to settle with the Collector of Taxes and Trustee.

Ordered that a former order for a road leading from the Rhea-Roane County line at or near where John Majors now lives passing Absolam Majors house and John Thompson Srs so as to intersect the old Federal Road at any place between Stephen Wintons and William Wests be revived and that Joshua Renfroe, Jeremiah Riddle, Samuel Baker, Isham Lackey, Absolam Majors, John Thompson Senr. and James Blackwell be appointed a Jury of View to mark and lay off the same.

(p. 155)   Court proceeded to the appointment of a Sheriff for the next two years "and on counting the ballots it appeared that Woodson Francis had a majority of the Court, And having taken the necessary oaths prescribed by law entered into and acknowledged the following bond, to wit:

50

"Know all men by these presents that we Woodson Francis, William S. Leuty, Robert Bell, Azariah David, Mumford Smith, and Richard Haslerig, all of Rhea County and State of Tennessee are jointly held and firmly bound to his Excellency William Carroll esquire Governor in and over the State of Tennessee and his successors in office or eithers assigns in the sum of five thousand dollars the which payment well and truly to be made and done we bind ourselves our heirs executors administrators and assigns firmly by these presents sealed signed and dated as follows to wit:

"The conditions of the above obligation is such that whereas the above bound Woodson Francis has this day been appointed by the Court of pleas and quarter Sessions Sheriff for the next insuing two years in and for said county. Now if the said Woodson Francis shall faithfully execute the said office of Sheriff for the aforesaid county of Rhea for the aforesaid term of next insuing two years from the date of these presents in all things appertaining to his said office of sheriff and shall moreover pay and satisfy as the law requires all monies that by him may be collected in virtue of said appointment to the proper office or person to which by law the said monies ought to be paid without default of any kind or delay in him as sheriff or in and of any failure in the compliance with the above conditions this Bond shall be recoverable in its fullest extent and in full force and virtue. . . ."

(p. 156) And the said Woodson Francis with his securities entered into the following Bond: "Know all men by these presents that we Woodson Francis, William S. Leuty, Robert Bell, Azariah David, Mumford Smith, and Richard Haslerig . . . in the sum of five thousand dollars . . .

"The conditions of the above obligation is such that whereas the above bound Woodson Francis has this day been appointed Collector of the State and County Taxes for the State and County aforesaid . . . Now if the aforesaid Woodson Francis . . . shall faithfully collect the taxes in and of said county which may become due and owing said State and county . . . and without delay or default pay over all of said taxes at the time respectively when by law they shall become due and payable to the State or county Treasurers then this obligation to be void otherwise in case of any failure therein this Bond to have full force and effect."

Thomas Cox appointed Coroner for two years by the Court; bond for $1000 with Miles Vernon and Jacob Slover, his securities.

(p. 157) Bond of Thomas Cox.
William Given resigned as Justice of the Peace.
Thomas Price resigned as Justice of the Peace.

(p. 158) Woodson Francis, Sheriff, returned list of Jurors summoned to attend at this session (see list on page 41) out of whom the following Grand Jury was elected: Robert Love, John Walker, William Wann, William Ingle, Walter R. Paine, Jeremiah Washam, James Nail, Elias Majors, William McDonald, Absolam Majors, Micajah Howerton, William Silliven, and Miles Vernon. Robert Love appointed foreman and David Shelton a Constable to attend said jury.

There remained of the original pannel: James McCance, Allison Howard, Francis Reevely, John Smith, and Rezin Rawlings.

(p. 159) Settlement returned by William Kennedy and William Johnson, Commissioners appointed to settle with William Lewis and Samuel Craig, Admrs of John Shafer:
To the amount of the estate of John Shafer, dec'd $ 1362.62½
Cr pr Contra
By receipt of Henry Heniger pr John Shafer drawn on
        power of attorney $ 41.55

By John Robinson's Receipt paid on said power		
from John Henniger	28.57½	
By Henry Hennegar's Receipt on said power	53.22	
Amount drawn for John Shafer		123.34½
By Nancy Shafers Receipt for	51.01	
By John Bowlings Receipt husband of Nancy Shafer	22.00	
Amount drawn by and for Nancy Shafer		73.01
By the receipt if widow Shafer	120.00	120.00
By the receipt of William Lewis Jun, Gdn for Sally		
Shafer, one of the legatees	2.34	2.34

Proven accounts &c

By Henry Collins acct pr season of three mares	10.00
By Hiram Hennegar ditto pr labor done	8.50
By ditto on affidavit of a proven account from	
Barefoot Armstrong lost	1.50
By amount paid James C. Mitchell for damages done his	
plantation while in occupancy of J. Shafer	10.00
By receipt of the Amt of a Judgment that Col. John Rice	
obtained vs the Admrs of said estate	12.37½
By Henry Hennegars receipt in behalf of John Hennegar	14.00
By a Receipt D. Gwin D. Shff of Green County for John	
Shafer Sen. tax for 1816	2.52
By Henry Hennegars receipt in behalf of John Shafer Sen	
by John Henderson Sen.	1.00
By Woodson Francis, Shiff receipt pr account of Jacob	
Brown for making J. Shafers coffin and costs	12.37½
By a note for $2.00 and $1.50 costs the note sworn to	
having been previously paid by Jacob Henneger	3.50
By three notes amt $14.50 & cost $3.12½ lost by insol-	
vency certified by John Moore esqr.	17.62½

(p. 160)

By Samuel Craigs account for expenditures and Services		
rendered the Estate	68.00	
By William Lewis Administrators do pr ditto	60.00	
By one day Settling with the Commissioners	1.00	
By the Commissioners receipt for services in Settlement		
two days each at $2 per day each	4.00	
Amount of expenditures Services		226.39½

Amount of unsettled Notes on hand as follows, viz Since paid

One Note on James C. Mitchell for $200 due 27th Dec 1822	
which Note tho Inventoried was proven to the	
Commissioners to have been previously paid	200.00
By the receipt of James C. Mitchell for the distributive	
Shares of Mary McGill and Jacob Shafer	202.53
By the receipt of Daniel Rawlings, Clk of Rhea County	
for cost on the administration of said estate	10.25
By Jonathan Fines receipt of 16th Sept 1822 as	
Guardian of the heirs	219.47
By William Lewis for Guardian for Sally Shafer	
6th February 1821	100.12½
By Woodson Francis receipt for cost 4th Feb 1822	1.87½
By cost of an exemple on record 29th Sept 1821	1.70
By the Commissioners service in settlement with the Admrs	10.00
By Jonathan Fines Receipt dated 18th Dec 1823	
pr two Notes amounting to	93.90

By Thos Shafers Receipt for part of John Bolins legacy   25.00

Total Amount paid $ 1409.94

Total Amount paid	$ 1409.94
	1362.62½
Overpaid	47.31½
Commissioners additional Services in completing Settlement	
$2.00 each	4.00
	$ 51.31½

(p. 161) Justices on bench (9th February)— William Kennedy, Thomas Cox, John Rice, and John Cozby. (NOTE— first names were included from this page onward).

John Love permitted to keep an Ordinary for one year.

James Lillard resigned as Justice of the Peace.

State VS William H. Douglass. Defendant made default; his security, Samuel Romines, also made default. State to recover $500 from Douglass and Romines, the amount of their recognizance bond.

State VS Sashwell McClure. Defendant made default; his securities, Samuel Murphey and Thomas Camp, also made default. State to recover $500 from defendants and securities.

(p. 162) State VS Sashwell McClure, Samuel Murphey, and Thomas Camp (Nos. 1343, 1344,1345). "Came the defendants and on the affidavit of Sashwell McClure, one of the defendants, and on motion the forfeiture this day entered against the defendants is set aside, and the defendants and Jesse Matthews and Elijah Collins confess judgment for the costs."

State VS Sashwell McClure. Came the defendant, Jesse Matthews, and Elijah Collins and acknowledged themselves indebted to the State for $500 ($250 McClure and $150 each Matthews and Collins) that the said McClure will make his appearance at the next session of this Court.

William McCormick VS Jesse Matthis (No. 1346). Came the defendant by attorney and upon his motion the plaintiff in this cause is non prossed; defendant to recover costs from plaintiff.

(p. 163) Orlando Bradley VS William Smith (No. 1347). Defendant confessed judgment for $50.41½ plus costs.

Edmund Whitfield and Needham Whitfield, Exrs of Needham Whitfield, dec'd by their attorney in fact Gaines Whitfield to Wright Smith. Deed of Conveyance for 188 acres; proven by Thomas J. Campbell and Return J. Meigs, subscribing witnesses; admitted to record.

John Parker permitted to keep an Ordinary for one year.

John Love permitted to keep an Ordinary for one year.

Grand Jury returned Bill of Indictment, State against Robert Beard for Petit Larceny, endorsed "a true Bill' by the foreman, Robert Love.

(p. 164) State VS Robert Beard. Defendant says he is not guilty. Jury (John Smith, Francis Reevely, Townly Riggs, Alexander McCall, James Kelly, William Hill, James Stewart, Orville Paine, Lewis Morgan, Washington Morgan, Thomas Eaves, and John Day) was respited until tomorrow morning.

Justices on bench (10th February)— William Kennedy, Thomas Cox, James Darwin, John Rice, and John Cozby.

Certificate for $3.00 issued to Joshua Hannah for a Wolf scalp.

(p. 165) State VS Robert Beard (No. 1348). Jury reports thay cannot agree; by consent a mistrial is entered. The Attorney General entered a Nolle proseque; Defendant and his security, Joshua Kelly, confessed judgment for the costs.

State VS William Hill (No. 1349). Defendant says he is not guilty.

Jury (John Parker, William McCormick, Robert Smith, Eli Renno, John Alexander, Daniel Swan, James Purser, John Smith, Francis Revely, James McCanse, Allison Howard, and Abraham Miller) finds the defendant guilty as charged; fined 50¢ and costs.

Moses Thompson VS George Gordon. On petition of Defendant a Certiorari and supercedas is awarded him to bring this cause into Court from before the justice on his entering into bond and security as the law directs.

(p. 166) State VS Jeremiah Carver, Josiah Thompson & Moses Thompson. Defendants made default by not appearing when called; State to recover $500, the amount of their recognizance.

Thomas Murphrey VS Allen Kennedy (No. 1350). Came the parties by their attornies and a jury (John Parker, John Alexander, Daniel Swan, John Smith, Francis Reevely, James McCanse, Allison Howard, Townly Riggs, Isaac Braselton jr. Abraham Miller, Eli Renno, and Robert Small) sworn to enquire of the damages "do say they assess the plaintiffs damage to one hundred and twelve dollars and seventy five cents in Tennessee Bank Notes." Plaintiff to recover damages plus costs expended.

Carson Caldwell deposited in the hands of the Clerk of this Court $6.25 a fine collected by him from Catharine Barns, a single woman, for refusing to declare the father of her bastard child.

(p. 167) William Ainsworth VS John Parker (No. 1351). Came the parties by their attornies and a jury (William Carter, John Alexander, Daniel Swan, John Smith, Francis Reevely, James McCanse, Allison Howard, Townly Riggs, Isaac Braselton Jr., Abraham Miller, Eli Renno, and Thomas Piper) which finds the defendant not guilty of the traver and conversion as the plaintiff complained. Defendant to recover costs from plaintiff.

Vincen Oden VS Meredith Brogdon. On motion of the Defendant, a Commission is awarded him to take the deposition of Joseph Roberts to be read as evidence in this cause, "upon giving the plaintiff one days notice of the time and place of taking the same."

John Love who on yesterday obtained a Licence to keep a house of Ordinary in this County on condition he would give bond and security, came into Court and entered into bond and security and took the oath prescribed by law.

Ordered that John Rice, Admr. of estate of David S. Williams, dec'd, have the further time of three months to make report of the same.

Grand Jury returned a Bill of Indictment, State against Orlando Holland for an assault and battery.

(p. 168) Isaac Braselton VS William Murphree & William Lewis. Came the parties by their attorneys and a jury (John Alexander, Daniel Swan, John Smith, Francis Reevely, James McCanse, Allison Howard, Townly Riggs, David Leuty, Abraham Miller, Eli Renno, and Thomas Piper) which says "the defendants has not well and truly paid the sum of Sixteen hundred dollars the debt in the declaration mentioned as they in their first plea have aledged and the jurors aforesaid upon their oaths aforesaid do say the plaintiff did loose the land mentioned in his declaration and the condition of the bond of said defendants by an older or prior title and they do assess the plaintiffs damage by reason thereof to ninety two dollars besides the sum of eight hundred dollars which sum they do find to be due to the said plaintiff upon the Bond declared upon in his declaration."

On the petition of John Day and John Madden they signifying their intention of erecting Iron works in this County on Richland Creek. Ordered that James Stewart, Joshua Tindle, Lewis Morgan, Washington Morgan, Henry Airhart, John Jack, George Manis, William Smith, John Able, James Coulter, Orville Paine, and Robert Parks be appointed a Jury of View to lay off adjacent to the said contemplated ironwork, 3000 acres of unapropriated land unfit for cultivation for the use of said works as the law directs.

(p. 169)   Justices on bench (11th February)— William Kennedy, Carson Caldwell, John Rice, and James A. Darwin.

Jesse Matthews VS William McCormick (No. 1352). Came plaintiff by his attorney, Return J. Meigs; defendant fails to appear and prosecute his appeal. Plaintiff to recover from McCormick and Gilbert Kennedy, his security, the sum of $10.00 plus interest and costs.

Isaac Braselton VS William Murphree & William Lewis (No. 1353). Came the parties by their attornies; adjudged that the Demurre to the third plea of the defendant be sustained. Considered by the Court that the plaintiff (upon the finding of yesterdays jury) recover of the defendants the sum of $800 debt and $92.00 damages sustained by said plaintiff by the detention of the debt, plus costs.

James C. Mitchell for the use of Seabourn Jones VS Thomas Hopkins (No. 1354). Came the parties by their attornies; adjudged by the Court that

(p. 170)   the demurre to the plaintiffs declaration be voided(?); judgment against the defendant for $817.16 2/3 debt and $121.00 damages.

William S. Leuty VS Samuel Holland (No. 1355). Attachment. Came the plaintiff by attorney and the defendant called to defend this suit and replevy the property attached, made default. Judgment entered against defendant for $426.00½ debt and $38.00 interest. It appearing that attachment had been levied upon three negroes, the property of the defendant, ordered that said negroes be sold for satisfaction of the debt and interest.

State VS Anson Dearmon (No. 1356). Bastardy. Came the attorney general and defendant by attorney; John Parker security for defendant in sum of $500; void on condition the defendant
(p. 171)   "do save harmless the County of Rhea from any charge in the support and maintainance of a bastard child begotten upon the body of Jane Houp by the said Dearmon. . ." Ordered that Dearmon pay unto the said Jane Houp the sum of $20 for one year to commence from the birth of said child for its support and maintainance to be paid Quarterly.

MAY TERM 1825

(p. 172)   Court of Pleas and Quarter Sessions met at the Court House in Washington on first Monday and 2nd day of May 1825. Justices on bench— William Smith, John Robinson, Jesse Thompson, Randolph Gibson, Frederick Fulkerson, Carson Caldwell, John Rice, Crispein E. Shelton, Daniel Walker, John Cozby, Azariah David, Stephen Winton, and William C. Wilson.

Patrick Martin appointed overseer of road in place of John Jones, resigned.
John D. Williams overseer of road in place of Samuel P. Stewart, resigned.
Samuel F. Swan and Edward Stewart, hands working under John Rodgers and Jacob Garrison, overseers, are taken from said Rogders and Garrison and are to work on the mountain road under James Walker, overseer.
Larkin Butram appointed overseer of road in place of Jacob Rigney.
Woodson Francis, Henry Airhart, Henry Collins, Abraham Howard, and Samuel Howard appointed a Jury of View to lay off and turn the road round James Coulters Spring.
Ordered that Washington Morgan, overseer, work on that part of the road from John Jacks old Shop to the forks of the road on the top of the hill in addition to what he now works.

(p. 173) Ordered that the Jury of View to lay off 3000 acres for the purpose of erecting an Ironwork be revived.

Return J. Meigs appointed Attorney General protem for this Term.

Randolph Gibson resigned as a Justice of the Peace.

Certificate for $3.00 issued to Oliver Pike for a Wolf scalp.

Ordered that Leonard Brightwell, overseer of road from Fraziers Ferry to Frenches Mill, work on said road from Mud Creek to where said road intersects with the Washington Road and that all the hands in the following bounds work under him: Beginning where said road crosses Mud Creek, thence along said road to where it intersects the Washington Road, then a direct line to Richland Creek, then down the creek to the River, then up the River to where John Singleton now lives, then to the beginning, so as to include said Singleton, James Jacobs, Francis Reavely, and John Bowlen.

On motion of Woodson Francis, James C. Francis was admitted to swear in as deputy Sheriff for the County.

Henry Collins, William Johnson, and Samuel Logan appointed Commissioners to settle with Matthew Hubbart and Abigail Ferguson, Admr. and Admrx. on estate of Robert Ferguson, dec'd.

(p. 174) John Roddy to John Chatten. Deed of Conveyance for 320 acres; acknowledged by Grantor; certified for registration.

Richard G. Waterhouse to James Montgomery. Deed of Conveyance for 120 acres; acknowledged by Grantor; certified for registration.

Woodson Francis, Sheriff, to Samuel Howard. Deed of Conveyance for 180 acres; acknowledged by Grantor; certified for registration.

Richard G. Waterhouse to William Kennedy. Deed of Conveyance for 294 acres; acknowledged by Grantor; certified for registration.

William Goad & Thomas G. Goad to William Kennedy. Deed of Conveyance for 60 acres; proven in part by Matthew Hubbart, a subscribing witness; certified for further probate.

Pleasant Miller appointed a Constable in Capt. White's Company; bond with William Miller and Henry Collins, his securities.

Henry Henry allowed $3.00 for attending three days on the Circuit Court at March Term 1825.

(p. 175) Woodson Francis, Sheriff, allowed a credit with the County Trustee for the following sums which by law he could not collect from the following persons: Isaac Crow, David S. Williams, William Martin, Randolph Smith, William H. Duglass, George Gothard, Zoaf Jackson, Francis Monday, Benjamin Rogers, Henry Tindle, John Henderson, William Orr, and James Dunn (all charged with 56¼¢).

Ordered that jurors be allowed 50¢ per day for 1825 to commence from the first of January.

Thomas Little to record his live stock mark: a half crop under each ear.

Grief Howerton appointed Guardian of William Johnson, Ann Johnson, and Lucinda Johnson, infant children of James Johnson, dec'd; bond with Thomas Woodward, his security, for $450.

Asahel Johnson allowed $1.31¼ for one white poll and 1 Black poll paid tax for in 1824 which by law he was not entitled to pay.

William Ferguson appointed overseer of road from Jacob Becks to Waltons Ferry; hands to work under him: Henry Beck, Thomas Godbehere, James Carnahan, George W. Riggle, Thomas Anderson, and John Ferguson.

Ordered that a former order for a road leading from Kellys Ferry up Goodfield Creek near Thomas Cox's Mill so as to intersect the road leading from Rosses Ferry be revived and that Miles Vernon, Samuel Looney, Samuel Tillery, Thomas Lucas, David Blevins, John Igou, Robert Elder, and Stephen Moore are appointed a Jury of View to lay off and mark said road.

(p. 176) James Cowan, Admr. on estate of Polly Lauderdale, dec'd, returned an inventory of the estate:
1 Draft No. 2634, dated March 22nd 1825, for the sum of $262.76 by Thomas T. Tucker, Treasurer of the United States, on the Cashier of the Branch Bank of Tennessee of Nashville in favour of James Cowan, esqr. administrator of all & singular the goods and chattles, rights & credits of Polly Lauderdale, deceased. $262.76
        Ordered that the road as reported by the Jury of View appointed at last Sessions from John Majors to intersect the old Federal Road at or near Stephen Wintons be established as follows: beginning at the County line near John Majors passing his house, thence to Absolam Majors, thence by John Thompsons Senr., and thence so as to intersect the old Federal Road at Stephen Wintons; Absalom Majors appointed overseer; to have the following hands to work under him: all the hands from Mark Massays between the river and the big ridge to the County line and all the hands subject to work on the road at John Thompsons, Hiram Mahaffe, William Day, and James Lawrence.
        Ordered that the road as reported by the Jury of View from Prices Ferry to the Town of Athens be established as follows: from Prices Ferry to Avary Hannars then with or near the now used road to (blank) then with or near said trace, intersecting the Federal Road so on with said road to intersect the McMinn County Road; Robert Hagan appointed overseer; to have all the hands in the poor Valley below Whites Mill to Joshua Atchley and all the hands south of said Valley including Sams to the County line, Also Jacob Price to work under said Hagan.

(p. 177) Jurors appointed for next term of this Court:

William McDonald	Bryan McDonald	John Day	John B. Swan
Jacob Garrison	John Walker	Peter Minnick	David Leuty
Adam Cox	Samuel Montooth	Walter Edwards	Alexander McCall
William Cumpton	Orville Paine	Isaac Mahan	Addison Riggs
Joseph McDaniel	David Roper	Peter Fine	John Hall
Elijah Wyatt	Robert Carr	William Woodward	Robert Bolton
David Shelton, a Constable to attend said Court			Jacob Brown

Jurors appointed for next term of Circuit Court:

Cain Able	William Howard	Robert Locke	Matthew Inglish [Eng-
Moses Thompson	Daniel Walker	John Robinson	Allen Kennedy lish]
Robert Pharis	Gideon Ragland	Cumberland Rector	Jonathan Fine
John Lewis	Capt. Henry Collins	Samuel Gamble	John Ferguson
Samuel McDaniel	William M. Smith	John Leuty	Daniel M. Stockton
Wilson Kilgore	Avery Hanna	Robert Parks	Matthew Hubbart
David Shelton, a Constable to attend said Court			Lewis R. Collins

        Samuel Beershears appointed overseer of road in place of John Benson, removed.
        The last Will and Testament of William Gamble, dec'd, was produced in Court and proven in part by oath of Samuel Gamble; ordered to lay over for further probate.
        William Walker, one of the executors named in the Will of George Walker, dec'd, took the oath of executor and entered into bond with Richard Manley, his security for $5000.

(p. 178) Joseph Thompson appointed overseer of road from Suay Creek to the McMinn County line on the Morganton Road in place of William Wann.
        Ordered that the road as reported by the Jury of View from Tennessee River on the land belonging to James Montgomery to the Blue pond to intersect the

road leading from Washington to Henry Collins be discontinued as Said Montgomery would retain to himself the controle of the said road and not let it pass through his land only under such conditions as the Court would not agree to.

Robert Bell, Crispeon E. Shelton, and Abraham Howard, Commissioners appointed to settle with William Smith and James Cowan, Exrs. of last Will and Testament of William French, returned their settlement:

Inventory of Sale 14th Dec 1820	Debit No. 1		713.32
Ballance due on Thomas Howels Note	" " 2		105.00
Inventory of Sale 4th April 1822	" " 3		322.39 3/4
Inventory of sale of Negroes 26th Oct 1822	" " 4		1050.00
			2190.72
Amount of Wm Alexanders Note			9.17½
			2199.89½
A Jurors Certificate for 3 days			1.50
			2201.39½
	Credit		2105.92½
	Balance due the Estate		95.47

Voucher	Paid		Voucher	Paid	
1	Smith & Cozby	80.02½	18	Thomas James junr	19.50
2	Benjamin C. Stout	48.00	19	Wm B. Lauderdale	11.66 2/3
3	Daniel Rawlings	35.57	20	Daniel Henderson	16.00
4	William S. Leuty	24.68 3/4	21	Benjamin McCarty	29.00
5	Patrick Martin	41.50	22	James McCampbell	25.00
6	Charles Ryon	7.50	23	Hiram A. Defriese	7.00
7	James Payne	4.12½	24	William S. Leuty	185.64
8	Abraham Howard	80.00	25	Mrs. French	5.00
(p. 179)			26,27	Tax for 1822 & 1824	8.00
9	Woodson Francis	519.88½	28	Isaac Benson	.98½
10	Woodson Francis	6.50	29	Abraham Howard	6.86½
11	Abraham Howard	3.15	30	William Lyon	589.25
12	Lewis Morgan	9.00	31	paid the Estate	142.50
13	Daniel Henderson	5.32	32	Tax for 1825	2.25
14	Geo W. Churchwell	5.00	33	Taxes for 1821 & 1823	5.25
15	Edward Gray	8.00	34	Cain Able	96.00
16	Spencer Jarnagin	7.50			
17	David Ragsdale	8.00			2043.61 3/4

Credit by balance of Notes due from Forbes & Ketchum		25.00
" by a Note due from James Cowan		6.18 3/4
" by ballance Note due from Ragsdale and Morgan		11.12
" by deficiency of Corn sold to Col. Turk		20.00
		2105.92½

(p. 180) Justices on bench (3rd May)— William Smith, Stephen Winton, Azariah David, and Crispien E. Shelton.

Woodson Francis, Sheriff, returned a list of Jurors summoned to appear at this Term of Court (see list on page 46) out of whom the following Grand Jury was elected: John Acre, Peter Fine, Tavner Masoner, Edward Templeton, Benjamin McCarty, William Howard, Robert Taylor, William Locke, Henry Hackworth, Byram Breeden, William McCarty, Roger Reece, and Joshua Kelley. William Howard appointed foreman and David Shelton, Constable to serve the Grand Jury.

There remained of the original pannel: William Carnahan, Jacob Beck, Bartholomew Gwin, James Snelson, and William Lea.

Woodson Francis, Sheriff, to William Blythe. Bill of Sale for one negro woman, one negro girl, and one negro boy; acknowledged by Francis; certified for registration.

58

(p. 181)   Charles Gamble VS Isaac Clement & John Clement (No. 1357). Plaintiff dismisses his suit and confesses judgment for costs.

John Holland VS John Angland (No. 1358). Plaintiff dismisses his suit; defendant confesses judgment for the costs.

Robert Brabson for use of James Thompson VS Michael W. Buster (No. 1359). Came the parties by their Attornies and a Jury: William Carnahan, Jacob Beck, Bartholomew Gwin, James Snelson, William Lea, John Angland, David Right, Jesse Poe, Ruben Freeman, William Smith, Charles Smith, and James Montgomery. Jury says the defendant has not paid the debt in the declaration not any part thereof; plaintiff to recover $134 debt and $4.69 damages plus costs.

William Blythe & Thomas Hopkins to John Locke. Bill of Sale for a negro boy named Daniel; acknowledged by Blythe and Hopkins; certified for registration.

(p. 182)   Miller Francis VS Mumford Smith (No. 1360). Came the parties by Attornies and a Jury: James Montgomery, Jesse Poe, Jacob Beck, James Snelson, David Right, John Angland, Ruben Freeman, William Smith, Charles Smith, Bartholomew Gwin, William Carnahan, and William Lea. Jury says the defendant "hath well and truly paid the debt in the plaintiffs declaration" except the sum of $81.72. Plaintiff to recover the debt and $2.04 damages plus costs.

Vincen Oden VS Merideth Brogdon (No. 1361). Came the parties by Attornies and a Jury (same as above) who says the Defendant is not guilty of the trover and conversion as the plaintiff complained. Defendant to recover costs of plaintiff.

Jesse Poe VS William M. Smith. Plaintiff has leave to amend the warrant in this cause so as to read, Jesse Poe Admr. of William Lewis, dec'd, and that he pay the cost of this amendment.

Stephen Winton, Benjamin Maxwell, and Daniel McPherson appointed Commissioners to settle with Joseph Mee, Exr. of last Will and Testament of Isaac Rice.

(p. 183)   Henry Welker VS James G. Martin. Leave is granted the Plaintiff to amend the original writ in this cause to read, Henry Welker assignee of James C. Mitchell, and that plaintiff to pay costs of amendment.

Moses Thompson VS George Gordon. Upon motion of plaintiff by attorney, a rule is granted him to dismiss the petition for Certiorari and Supercedence in this cause.

Alexander Forbes VS Abraham Bryson (No. 1362). Came the plaintiff by his attorney William C. Dunlap; appears to satisfaction of Court that plaintiff has paid $14.37½ as security for the defendant. Plaintiff to recover debt plus costs.

Alexander Forbes VS Jackson Wherry (No. 1363). Came plaintiff by attorney W.C. Dunlap; appears to satisfaction of Court that plaintiff has paid $11.60, the defendants part of a note given jointly by the plaintiff and defendant. Plaintiff to recover debt plus interest and costs.

(p. 184)   Elisha Kirklin VS John Rice & others. Came the parties by Attornies and after agrument had the demurrer to the plaintiffs declaration is overruled and that the plaintiff have judgment against the defendant in this behalf, a writ of inquiry awarded plaintiff (by a jury) to inquire into the damages.

Moses Thompson VS George Gordon. Parties by attornies agreed that all matters in this dispute be referred to final determination of George Gillespie, James Preston, Jesse Roddy, William T. Gillenwaters, and Arthur Fulton, who are to meet at the house of Frederick Fulkerson.

Declaration in order to be placed on the Pension list under the Act of the 18th March 1818.

"On the 3rd day of May 1825, personally appeared in open Court of Pleas and Quarter Sessions, it being a Court of Record, Thomas Moore resident in said County aged 73 Years who being first duly Sworn according to law doth on his oath make the following declaration in order to obtain the pension made by the act of Congress of the 18th March 1818 and the first May 1820; that he the said Thomas Moore entered the Army for three Months as a substitute for Wm Deale the day and year is forgotten, & my pocket book was lost and my discharge with it in the State of North Carolina in the company commanded by Captain Cazy Bulk, before he reached Charleston it was taken by the british, & the company he belonged to never joined its Regiment, he was then discharged & returned home, he volunteered immediately under captain William Bennett & Samuel Gray Lieutenant & continued to serve untill discharged at the battle of Cowpens after having his thumb cut off by a bullet & also received a wound in the thigh which rendered him unable to perform service. He was in the battle of Gates defeat at Ruges Mill at Guilford Court house Kings Mountain & the Cowpens where he was wounded as above. He hereby relinquishes every claim whateaver

(p. 185) to a pension except the present, that his name is only on the roll in North Carolina the reason he has not applied for a pension before he is very poor, ignorant & had no knowledge of the provisions of the acts of Congress and in pursuance of the act of the 1st May 1820, I do Solemnly swear that I was a resident citizen of the United States on the 18th day of March 1818 and that I have not since that time by gift, sale or in any manner disposed of my property, or any part thereof with intent thereby so to deminish it as to bring myself within the provisions of an act of Congress entitled an Act to provide for certain persons engaged in the land & naval service of the United States in the Revolutionary war passed on the 18th day of March 1818, and that I have not nor has any person in trust for me any property or securities contracts or debts due to me nor have I any income other than what is contained in the schedule hereto annexed & by me subscribed.

"There has been no changes in my property since 1818, 18th March. I have no real estate by occupation a farmer & by my wounds, age & diseases have become entirely unable to pursue it or to maintain myself, my wife has been dead 6 years, I live with my son, who is very poor and has a wife & ten children, he rents land to work & is hardly able to live.

Schedule— One bed $ 5.00
Tin pan & bucket .75
Axe & hoe 2.00
$ 7.75   his
Thomas X Moore
mark

Sworn to and declared on the 3rd day of May 1825 in open Court, James Berry Clk. The foregoing declaration being read to the Court and it appearing to the satisfaction of the Court that the facts set forth in the declaration are true as also the amount exhibited in the said schedule above annexed and the same was ordered by the Court to be recorded and certified."

Allen Kennedy, Richard Haslerig, and David Caldwell, Commissioners appointed to settle with Andrew Evans, Admr. on estate of William Floyd, dec'd, returned their settlement:
A. Evans Dr for amt sales $ 98.35½
Cr by Notes & accounts by him lifted 98.35½

(p. 186) Cain Able VS Spencer Benson jun. (No. 1364). David Shelton, Constable, returned a Fieri Facias issued by William Smith, Justice, for $18.12½; levied on 100 acres of land on which Spencer Benson jun now lives adjoining the lands of John Able, Robert Cozby, Spencer Benson Senr, and William Biace. Upon motion of Plaintiff by his attorney George W. Churchwell, ordered that the land be sold.

Eli Ferguson to John H. Beck. Deed of Conveyance for 130 acres; proven in part by Spills Be Dyer; certified for further probate.

Nimrod Pendergrass to David Ragsdale. Deed of Conveyance for 50 acres; proven in part by William Smith; certified for further probate.

Grand Jury returned Bills of Indictment: State against John Harral for Pettit Larcany; State against Celia Angland for Assault and Battery. Endorsed a true bill by the foreman, William Howard.

(p. 187) Justices on bench (4th May)— William Smith, Azariah David, Stephen Winton, and Crispein E. Shelton.

State VS Orlando Holland (No. 1365). Return J. Meigs, Attorney General protem; defendant says he cannot gainsay the charges; fined 50¢ and costs.

Joseph Windle & George W. Sevier VS Thomas Hamilton. On petition of the defendant a Certiorari and supersedas is awarded him to bring this Cause into Court from before the Justice on his entering into bond and Security.

Archabald Sevier VS Thomas Hamilton. On petition of the defendant a Certiorari and supersedas is awarded him to being this Cause into Court from before the Justice on his entering into bond with Security.

State VS Celia Angland. Came Temperance Sego and acknowledged herself indebted to the State in the sum of $250 and John Holland the sum of $250; void on condition that Temperance Sego appear at next Court and give evidence against Celia Angland.

(p. 188) State VS David Leuty. Defendant together with Michael W. Buster and John Walker acknowledge themselves indebted to State for $1000 (Leuty $500 and Buster & Walker $250 each); void on condition that defendant makes his appearance at August Sessions "to then and there abide by what further order or decree the said Court may make in this cause respecting bastardy and not depart the Court without leave and that he in the mean time save harmless the County of Rhea from all charges that may likely be charged to said County by the birth and maintainance of a child begotten by said defendant on the body of Margaret Woodson, late Margaret Leuty, not yet born."

State VS Jeremiah Carver, Moses Thompson & Josiah Thompson (No. 1366). Sci Fa. Defendants Moses & Josiah Thompson surrendered Jeremiah Carver in discharge of themselves and the forfeiture entered against them on their recognizance is set aside upon the payment of costs. Jeremiah Carver to appear at next Court to answer a charge of Petit Larceny.

(p. 189) State VS Sashwell McClure (No. 1367). Nolle proseque entered in this cause; County to pay costs.

Orville Paine VS John Rice & John Robinson. Appeal taken in this cause at November Sessions 1824 to the Circuit Court was dismissed by said Court; Clerk of this Court to issue an execution against the defendants and their securities according to the judgment heretofore given in this cause.

(p. 190) John Howard VS William Gwin (No. 1368). Rezin Rawlings appeared and declared that he was indebted to the Defendant for $4.67½; considered by the Court that the plaintiff recover against the Garnishee Rezin Rawlings $4.67½.

State VS Celia Angland. Came John Angland and acknowledged himself indebted to State for $500; Thomas Brown, John Rice, Robert Parks, Thomas Kelly, Woodson Francis, and Alexander Forbes acknowledged themselves indebted to State for $250 each; void on condition that Celia Angland make her personal appearance at the next session of this Court.

State VS Aquilla Parker (No. 1369). Return J. Meigs, Attorney General protem; defendant says he is not guilty; jury (James Stewart, Edmund Bean, George

Manas, William Lewis, John Parker, Rezin Rawlings, William Lowrey, Willie Lewis, John Angland, Orville Paine, William Hill, and Vincen Oden) finds the defendant guilty as charged; fined $1.00 and costs; James Kelly security for payment.

(p. 191)   Vincen Oden VS Meredith Brogden. Came the plaintiff by his attorney and on his motion a rule is granted on the defendant to shew cause why a new trial should not be granted him in this cause.
        Grand Jury returned Bills of Indictment: State against Jeremiah Carver for Petit Larceny; State against Absolam Barnes for keeping a tipling house. Also a presentment, the State against Joseph McDaniel for an assault and battery.
        State VS John Harrel. Petit Larceny. Return J. Meigs, Attorney General protem; defendant says he is not guilty; jury (William Carnahan, Jacob Beck, Bartholomew Gwin, James Snelson, William Lea, John B. Hood, Daniel Holland, David Leuty, James Montgomery, Alexander McCall, Hastin Poe, and George Henry) retired to consult of their verdict under the care of an officer. Court adjourned until tomorrow morning.

(p. 192)   Justices on bench (5th May)— William Smith, Stephen Winton, C.E. Shelton, and A. David.
        John Dudley VS James G. Martin (No. 1370). Plaintiff by attorney dismisses suit; defendant to recover his costs from plaintiff.
        Vincen Oden VS Meredeth Brogden. Rule for new trial is discharged.
        State VS John Harrald. Jury returned and declared they could not agree. Cause is continued until next session.

(p. 193)   State VS John Harrald. Defendant acknowledged debt to State for $500; William Harrald and Samuel Harrald, his securities, indebted for $250 each; void if he appears at next session to answer charge of petit larceny.
        State VS John Harrald. James Stewart and Jacob Beck acknowledged they are indebted to State for $500 each; void on condition they appear at next session and give evidence in the above suit.

(p. 194)   State VS Jeremiah Carver. Came Joseph McCall and acknowledged himself indebted to State for $500; Alexander McCall for $250. Void on condition that Joseph McCall make his appearance at next session and give evidence.
        All causes not tried at this term are ordered to be continued until next Court.

AUGUST TERM 1825

(p. 195)   Court of Pleas and Quarter Sessions held on first Monday and first day of August 1825. Justices on bench— William Smith, Daniel Walker, John Robinson, John McClure, John Cozby, Frederick Fulkerson, Thomas Cox, William Kennedy, Jonathan Fine, William M. Smith, John Rice, Arthur Fulton, Jesse Thompson, James A. Darwin, and Azariah David.
        Woodson Francis, Sheriff, to Ralph B. Locke. Deed of Conveyance for 200 acres; acknowledged by Grantor; certified for registration.
        Woodson Francis, Sheriff, to John Locke. Deed of Conveyance for 100 acres; acknowledged by Grantor; certified for registration.
        William B. Lewis, atty in fact for Exrs of Wm T. Lewis, dec'd to Isaac Lewis. Deed of Conveyance for 100 acres; proven by James C. Mitchell and William Lewis, subscribing witnesses; certified for registration.
        John Able appointed overseer of road in place of William Buyse.
        Gilbert Kennedy appointed overseer of road in place of Edward Templeton.

(p. 196)   Alexander Coulter appointed overseer of road in place of Willie Lewis.

John Stewart appointed overseer of part of Rosses Ferry Road to commence where said road leaves Prices Ferry Road and to extend to where Andrew Kincannon now lives; to have hands in following bounds: to include James Lillard on Goodfield and to run up said Goodfield Creek to the County line then with the line to include Asa Rowden, then to the beginning of said road so as to include Jonathan Collins, then with the dividing ridge between Tennessee River and Goodfield and Sewee Creek so as to include William Parker.

The last Will and Testament of Lyddia Roddy dec'd was produced and proven by oath of William Givens, the subscribing witness thereto who says he saw Lyddia Roddy sign seal publish and declare the said instrument of writing to be her last Will and Testament and that he believed she was of perfect sense and memory at the time, and that he subscribed his name as a witness in her presence and at her request; ordered to be recorded.

John Lea, executor named in last Will and Testament of Lyddia Roddy, took the oath and entered into bond with his securities, Woodson Francis and James C. Mitchell, for $2000.

David Shelton permitted to keep a house of Ordinary.

James F. Bradford produced his Licence as a practicing attorney.

(p. 197)   Samuel Beshears appointed overseer of road from David Sheltons towards Blythes Ferry to the hollow leading into Tennessee River immediately below Robert Bells meadow and that all the hands in Cramers Cove and all the hands living between said road and the little mountain excepting Washington Morgan and including Reuben Jackson, also all the hands between said road and Richland Creek as far down as the lower line of Lauderdales land be subject to work under him.

Ordered that the order made at last February Session appointing Miles Vernon, Samuel Looney, Samuel Tillary, Thomas Lucas, and David Blevins a Jury of View to lay off and mark a road from Kellys Ferry up Goodfield Creek near Thomas Cox's Mill &c. be revived.

Samuel F.D. Swan resigned as Constable.

William Goad & Thomas G. Goad to William Kennedy. Deed of Conveyance for 60 acres was proven in part by William Johnson (already proven by Matthew Hubbart at May session); certified for registration.

Byram Breeding released from payment of poll tax for this year, he being over the taxable age.

Elijah Runnels allowed $45.00 for keeping Mary Owens for 12 months.

On application of Elijah Runnels, he undertakes to keep Mary Owens, a poor person, for 12 months for $45.00.

(p. 198)   Samuel Looney appointed overseer of road in place of David Roper.

Ordered that William Ferguson, overseer of road from Waltons Ferry to Jacob Becks, have in addition to his former hands John Ferguson and Edward Wassun and all the hands from a straight line from Jeremiah Able to Samuel Fergusons on Wolf Creek and all the hands from that line to the head of Wolf Creek to work under him.

On petition of John Farmer, he having Iron works established in Rhea County, it is ordered that Thomas Price, James Price, John Stewart, Peter Fine, John Bailey, Bartholomew Gwin, Avery Hannah, Robert Kerr, Micajah Clack, Thomas Atchley, William Miller, Reuben Dowel, William Tillary, Williamson Todd, Clayton Stockton, James Stockton, and Daniel M. Stockton be appointed a Jury of View to lay off adjacent to the said works 3000 acres of unapropriated land unfit for Cultivation for the use of said works as the law directs.

Last Will and Testament of William Gamble produced and proven by oath of David Campbell, one of the subscribing witnesses, it having been proven at the

May session by the other witness, Samuel Gamble. Ordered to be recorded.

Robert Gamble, George Russell, and Mary Gamble, Exrs. named in last Will and Testament of William Gamble, took oath and entered into bond with securities Wright Smith, John Cozby, and Charles Gamble for $4000.

(p. 199) On affidavit of Woodson Francis, ordered by the Court that John Rice esqr. issue an alias fi fa in favor of Alexander Ferguson against Benjamin Johnson and Reuben Freeman, the execution heretofore issued being lost or mislaid and no return having been made of said execution.

William Cumpton is released from further attendance as a Juror at this session; Isaac Mahan and Jacob Garrison also released from attendance.

Ordered that the order made at the last February Session of this Court appointing Miles Vernon guardian for the heirs of David Hill, dec'd, be amended to read as follows: Miles Vernon is appointed by the Court Guardian of James Hill, Rebecca Hill, Melvina Hill, and William Hill infant children of David Hill, late of the County of Sevier in this State, deceased who entered into bond with Thomas Price and Jacob Slover his securities for $1000.

Joseph Barr atty in fact for William McCamey Barr to William Noblet. Bill of Sale for a Negro girl; acknowledged by Joseph Barr; certified for registration.

The Court having failed to appoint inspectors for the next election and the Sheriff having summoned Crispien E. Shelton, Daniel Walker, and Carson Caldwell to inspect the election at Washington;

Arthur Fulton, George Gillespie, and Frederick Fulkerson inspectors at the Piney Precinct;

Samuel McDaniel, James Wilson, and William C. Wilson at the Sewee Princinct (Court approves of said appointments).

Robert Gamble, George Russell, and Mary Gamble, Exrs, returned an inventory of the property belonging to the estate of William Gamble; ordered to be recorded.

(p. 200) On petition of Isaac Baker, James Walton, Thomas McCarty, Benjamin McCarty, and William McCarty, they signifying their intentions of erecting Salt works in this County in the bounds of the 18th Section of fractional Township the 3rd West of the meredian in the Hiwassee district. Ordered that George W. Riggle, John Riggle, Thomas Anderson, Wilson Putman, Morris Putman, Mark Hardin, Joseph Harden, John Richardson, John Miller, Samuel Riddle, Randolph Gibson, Josiah Fike, Williamson Todd, William Beerman, Jesse Reese, James Reese, John Huff, and Benjamin Putman be appointed a Jury of View to lay off adjacent to the said contemplated works 3000 acres of unapropriated land unfit for cultivation for the use of said works.

Orlando Bradley appointed Constable in Capt. Jacob Brown's Company; bond with Miller Francis and Frederick Fulkerson.

Jurors appointed for next session of this Court:

Benjamin F. Jones	William Carter	Samuel Garwood	Abraham Davis
William Humbart	William Johns	Bruten Peters	Jesse Day Senr
Edmund Howerton	Benjamin Allen junr	Isaac Masoner	Brinkley Hornsby
Thornton Creed	Robert Walker	John Kelley	John Chateen
William Blackwood	Leonard Brooks	John A. Smith	George Preston
James Snelson	Samuel Frazier	Samuel Hackett	William Lauderdale
David Shelton, Constable to attend Court			John Hill

The Indenture heretofore entered into between Cain Able and Abraham Howard, Chairman of Court, binding Margaret Booker to said Able is disolved by order of the Court satisfactory reason having appeared to the Court that the same should be done.

64

(p. 201) State of Tennessee, Rhea County. Original Claim. August Term 1825.
"On this 1st day of August 1825 personally appeared in open Court being a Court
of Record for the County aforesaid Joseph Axhly or Atchley he was called by both
names at the time of his service resident in said County 78 years who being duly
sworn according to law doth on his oath make the following declaration in order to
obtain the provision made by the acts of Congress of the 18th March enlisted for
the term of nine months on the day of March in the year 1775 in the State of New
Jersey in the Company commanded by Captain Gallaway in the Regiment Commanded by
Maj. John Dunn & Col Herd in the line of the State of New Jersey continental
troops Genls Lee Milenburg & Genl Washington that he continued to serve in the
said Corps untill he was discharged on North River in the State of New York, that
he hereby relinquishes every claim whatever to a pension except the present that
his name is not on the roll of any State except New Jersey & that he served 6 Months
in Virginia & when Cornwallis was defeated & the following are the reasons for not
making earlier application for a pension. I am poor and ignorant & did not know
how or in what manner to apply and in pursuance of the act of the 1st May 1820,
I do somemnly swear that I was a resident citizen of the United States on the 18th
day of March 1818 and that I have not since that time by gift or sale or in any
manner disposed of my property or any part thereof with intent thereby so to di-
minish it as to bring myself within the provisions of an act of Congress entitled
an act to provide for certain persons engaged in the land and naval service of the
U.S. in the Revolutionary war passed on the 18th day of March 1818, and that I
have not nor has any person in trust for me any property or securities contracts
or debts due to me nor have I any income other than what is contained in the
Schedule hereto annexed and by me Subscribed.

One mare & Colt, 13 years old		$ 30.00
3 Cows & one Calf		15.00
7 Hogs		4.00
1 Bed		4.00
2 Biggins & 1 pail		.50
8 Chickens		.25
(p. 202)	Cupboard ware	1.50
	his	$ 63.75

Joseph X Atchley
mark

"I am by occupation a farmer & entirely unable to pursue it from age & disability
pains & diseases. I have a wife 60 years old weak & feeble & cannot work, my
son Moses is 17 years old crippled & unable to do any thing, my daughter Therse
16 years old & a little boy 10 years old & I cannot live without the charity of
the Government, I have not made any change in my property since March 1818.
Sworn to & declared on 1st August 1825. James Berry, Clerk.
"The foregoing declaration being red to the Court and it appearing to the satisfaction of the Court that the facts set forth in the declaration are true as also
the amount exhibited in said Schedule above annexed and the same was ordered to
be recorded and certified."
        The Jury of View appointed at May Sessions to lay off 3000 acres for
the use of Iron works intended to be erected by John Day and John Madden on Richland Creek made report: "find that there are 3000 acres along and adjoining the
lines of Jesse Witt their own Robert Hood and Lewis Morgan on both sides of Richland Creek in Rhea County thence up the Creek northwardly and on the mountain for
compliment we find that the said compliment of land may be run out in a square or
an oblong unfit for cultivation. . ." Confirmed by Court and ordered to be recorded.
        Isaac West released from payment of Tax on 100 acres of land for 1821,
he having been charged with 100 acres more than he ought to have been on the Tax
list.

(p. 203) Thomas Price and John Robinson, Commissioners appointed to settle with Daniel Walker, Exec. of last Will and Testament of Jeremiah Duncan, dec'd, returned the following settlement:

To amount of Sales returned at August Session 1820 as pr Clerks certificate	1840.34
Ditto Amount of Sales Made 5th Sept 1820	156.25 3/4
Ditto February Sessions 1821	108.35
Ditto Cash returned in first Inventory	59.00
To Amount of Notes returned in Same	606.81 3/4
	$ 2770.76
Balance due to Executor	116.72 3/4
	2887.48 3/4

Contra Cr

By amount of proven accounts Receipts and other Vouchers settled for 29th July 1824	$ 2104.94 ½
By Haleys proven account	32.50
Ditto Jonathan Fine order in favor of Rawlings	24.96
Ditto By Hiram Wolleys Voucher	50.00
Ditto Ditto	14.00
Ditto Ditto	16.50
Counterfeit dollar of Estate proven back	1.00
Sheriffs Receipt for Tax	11.62 ½
Monies expended and provisions provided for support of heirs Also work and labor performed in making a crop	63.94
Ditto 2 days Settlement	2.00
Esqr. Robinson Comm 2 days	2.00
Tho Price Commissioner 2 days	2.00
William Murphrees Note not collected	40.00
One ditto on Same not collected for	10.00
One ditto on Same for	225.00
One ditto on Same for	70.00
One ditto on Robert King for	20.00
Ballance of J. Harwoods Note	14.55
Ballance Rutherfords Note not collected	12.50
By error in the Credit G.W. Lewis Note	54.00
By 5 pr ct commission on $2319.46 3/4	115.97
	$ 2887.48 3/4

(p. 204) State VS John Witt. Bastardy. Ordered that the defendant pay to Dorcas Taylor $15.00 quarterly for the ensueing year for the maintainance of a bastard child begotten by the said defendant upon the body of Dorcas Taylor.

Stephen Winton appointed to take the list of taxable property and polls in Captain Baker's Company.

(p. 205) Justices on bench (2nd August)— Daniel Walker, Jesse Thompson, John Robinson, and William M. Smith.

Woodson Francis, Sheriff, returned a list of Jurors summoned to appear at this term (see list on page 56; difference in the two lists was Robert Montooth instead of Samuel), out of which a Grand Jury was elected: Addison Riggs, Robert Carr, John Day, Bryan McDonald, Jacob Brown, Robert Bolton, Elijah Wyatt, John Hall, David Roper, Joseph McDaniel, Walter Edwards, Robert Montooth, and David Leuty. John Day appointed foreman and David Shelton a Constable to attend the Grand Jury.

There remained of the original pannel: Peter Fine, William McDonald, John Walker, Alexander McCall, Peter Minnick, John B. Swann, William Woodward, and Orville Paine.

On application of Allen Kennedy, he is appointed guardian of Mary Kennedy; bond with Rezin Rawlings, his security, for $1200.

(p. 206) Peter Fine is released from further attendance as a Juror at this Term.

Cornelius Milliken, Admr. of Isham Gann, dec'd, VS William Blythe (No. 1371). Defendant confessed judgment for $121.43 3/4 debt plus costs.

Cornelius Milliken, Admr. VS Henry Airhart & James Stewart (No. 1372). Defendants confessed judgment for $92.43 3/4 debt plus costs.

Elisha Kirkland VS John Rice, Henry Collins, & Elijah Rice (No. 1373). Cause heard by jury (William McDonald, John Walker, Alexander McCall, Peter Minnick, John B. Swan, William Woodward, Orville Paine, Thomas Henry, Abraham Miller, David Blevins, Solomon Nediffer, and Samuel Looney) which says the defendants have not paid the debt of $220.00 in the plaintiffs declaration nor any part of it; plaintiffs damages assessed to $12.10. Defendants to pay debt, damages, and costs.

(p. 207) State VS Joseph McDaniel (No. 1374). Defendant says he cannot gainsay the charges; fined 25¢ plus costs.

McGhees & McCarty, assignees &c VS John Clement & Isaac Clement (No. 1375). Defendants having failed to file any plea to the plaintiffs declaration, judgment is entered against them for $137.61 debt and damages plus costs.

James Kelly VS Aquila Parker (No. 1376). Motion on security. Came the plaintiff by attorney and a jury (same as above) to enquire whether James Kelly (p. 208) was security for and paid as such security money for the said defendant. Jury finds that Kelly paid $47.30; to recover said amount from defendant plus costs.

James Thompson VS Robert Brabson (No. 1377). On motion of the defendant, ordered that the pleadings in this cause be opened and that the defendant have leave to file a plea of set off upon the payment of the costs of the present term; cause continued until next term.

Henry Welker assignee &c VS James G. Martin (No. 1378). Defendant withdraws his plea of payment to the plaintiffs declaration and says he cannot gainsay the plaintiffs demand against him for $255.25 and damages; also costs.

(p. 209) State VS John Stewart (No. 1379). Defendant says he cannot gainsay the charges; fined 25¢ and costs.

Jesse Poe, Admr &c. VS William M. Smith. Appeal. Came the parties by their attornies and a jury (same as above) which after hearing the evidence retired to consult of their verdict; respited until tomorrow morning.

Grand Jury returned presentments: State vs Isaac Clement for an affray; State vs Thomas D. Paine for an affray; State vs David Hounshell for an affray; State vs John Fooshee for an assault and battery.

(p. 210) Justices on bench (3rd August) — Daniel Walker, Jesse Thompson, John Robinson, and William M. Smith.

State VS William H. Duglas & Samuel Romines (No. 1380). Defendants made default; it appearing to the satisfaction of the Court that two writs of Sci fas had issued in 1825 (one from Feb Session and one from May Session) requiring them the said defendants to come and shew cause if any they had why a conditional forfeiture for the sum of $500 entered up against them should not be made absolute. Therefore considered by the Court that the State recover the said forfeiture from the defendants, plus costs.

State VS David Leuty. Came the defendant and his securities, George Henry Sr. and John Parker, acknowledge themselves indebted to the State for $500; void on condition that the defendant appear at the November Session, and "there abide by what further order or decree the said Court may make in this cause respecting bastardy and he in the meantime same harmless the County of Rhea from all charges that may likely be charged to said County by the birth and maintainance of

2

a child begotten by said defendant on the body of Margaret Woodson (late Margaret Leuty) not yet born."

Grand Jury returned the following presentments: State vs Jacob Brown for an affray; State vs Flemming Manley for an affray; State vs John A. Smith for an affray; State vs James L. Cobbs for an affray.

(p. 211) State VS Celia Angland (No. 1381). Thomas J. Campbell, Atty General; defendant says she is not guilty; jury (Joshua Mosely, Josiah Thompson, Leonard Brooks, Thomas Piper, Richard Waldrid, James Stewart, Absolam Barnes, Joseph Harwood, George Henry Sen., Barefoot Armstrong, Jesse Poe, and Matthew Hubbart) says the defendant is guilty as charged; fined 25¢ and costs. John Angland security for payment of fine and costs.

State VS Jacob Brown (No. 1382). Defendant says he cannot gainsay the charges; fined 25¢ and costs.

State VS John Herral. Petit Larceny. Defendant made default; considered by Court that he forfeit $500, the sum in the recognizance, unless he shall shew cause to the contrary at the next session of this Court.

(p. 212) State VS William Harrel & Samuel Harrel. Securities for the appearance of John Harrel. Called upon to bring into Court the body of John Harrel, came not but made default; for this they are to forfeir to the State $250 each.

State VS Jeremiah Carver. Petit Larceny. Defendant came not but made default; to forfeit $500 recognizance bond plus costs.

State VS Moses Thompson & Josiah Thompson. Securities for appearance of Jeremiah Carver. For default, they are to forfeit $250 each.

(p. 213) State VS John Foushea (No. 1383). Defendant says he cannot gainsay charge against him; fined 25¢ and costs.

State VS Absolam Barns (No. 1384). Tipling House. Defendant says he is not guilty; jury (William McDonald, John Walker, John B. Swan, William Woodward, Orville Paine, Solomon Nediffer, Joshua Mosely, Richard Waldrid, David Blevins, John McClanahan, Jesse Poe, and Samuel Looney) finds him guilty as charged; fined $1.00 and costs.

(p. 214) Jesse Poe, Admr, &c VS William Smith. Appeal. Jury heretofore sworn in this cause and was respited until today, returned into Court and say they cannot agree; jurors are discharged and cause is continued until next session.

Report from Jury of View to lay off 3000 acres for the use of the Iron Works established by John Farmer: "In conformity to an order . . . we have proceeded to examine and condemn the following sections and quarter sections of land that are unfit for cultivation for the use of John Farmers Iron works in Rhea County on Soowee Creek which are numbered as follows to wit: Northwest quarter of Section 19, Range second west of the meridian and first township, Being part of his Ore bank. Section first third Range West 2nd fractional Township. Southwest and northwest quarters of Section 12, Range 3 west, second fractional township. Southwest and northeast quarters of section 25 same range and Township, Northwest quarter of Section 36 in the same range and Township. Southeast quarter of section 35 in the same range and Township. Southeast and Northeast quarters of Section 14 in same Range and Township, and Southeast quarter of Section 24. . ." Confirmed by Court and ordered to be recorded.

(p. 215) "Mary Walkers declaration of Intention was this day duly proven in open Court by the oaths of Thomas J. Campbell and Elihu Barclay, the subscribing witnesses thereto and the same was ordered to be certified for Registration."

Jesse Poe, Admr. &c VS William M. Smith. A commission is awarded the plaintiff to take the deposition of Abraham Parker in State of Alabama by giving the defendant 30 days notice of the time and place of taking the same.

  Samuel Hoskins VS John Rice. Commission is awarded to take depositions generally by giving the oposite party 10 days notice of the time and place of those taken within the County and 20 days notice of those taken in the State and 30 days notice of those taken out of the State.

  James Thompson VS Robert Brabson. Commissions awarded to take depositions generally; 10 days notice in the County; 25 days notice out of the County.

  State VS James L. Cobbs. Defendant acknowledged himself indebted to the State for $250; David Leuty also indebted for $250; void if Cobb makes his appearance "here from day to day and answer the Charge of the State to be exhibited against him for an affray and not depart the Court without leave."

(p. 216) State VS Flemming Manley. Defendant indebted to State for $250; also William Walker for $250; void if Manley makes his appearance from day to day to, answer a charge of the State for an affray.

  State VS Collier Johnson (No. 1385). With consent of the Attorney General and the Court a Nolle proseque is entered in this cause; County to pay costs.

  State VS James L. Cobbs. Defendant comes into Court and acknowledges himself indebted to the State for $250, and John Day and David Leuty in the sum of $125 each; void on condition that Cobbs makes his appearance at next Court.

  State VS Flemming Manley. Defendant and Jesse Poe acknowledged themselves indebted to State for $500; void on condition Manley appears at next term of Court.

(p. 217) Henry Collins, William Johnson & Samuel Logan, Commissioners to settle with Matthew Hubbart and Abigail Ferguson, Admr. & Admrx. of Robert Ferguson, dec'd, returned settlement; received and ordered to be recorded.

  William Walker, Exr. of last Will and Testament of George Walker, dec'd, returned inventory and account of sales of said estate; ordered to be recorded.

(p. 218) Justices on bench (4th August) — Daniel Walker, John Robinson, and William M. Smith.

  William L. Bradley et al VS William Lewis. On petition of the defendant a Certiorari is awarded him to bring this cause into Court from the Justices record filed in the Clerks office of Rhea County on his entering into bond and security as the law directs. From which opinion of the Court the Plaintiffs Excepts in law and filed reasons for the same.

  All causes not tried at this term are ordered to be continued until next Court. Court adjourned.

NOVEMBER TERM 1825

(p. 219) Court of Pleas and Quarter Sessions met on the first Monday and Seventh day of November 1825 at the Courthouse in Washington. Justices on bench— Jonathan Fine, William M. Smith, John McClure, John Robinson, Carson Caldwell, James Wilson, Crispein E. Shelton, Jesse Thompson, Daniel Walker, James McDonald, James A. Darwin, and John Cozby.

  Benjamin F. Jones appointed overseer of road in place of William Gray.

  The road as reported by the Jury of View appointed at last session from Kellys Ferry up Goodfield Creek near Thomas Coxes Mill &c. to be established as follows: Beginning at Kellys Ferry, thence by John McDaniels, thence by Cox's Mill, thence by Lucas' Mill, thence by Igous, thence by Vernons, thence by Tillerys, thence to intersect the Ross's Ferry Road above Tillerys.

  On application of John Smith Sr., he is appointed administrator of the estate of Evan Evans, dec'd; bond for $1200 with Robert Parks and James Kelly, his securities.

On motion of John Smith, Sr., Admr. on estate of Evan Evans, ordered that Robert Parks, James A. Darwin, and Woodson Francis are appointed commissioners to lay off a years provisions for the widow and children of Evan Evans.

(p. 220) On application of Spencer Benson Jr., ordered that he keep Mary David one year for $30.00

John Smith, Admr. on estate of Evan Evans, returned an inventory of said estate; received and ordered to be recorded.

The last Will and Testament of Philip Harmon, dec'd, was produced and proven by oaths of George Ramsey and Thomas M. Harp, subscribing witnesses.

Edward Templeton, Executor named in will of Philip Harmon, took the oath and entered into bond for $500 with George Ramsey and John Fitzgerrel, securities.

Richard G. Waterhouse & Enoch Parsons to Lewis Wilkerson. Deed of Conveyance for 150 acres; proven in part by Jeremiah Howerton; certified for further probate.

Richard G. Waterhouse & Enoch Parsons to Roger Reece. Deed of Conveyance for 200 acres; proven in part by Jeremiah Howerton; certified for further probate.

(p. 221) John H. Beck to Matthew Hubbart for use of Elias Ferguson. Deed of Conveyance for a certain undivided moiety or childs part of a tract of land; acknowledged by Grantor; certified for registration.

William Howard appointed overseer of road in place of Mansion Howard.

John Alexander appointed overseer of road in place of Lewis Wilkerson.

Thomas Breeding appointed overseer of road in place of Boldin Fine.

David Ragsdale allowed $40.00 for keeping Mary David 12 months.

George W. Riggle appointed a Constable in Capt. Riggle's Company; bond with Jonathan Fine and Adam W, Caldwell, his securities.

Isaac Baker appointed a Constable in Capt. Baker's Company; bond with Henry Collins and Woodson Francis, his securities.

(p. 222) William S. Russell appointed a Constable in Capt. Brown's Company; bond with Jesse Poe and Samuel Looney, his securities.

James Walker appointed a Constable in Capt. Swan's Company; bond with Jesse Thompson and Moses Thompson, his securities.

Anson Dearmon appointed a Constable in Capt. Brown's Company; bond with Lewis Wilkerson and John Parker, his securities.

John Robinson, James Wilson of Yellow Creek, and William Smith of Yellow Creek are appointed Commissioners to settle with William Walker, Exr. of last Will and Testament of George Walker, dec'd.

Charles White released from payment of Tax on two negroes for 1825, he having been charged with the same by mistake.

Eli Ferguson to John H. Beck. Deed of Conveyance for 130 acres heretofore proven by oath of Spills B. Dyer; proven this day by Lewis Wilkerson the other witness; certified for registration.

On application of Woodson Francis, Henry Collins is admitted to swear in as deputy Sheriff for Rhea County.

(p. 223) Thomas J. Campbell, Solicitor, allowed $40.00 for exofficio services.

Woodson Francis, Sheriff, allowed $50.00 for exofficio services.

James Berry, Clerk of this Court, allowed $40.00 for Exofficio services for 1825 and $25.00 for making out the Tax lists for the same year.

Reuben Freeman appointed overseer of road leading from Washington to Mrs. Lauderdales to begin at the line of the Town at the head of the Town Spring and work to where the road leading from Kellys ferry intersects said road and that he have the following hands to work under him: all this own hands and all the

hands belonging to Allen Kennedys possessions in the Southern Liberties, all the
hands belonging to the place where James G. Martin had his quarter, Cornelius
Myors, James P. Miller, Walter R. Paine, and Michael Stoner,

Ordered "that the Clerk make out the Tax list taken by Stephen Winton in
Captain Bakers Company and by him returned to Court this day in the same manner
and return the amount of the same as he has heretofore done with the Tax lists of
this County."

Orville Paine allowed to enter his taxable property and polls on the
Tax list returned to Court this day by Stephen Winton, said Paine having neglected
to make return of the same at the proper time which taxable property & polls is as
follows: 200 acres of land, one white poll, and one stud horse at $4.00.

(p. 224) Ordered that James Stockton, overseer of road from William Prices line
to Souey Creek crossing the road above William Millers have to work under him in
addition to his former hands William Miller, Pleasant M. Miller, Robert Carr,
Micajah Clack, Moses Wyott, Elijah Wyott, Levy Thrailkill, and Nicholas Frailey.

William Runyon appointed overseer of road from Kellys Ferry up Goodfield
Creek to where said Road intersects the Rosses Ferry Road; hands: Joseph McDaniel,
Sabred Martin, Jonathan Stanly, Cyrus Quiet, James Kelly and all the hands belong-
ing to Samuel Looneys bounds to help cut out said road.

Jury of View appointed at last session to lay off 3000 acres of unappro-
priated land for the purpose of erecting Salt works by Isaac Baker, James Walton,
Thomas McCarty, Benjamin McCarty, and William McCarty made the following report:
"Beginning at the 8th section 3rd fractional township, Range 2nd west of the Meridian line, Section 18th north east, north west & south west quarters of said section, 18th Section 19th north west quarters south west quarter & south east quarter of section 19, 17th section quarters north east & south east quarters, 20th
Section all in fractional Township and Range 2nd Range 3rd Fractional Township 1st
North East & South East quarters of Section 13th, North East quarter of Section
24 . . ." Report was received and confirmed by the Court; ordered to be recorded.

(p. 225) Benjamin Bond, John Roddy, Vaden H. Giles, Jesse Martin, William McCormick, William Blackwood, and Isaac Mahan appointed Jury of View to lay out a road
the nearest and best way from James McDonalds Ferry to intersect the Calhoun Road
at the McMinn County line.

Orlando Bradley resigned as a Constable.

Henry Henry allowed $9.00 for attending the Courts three days each as a
Constable.

John Lea, Deputy Sheriff, allowed $8.87½ for money paid by him to John
Love and John Day for supper, Lodging & breakfast for two sets of Jurors.

Joseph Love and William T. Gillenwaters allowed $10.00 each for settling
with the Collector and Trustee of Rhea County for 1824.

On motion of James A. Darwin, ordered that the Indenture entered into
between him and the Chairman of the Court binding James Madison Chapman be canceled and made void. On motion of William Woodward, he is permitted to take said
James M. Chapman on the same terms the said Darwin had him from this time.

(p. 226) On motion of Jeremiah Howerton, ordered that the Indenture entered into
between him and the Chairman of the Court binding Benjamin Chester be canseled
and made void.

Jurors appointed for next session of this Court:

Peter Daniel	Jacob Garrison	Samuel Price	James Price
Mantion Howard	David Day	Jacob Bryson	Merideth Cox
Benjamin Bond	Thomas Harp	William Woodward	Charles Woodward
John Barnett	Kennedy Cooper	James Taylor	Thomas Marshal

Allen Kennedy	Joseph Rice	John Martin	William Lowrey
Edmund Bean	John Parker	Samuel McDaniel	Thomas B. Swan
Abraham Cox. a Constable to attend Court			Anson Dearmon

Jurors appointed for next term of Circuit Court:

Roger Reese	Moses Paul	Robert Bell	John Cozby
John Roddy	James Carrell	Abijah Boggs	Patrick Martin
Samuel Igo	William Moore	David Campbell	Abraham Miller
James Coulter	Joseph Love	James Montgomery	James Lillard
Robert Bell Jun.	Pulaski Poe	John Day	Archabald Taylor
Matthew Hubbart	James A. Darwin	Jonathan Fine	William Kennedy
David Shelton, a Constable to attend Court			Frederick Fulkerson

James Wilson & Nancy Wilson to Moses Kirpatrick. Deed of Conveyance for 130 acres dated 12th December 1822 lying in Monroe County, Kentucky; acknowledged by James Wilson and Nancy (after being examined separately). Certified for registration to Kentucky.

(p. 227) Thomas Arthur Jr. assignee of Rowlen Brown VS James Kirkpatrick (No. 1386). Defendant says he cannot gainsay the plaintiffs demand for $134.37½ debt and damages plus costs.

Robert Parks VS Orville Paine (No. 1387). Defendant dismisses appeal and confesses judgment for costs.

(p. 228) Justices on bench (8th November)— Carson Caldwell, William M. Smith, John McClure, James McDonald, James A. Darwin, Azariah David, Daniel Walker, William Smith, John Robinson, and John Cozby.

Woodson Francis, Sheriff, returned a list of Jurors summoned to appear at this Court (see list on page 63) out of which a Grand Jury was elected: John Hill, Leonard Brooks, Brinkley Hornsby, James Snelson, Samuel Garwood, Benjamin F. Jones, William Carter, John Chatten, Bruten Peters, William Lauderdale, Thornton Creed, Benjamin Allen Jun., and Samuel Frazier. John Hill appointed foreman and David Shelton a Constable to serve the Grand Jury.

There remained of the original pannel: Jesse Day Sr., Samuel R. Hackett, William Blackwood, Edmund Howerton, John Kelley, Isaac Masoner, Abraham Davis, William Humbart, and Robert Walker.

(p. 229) Daniel Rawlings to William Lauderdale. Deed of Conveyance for 114 acres; heretofore proven by Benjamin C. Stout; this day proven by John Henniger; certified for registration.

On motion of John Day, ordered that an orphan boy named Charles Coats be bound to the said John Day to live with him after the manner of a bound apprentice for five years and two months; at the end of that time the said Day is to give him two good suits of coarse clothes and one fine suit and during his apprenticeship to instruct or cause him to be instructed in the art and mastry of the blacksmith business and to give him three months schooling in said five years and two months.

John Rice successor &c for the use of Jane Lawson VS David Ragsdale. Came the parties by attornies and agree and with the assent of the Court a Commission is awarded the Defendant to take the deposition of David Henderson before John Russell esqr. a Justice of the Peace in Hamilton County by giving the plaintiff ten days notice of the time and place of taking the same.

Jesse Poe, Admr. of William Lewis dec'd VS William M. Smith. Commission awarded Defendant to take the deposition of Abraham Parker in Alabama.

Andrew Evans VS Jesse Reese. Commission awarded the Plaintiff to take the deposition of Elizabeth Floyd de bene esse at the house of Andrew Evans.

(p. 230) William Johnson, Trustee of Rhea County, allowed $127.50 in his settlement with the Commissioners.

72

Joseph Galbreath and Patrick Martin surrender the guardianship of the minor children of James Galbreath.

William S. Leuty VS Jacob Slover. "The Sheriff of Rhea County having failed to take security for the appearance of the said Defendant the Plaintiff by his attorney notifies the said sheriff that he holds him as appearance bail as prescribed by law."

William Runyon VS Woodson Francis. "The Coroner of Rhea County having failed to take security for the appearance of the said defendant the Plaintiff by his attorney notifies the said Coroner that he holds him as appearance bail as prescribed by law."

William S. Leuty VS Benjamin McKenzie (No. 1388). Plaintiff dismisses his suit and confesses judgment for the costs.

Court proceeded to appoint a Trustee for the County for the next two years. Carson Caldwell, Crispein E. Shelton, and Jonathan Fine esquires in nomination and upon balloting and counting out the ballots, Caldwell had 6, Shelton had 5, and Fine had 1 vote; whereupon Carson Caldwell was pronounced duly elected Trustee. Caldwell entered into bond with Thomas Cox, John McClure, James Kelly, and Edmund Bean.

(p. 231) John Dudley for the use of James King VS James G. Martin (No. 1389). Came the parties by their attornies and a jury (William Runyan, Lewis Wilkerson, Elias Majors, Jesse Day, Samuel R. Hackett, William Blackwood, Edmond Howerton, John Kelly, Isaac Masoner, Abraham Davis, William Humbart, and Robert Walker) which says the Defendant did assume and undertake in manner and form as the plaintiff in declaring hath complained against him, and they do assess the plaintiffs damage by reason thereof to the sum of $107.00 (also the costs).

Stephen Plumley VS Thomas B. Swann (No. 1390). Covenant. Came the parties by their attornies and a jury (same as above) which says that the defendant has not well and truly kept and performed his covenant as the plaintiff declares. Plaintiffs damages assessed at $94.06¼ (plus costs).

(p. 232) Justices on bench (9th November)— James McDonald, John McClure, William M. Smith, and Carson Caldwell.

State VS David Hownshell (No. 1391). Defendant says he cannot gainsay the charges; fined 50¢ and costs.

State VS Nathan Blackwell (No. 1392). Defendant says he cannot gainsay the charges; fined 50¢ and costs; James Blackwell security for payment.

(p. 233) State VS Thomas D. Paine (No. 1393). Defendant says he cannot gainsay the charges; fined 50¢ and costs; William Blackwood security for payment.

State VS Isaac Clements (No. 1394). Defendant says he cannot gainsay the charges; fined 50¢ and costs; William Blackwell security for payment.

State VS James L. Cobbs (No. 1395). Defendant says he is not guilty; jury (John Clack, James Kelly, William Hill, Jesse Day Sen, Samuel R. Hackett, William Blackwood, Edmund Howerton, John Kelley, Isaac Masoner, Abraham Davis, William Humbart, and Robert Walker) finds the defendant not guilty; County to pay costs.

(p. 234) State VS Flemming Manley (No. 1396). Defendant says he is not guilty; jury (John Hill, Leonard Brooks, Brinkley Hornsby, James Snelson, Samuel Garwood, Benjamin F. Jones, William Carter, John Chatten, Bruten Peters, William Lauderdale, Thornton Creed, and Benjamin Allen Jr.) finds the defendant guilty as charged; fined 50¢ and costs; William Walker security for payment.

State VS John A. Smith. Defendant says he is not guilty; jury (John Clack, James Kelly, William Hill, Jesse Day Sr, Samuel R. Hackett, William Blackwood, Edmund Howerton, John Kelley, Isaac Masoner, Abraham Davis, William Humbart, and Robert Walker) says it cannot agree; mistrial is entered and cause is continued until next session of this Court.

(p. 235) State VS Jeremiah Carver (No. 1397). On motion of the defendant, it is ordered that the forfeiture incurred by him be set aside upon payment of all the costs; whereupon came Mary Thompson and Josiah Thompson, securities for payment.
      State VS Josiah Thompson (No. 1398). On motion of the defendant, it is ordered that the forfeiture incurred by him as appearance bail of Jeremiah Carver be set aside upon the payment of all costs; Mary Thompson security for payment.
      State VS Moses Thompson (No. 1399). On motion of the defendant, it is ordered that the forfeiture incurred by him as appearance bail of Jeremiah Carver be set aside upon the payment of all costs; Mary Thompson and Josiah Thompson, securities for payment.

(p. 236) State VS John A. Smith. Came the defendant and acknowledged himself indebted to State for $250; John Whaley in sum of $250; void on condition that John A. Smith appear at next term of this Court to answer the States charge for an affray.
      William Runyon VS Woodson Francis. Commission is awarded Defendant to take the deposition of John Brigman in Bledsoe County, Tennessee.
      William Kennedy resigned as a Justice of the Peace.
      Ordered that the Grand Jury be discharged from further service this term.
      Windle & Sevier VS Thomas Hamilton (No. 1400). Came the parties by their attornies and a jury (William Carter, John Hill, Benjamin F. Jones, Benjamin Allen Jr., James Snelson, Leonard Brooks, Brinkley Hornsby, Samuel Garwood, William Lauderdale, Samuel Frazier, Bruten Peters, and John Chattin) which finds for the defendant; plaintiff to pay costs. Plaintiff prays an appeal to the next Circuit Court; granted.

(p. 237) Archabald Sevier VS Thomas Hamilton (No. 1401). Came the parties by their attornies and a jury (Anson Dearmon, Samuel R. Hackett, William Lewis, James Swan, Walter R. Paine, James Kelly, George Manor, George Ransom, John A. Smith, Jacob Brown, Thomas J. Campbell, and Elihu Barclay) which finds for the defendant; Plaintiff prays an appeal to the next Circuit Court; granted.
      William Randolph VS James Swan (No. 1402). Petition for Certiorari and supersedias. Defendant by attorney presented his petition; Court refused to grant prayer. James Swan by his attorney tenders his Bill of exceptions; Swan prays appeal to the next Circuit Court; allowed.

(p. 238) State VS David Leuty (No. 1403). Bastardy. Came Thomas J. Campbell and moved the Court to dismiss the present proceedings therein because the child charged to have been begotten by the said David Leuty was born in McMinn County; Court dismisses case and County to pay costs.
      David Leuty came into Court and filed his Petition as follows:
"The Worshipful, the Court of Common Pleas and Quarter Sessions in and for Rhea County now in session. The memorial and humble petition of David Leuty a citizen of the County of Rhea would respectfully shew to your worships that heretofore he unfortunately became bound in the solemn bonds of wedlock with a certain Margaret Woodson who bore to your memorialist three children in that estate, but owing to the immorality and depravity of uncontroled human nature producing effects unpleasant for your memoralist to think on much less willing at this time to mention he was compelled for the preservation of his peace and repose his character together with that of his little resing progeny by a petition filed before the Honorable Circuit Court for the County of Rhea to apply for and on the hearing of said application he obtained a disolution of the solemn rites of Matrimony with the then Margaret Leuty formerly Margaret Woodson, And

(p. 239) altho reluctantly compelled to this only alternative to maintain for himself and family a common Standing in the social compact Yet there remains Some what connect with this ever lemented incident of his life one more object that goes far to allay and exclude from the bosom of your Memorialist that little domestick happiness and comfort hoped for in a secluded retirement on the bosom of his little family on account of a little innocent inoffending infant brought into an unfriendly world by the unhappy and thoughtless connection with your petitioner and its mother since the dissolution of the Marriage rites. Your Memorialist therefore humbly petitions Your Worships as conservators of the peace harmony and morral order of the Social compact to extend to him the benefits of the provisions of the Statutes of our common Country by legitemating said child by the name of John Hess Leuty thereby to be made capable to inherent in common with your petitioners other children, this will authorize and encorage your petitioner to extend thereto that Fatherly care and protection necessary for the rearing encouraging and nurtureing said infant in the paths of moral honesty and integrety and nurtureing its youthfull mind in the fiar maxims and admonitions of its great Creator And your petitioner in duty &c.   David Leuty 8th Novr 1825
To which petition Margaret Leuty by her Attorney excepts."

John Barnett for the use of Love & Kennedy VS James C. Mitchell. "In this Cause time is allowed the Defendant to plead to the Plaintiffs Declaration so as not to delay the trial of the Cause."

(p. 240) Justices on bench (10th November) - James McDonald, William M. Smith, Carson Caldwell, and John McClure.

Joel K. Brown VS Elijah Rice (No. 1404). Petition for Certiorari and Supersedeas presented by Defendant; argument thereon being had and mature deliberation had, the Court refused to grant the prayer of the said Elijah Rice. Plaintiff to recover his costs from defendant.

Abraham Miller VS William Vaughn (No. 1405). Came the plaintiff by attorney and a jury (William Lewis, James Swan, Henry Henry, David Caldwell, William Johnson, Walter R. Paine, Jacob Brown, Thomas Hamilton, William Long, Joseph Rice, William Walker, and Robert Locke) which says that Abraham Miller was security for the said Vaughn and paid for him as such security $11.41. Plaintiff to recover $11.41 plus costs.

William M. Smith resigned as a Justice of the Peace.

Ordered that all causes not tried at this session be continued until next Court. Court adjourned.

FEBRUARY TERM 1826

(p. 241) Court of Pleas and Quarter Sessions met at the Courthouse in Washington on the first Monday and 6th day of February 1826. Justices on bench- George Gillespie, Carson Caldwell, Daniel Walker, Arthur Fulton, William Smith, Stephen Winton, James Wilson, William C. Wilson, John Robinson, Jonathan Fine, John McClure, Thomas Cox, Azariah David, John Cozby, James A. Darwin, Jesse Thompson, Crispein E. Shelton, and James McDonald.

On application of Thomas J. Campbell, Solicitor, James Berry, Clerk of this Court produced a Receipt from the Treasurer of East Tennessee for $319.20. Also a receipt from the Trustee of Rhea County for $15.41 3/4, the amount of fines and forfeitures collected by him.

Hopkins L. Turney produced his Licence as a practicing attorney of law.

John Smith, Admr. of estate of Evan Evans, returned an account of sales on 2nd December 1825.

Report of Robert Parks, Woodson Francis, and James A. Darwin, appointed Commissioners to lay off a years provisions for widow and children of Evan Evans, as follows: all the corn and fodder on the place and all the wheat, rye and oats, 10 fatening hogs, their crop of Cotton and flax and $30 out of the proceeds of the sale to procure salt, shoe leather and other necessaries for the support of the widow and children.

(p. 242) Samuel Gamble and Peach Taylor, having been appointed by the Legislature Justices of the Peace for Rhea County, produced their Commissions and took the oath of office.

William Smith appointed Chairman of this Court in place of John Rice, resigned.

Edward Templeton returned an inventory of the estate of Philip Harmon.

Thomas Price and Willis H. Chapman appointed Commissioners to settle with the Clerks of County and Circuit Courts.

John Blythe appointed overseer of road in place of William Seymore.

John H. Henderson appointed overseer of road in place of Archabald Taylor.

Benjamin F. Locke appointed overseer of road in place of William Moore.

Abijah Bogges appointed overseer of road in place of Joseph Thompson; to have in addition to Thompsons hands, William H. West, James Carrall, and James Gallant.

(p. 243) James Smith appointed overseer of road in place of Leonard Brightwell. To work road from Fraziers Ferry to Frenches Mill from Mud Creek to where said road intersects the Washington Road and that all the hands in the following bounds work under him: beginning where said road crosses Mud Creek, thence along said road to where it intersects the Washington Road, then a direct line to Richland Creek, then down the creek to the River, then up the River to where John Singleton now lives, then to the beginning, so as to include said Singleton, James Jacobs, Francis Reavely, and John Bowlen.

Jacob Runnels appointed overseer of road in place of Joseph Love, resigned.

William Fox appointed overseer of road in place of Joshua Hill.

Kennedy Cooper appointed overseer of road in place of Palatiah Chilton.

Jurors appointed for next term of this Court:

Bryan McDonald	Charles Witt	John Parker	Abner Casey
John Smith	James McCanse	Landon Rector	Charles Reevely
Edward Stokes	Palatiah Chilton	James Woodward	Isaac West
Elijah Wyatt	David Blevins	Micajah Clack	Henry Walton
James Carroll	Abijah Harris	Charles Ryon	William Walker
Jesse Day Sr.	Edward Templeton	Joseph McDaniel	John Roddy
Anson Dearmon, a Constable to attend Court			John Chatten

Frederick Fulkerson resigned as a Justice of the Peace.

(p. 244) The following Justices were appointed to take the lists of taxable property and polls (all of the free males over twenty one years of age) for 1826:

John Robinson	in Captain Riggle's Company
Jesse Thompson	in Captain Swann's Company
John Cozby	in Captain Hill's Company
Azariah David	in Captain Howard's Company
James A. Darwin	in Captain Lewis' Company
Samuel Gamble	in Captain Powel's Company
Thomas Cox	in Captain Cooley's Company
Peach Taylor	in Captain Miller's Company
James Wilson	in Captain White's Company
Stephen Winton	in Captain Baker's Company
William C. Wilson	in Captain Mee's Company

William Walker, Exr. of last Will and Testament of George Walker, dec'd, returned a settlement made with John Robinson, William Smith, and James Wilson, Commissioners appointed by the Court to make settlement.

Abraham Cox appointed a Constable in Capt. Cooley's Company; bond with Samuel Hackett and James Lillard, his securities.

(p. 245) Court proceeded to a classification of the Justices: William Smith, James Wilson, John McClure, Carson Caldwell, and Thomas Cox were drawn on the 1st Class for holding this Court for the trial of Causes.

Daniel Walker, Crispien E. Shelton, Samuel Gamble, Jesse Thompson, and George Gillespie on the 2nd Class.

John Cozby, Peach Taylor, James McDonald, Stephen Winton, and John Robinson on the 3rd Class.

James A. Darwin, Jonathan Fine, William C. Wilson, Azariah David, and Arthur Fulton on the 4th Class for the above purposes.

Ordered that Jurors be allowed 50¢ per day for this year.

William Smith, William S. Leuty, and John Locke, Commissioners appointed under the provisions of an Act entitled An Act authorizing the County Court of Rhea to lay a tax to build a new jail in said County, reported a plan for a jail as in said Act provided, together with the sum which in the opinion of said Commissioners would be necessary to be appropriated for the erection of said jail.

Ordered that a sum of $2000 be appropriated for the building of said jail, and that the sum of $666.66 2/3 be levied upon the taxable property and polls of the County for 1826, the sum of $666.66 2/3 be levied as aforesaid for the purposes aforesaid for 1827, and the sum of $666.66 2/3 be levied for 1828.

(p. 246) The said tax to be levied in the following proportion:

On each 100 acres of land	25¢
On each town lot	25¢
On each white poll	25¢
On each black poll	50¢

and that said tax be collected, accounted for, and appropriated as in said Act provided.

Ordered that the jury and poor tax for 1826 be of the same amount on the various articles of taxation as laid by this Court for 1825.

Thomas Cox, George Gillespie, Joseph Love, James Wilson, and Abram Cox appointed Commissioners to settle with the Bank Agent of Rhea County for the school funds in the hands of said Agent.

Joseph Love, Wyllis H. Chapman, George Mayo, James Berry, William Johnson (Col), John Locke, and Carson Caldwell appointed Trustees of Tennessee Academy.

It appearing to the satisfaction of the Court that from the refusal of a number of the Commissioners or Directors to act as appointed under the provisions of the Act of Assembly entitled An Act authorizing the County Court of Rhea to lay a tax to build a new jail in said County, that but the number of three remained to carry the provisions of said act into execution.

(p. 247) Ordered that Joseph Love and James Berry be appointed additional Commissioners or Directors for the purposes in said Act.

Ordered that the Indenture between the Chairman of this Court and Azariah David for binding Jane Myers be dessolved.

Azariah David resigned as a Trustee of Tennessee Academy.

James Henry to Joshua Tindle. Deed of Conveyance for 200 acres; proven by Woodson Francis and John Tindle; certified for registration.

Richard G. Waterhouse to Peter Majors. Deed of Conveyance for 47 acres; acknowledged by Grantor; certified for registration.

Richard G. Waterhouse to John Wasson. Deed of Conveyance for 114 acres; acknowledged by Grantor; certified for registration.

Richard G. Waterhouse to James Preston. Deed of Conveyance for 26 acres; acknowledged by Grantor; certified for registration.

(p. 248) Richard G. Waterhouse to Arthur Fulton. Deed of Conveyance for 50 acres; acknowledged by Grantor; certified for registration.
Richard G. Waterhouse to Roger Reese. Deed of Conveyance for 40 acres; acknowledged by Grantor; certified for registration.
Richard G. Waterhouse to Samuel Frazier. Deed of Conveyance for 193 acres; acknowledged by Grantor; certified for registration.
Richard G. Waterhouse to Wright Smith. Deed of Conveyance for 80 acres; acknowledged by Grantor; certified for registration.
Richard G. Waterhouse to Edward Gray and Patrick Martin. Deed of Conveyance for 100 acres; acknowledged by Grantor; certified for registration.
Richard G. Waterhouse to James Rogers. Deed of Conveyance for 155 acres; acknowledged by Grantor; certified for registration.
Richard G. Waterhouse to Farley Brady. Deed of Conveyance for 157 acres; acknowledged by Grantor; certified for registration.
Richard G. Waterhouse to Allen Kennedy. Deed of Conveyance for 214 acres; acknowledged by Grantor; certified for registration.

(p. 249) Richard G. Waterhouse to Matthew English. Deed of Conveyance for 125½ acres; acknowledged by Grantor; certified for registration.
Woodson Francis, Sheriff to Richard G. Waterhouse. Deed of Conveyance for 3275 acres; proven by oaths of William Smith and Henry Collins; certified for registration.
Richard G. Waterhouse & Charles McClung to Byram Breeden. Deed of Conveyance for 80 acres; proven by John Rice and William Smith; certified for registration.
John McCoy to Joshua Mosely. Deed of Conveyance for 150 acres; proven by Samuel Snelson and James McCoy; certified for registration.
Charles McClung to James Thompson. Deed of Conveyance for 149 acres; proven by William Smith and John Rice; certified for registration.
Abijah Harris to Edward Gray. Deed of Conveyance for 100 acres; proven by Grantor; certified for registration.
John Hudson to James Blevins. Deed of Conveyance for 160 acres; proven by Grantor; certified for registration.
Thomas Scott & Sarah C. Scott to Martin Ferguson. Deed of Conveyance for an undivided part of 130 acres; proven by William Smith and John Rice; certified for registration.

(p. 250) Joseph Garrison appointed overseer of road in place of Robert Ferguson.
Ordered that the road as reported by the Jury of View be established: leaving the Athens Road near the Widow Blythes, thence along the old Calhoun Road by way of Isaac Mahans, thence crossing the creek below McCormicks Mill, thence on the old road so as to intersect the Calhoun Road at the McMinn County line. David Campbell appointed overseer of said road from Widow Blythes to Isaac Mahan; to have all the hands in the following bounds: all the hands between the road and Hiwassee River as high up the river so as to include James Cowans, then across to Isaac Mahans.
Isaac Mahan appointed overseer of said road from Mahans to the County line and have all the hands in the following bounds: from James Cowans up Hiwassee River to the County line, then up Prices Creek so as to include White at Hugh Murpheys old place, then across to James Lees so as to include Benjamin McKenzey and the sand Lee and then down the foot of the ridge to said Mahans.
Samuel Besheer overseer of road from Morganton to Blythes Ferry work on that part of the road as David Shelton has lately turned said road.

David Shelton allowed $3.00 for attending Circuit Court three days at last Term.

George Ramsey, Benjamin McKenzie, Thomas Harp, Allen Gentry, John Night, David Mahan, and Townley Riggs appointed Jury of View to lay off and mark a road the nearest and best way from Samuel McDaniels to Rosses Ferry.

(p. 251) On motion of Patrick Martin, Admr. on estate of James Galbreath and Jane Galbreath, ordered that John Russell, William Smith, and Robert Cozby be appointed Commissioners to settle with said administrator.

Ordered that James Berry pay over to the Trustee of Rhea County $6.25 that was deposited in his hands by Carson Caldwell at last February Sessions, money collected by said Caldwell from Catharin Barnes single woman for refusing to declare the father of her Bastard Child and that the Trustee accounts for the same as he does other fines and forfeitures.

James Smith VS Robert Mitchell (No. 1406). Debt. Plantiff by attorney dismisses suit; defendant confesses judgment for costs.

Jesse Thompson & wife & others to John W. Looney. Deed of Conveyance dated 6th February 1826, for an undivided parcel of land in Madison County, Alabama; acknowledged by Jesse Thompson and wife Jane W. Thompson & Thomas Thompson and wife Priscilla Thompson (Jane and Priscilla examined separately); certified for further probate.

(p. 252) Woodson Francis, Sheriff and Collector of public taxes, reported the following tracts of land & town lots as having been admitted to be returned for public taxes for 1825, that the same is liable to double tax and that the double taxes thereon remain due and unpaid, and that the respective owners or claimants thereof have no goods or chattels in this County on which he can detain for said double tax:

Number		Quarter Section	Township		Range	Acres
1407	Daniel M. Stogden [sic] & Wm Harmon	N.W.	19	2	1 W	160
1408	Mike Cellers	S.W.	20	2	1	160
1409	John Crow	N.E.	29	2	1	160
1410	Jesse Thompson	N.E.	2	F 3	2	160
1411	Charles Matlock	S.E.	15	F 3	2	160
1412	John H. Beck	S.E.	24	F 3	2	160
1413	William Wann	S.E.	27	F 3	2	160
1414	John Price	N.E.	7	F 3	2	160
1415	Henry Newkirk	N.W.	12	F 1	2	160
1416	Jno Ginans and Jno Homes	S.W.	1	1	2 W	160
1417	Warran Sams	S.E.	13	1	2	160
1418	Warran Sams	S.W.	34	1	2	160
1419	James Butram	N.E.	24	1	2	160
1420	Jno and Joseph Hurt	N.E.	26	1	2	160
1421	John Hurt	S.E.	26	1	2	160
1422	Joseph Chasten	S.E.	26	F 1	3	141½
1423	John Huff	N.W.	36	F 1	3	160
1424	James Isham and Wm H. Reece	S.W.	36	F 1	3	160
1425	Peter Fine	N.W.	24	F 2	3	160
1426	Duke Ward	N.E.	26	F 2	3	160
1427	D. Stockton & S. Binnich	N.W.	28	F 2	3	160
1428	D. Ward & A. Kincannon	N.W.	35	F 2	3	160
1429	Sanford Bridwell	S.W.	12	F 3	3	160
1430	J. Hunter	N.E.	19	F 2	3	6
1431	Samuel Looney	S.E.	6	F 3	3	160
1432	Sanford Bridwell	N.W.	12	F 3	3	160
1433	Joseph McCord	N.E.	21	F 3	3	160

(p. 253)

1434	James Whaley	S.E.	24	F 1	4	160
1435	William Blythe	S.W.	32	F 2	4	160
1436	Benjamin McKindre	N.W.	12	F 3	4	160
1437	Jno Knight	S.W.	12	F 3	4	160
1438	Austin L. Dunn	N.W.	23	F 3	4	160
1439	Jno Chattin & James McDaniel	N.E.	23	F 1	5	160
1440	Jno Were	S.E.	14	3	4	160
1441	Jno Were	S.W.	14	3	4	160
1442	J.C. Mitchell assignee of S. McDonel?	N.W.	3	3	2	160

1443 1 tract part of Grant No. 1347 for 5000 acres granted to Stokely Donelson
    & John Hackett lying pleasant Garden Valley   4360
1444 1 tract belonging to Rodger Reece on Vanns Spring Creek 165
1445 1 tract belonging to John Henrys heirs on E fork Richland Creek 103
1446 1 tract belonging to Mary Purcer in Morganton on Richland Creek 1
1447 1 tract belonging to Caswell Johnson on Richland Creek 100
1448 1 tract belonging to William S. Moore near Washington 2
1449 1 tract belonging to Asiel Johnston on Richland Creek 234
1450 Lot No. 7
1451 Lot No. 19   1456 Lot No. 50
1452 Lot No. 21   1457 Lot No. 51
1453 Lot No. 35   1458 Lot No. 52
1454 Lot No. 45   1459 Lot No. 54
1455 Lot No. 49   1460 Lot No. 55

(p. 254)   1473 Lot No. 69
1461 Lot No. 56   1474 Lot No. 70
1462 Lot No. 57   1475 Lot No. 71
1463 Lot No. 58   1476 Lot No. 74
1464 Lot No. 59   1477 Lot No. 78
1465 Lot No. 60   1478 Lot No. 79
1466 Lot No. 62   1479 Lot No. 80
1467 Lot No. 63   1480 Lot No. 81
1468 Lot No. 64   1481 Lot No. 82
1469 Lot No. 65   1482 Lot No. 85
1470 Lot No. 66   1483 Lot No. 86
1471 Lot No. 67   1484 Lot No. 87
1472 Lot No. 68   1485 Lot No. 88

    Also the following tracts of land returned for taxation by the respective
owners and not paid: Acres
1486 1 tract belonging to Philip Harmon on Richland Creek 14
1487 1 tract belonging to Frederick A. Ross on Tennessee River 2000

(p. 255) Judgment entered against aforesaid tracts.
1488 Josiah Fike returned 1 tract of land containing 160¼ acres
1489 Charles Gamble returned 1 tract containing 50 acres
    Fike and Gamble are released from the payment of double taxes.
    Woodson Francis, Sheriff, returned the following taxable polls as not
having been returned for the tax of 1825:
Richard Manly, 3 Black polls and 1 Stud Horse
Flemming Manly, 1 white poll
George Walker heirs, 4 black polls
Richard G. Waterhouse, 4 black polls
    Ordered that the Clerk enter the polls and stud horse on his list of
taxable property as prescribed by Act of Assembly.

80

(p. 256)   Justices on bench (7th February) — James Wilson, Carson Caldwell, Thomas Cox, and John McClure.

Woodson Francis, Sheriff, returned a list of Jurors summoned to appear at this session of Court (see list on page 70), out of which a Grand Jury was elected: Allen Kennedy, Peter Daniel, James Price, Merideth Cox, Benjamin Bond, Charles Woodward, John Barnett, Kennedy Cooper, James Taylor, Joseph Rice, William Lowery, John Parker, and Samuel McDaniel. Allen Kennedy appointed foreman and Anson Dearmon, a Constable to attend the Grand Jury.

There remained of the original pannel, Thomas Marshall.

Robert C. Gordon to Polly Park Colbert. Deed of Conveyance for 640 acres in Overton County; proven by George Gordon; certified for registration to Overton County.

(p. 257)   William Montgomery, Admr. of John A. Montgomery, dec'd VS Woodson Francis & William Johnson. Plaintiff dismisses suit and defendants confess judgment for the costs. (No. 1490)

Samuel Hoskins VS John Rice (No. 1491). Came the parties by their attornies and a jury (Thomas Marshall, Andrew Evans, David Leuty, William Walker, William Runyon, John Dunlap, Abner Majors, William Locke, Hasting Poe, Jesse Reece, William Lewis, and William Gwin) which finds for the plaintiff; damages set at $569.50. Plaintiff to recover damages plus costs.

Ruben Freeman VS William M. Smith & Cyrus Quiet (No. 1492). Anson Dearmon, Constable, returned a fieri facias issued by Carson Caldwell for $19.19 3/4; levied on half of a quarter section in Hiwassee District.

(p. 258)   And upon motion of the plaintiff by his attorney, Wyllis H. Chapman, the Court orders the land sold to satisfy the plaintiffs debt and the costs.

Thomas Marshall released from further attendance as a Juror at this Term.

Justices on bench (8th February) — James Wilson, Thomas Cox, John McClure, Carson Caldwell, and William Smith.

State VS Isaac Bullard (No. 1493). Peace Warrant. Came Thomas J. Campbell, Attorney General, and the Defendant "in his own proper person and the Prosecutor Isaac Mahan not further requiring sureties of the peace of the Said Defendant. . . . considered by the Court that the Defendant go hence without day upon the payment of the cost acrued upon said prosecution. Whereupon came the Defendant and confesses Judgment for the costs . . ."

Alexander Ferguson to Elijah Rice. Deed of Conveyance for Lot No. 8 in Town of Washington; proven by Joseph Rice and George W. Rice, subscribing witnesses; certified for registration.

(p. 259)   Alexander Ferguson to Elijah Rice. Deed of Conveyance for parcel of land adjoining the Town of Washington; proven by Joseph Rice and George W. Rice; certified for registration.

Joel K. Brown VS Elijah Rice (No. 1494). John Miller who was summoned as Guarnishee by the Sheriff, appears at present sessions to declare on oath what he owed to the defendant; declared that he was indebted to the defendant for $50. Plaintiff to recover against Guarnishee John Miller $14.54, the amount of the plaintiffs demand.

Jacob Brown VS Washington J. Dewitt (No. 1495). Motion on Security. Came the plaintiff by attorney and a jury (John Leuty, Barefoot Armstrong, Bruten Peters, David Ragsdale, John Witt, John A. Smith, William Walker, William Swenney, William Lauderdale, Pulaski Poe, William Walker, and Andrew Evans) which says that Jacob Brown was security for Washington J. Dewitt and paid for him as security $43.06. Plaintiff to recover from defendant sum and costs.

(p. 260)   State VS John A. Smith (No. 1496).   Defendant says he is not guilty;
jury (Thomas Marshall, Elias Majors, Barefoot Armstrong, Bruten Peters, John Witt,
William Walker, William Swiney, William Carter, William Walker, Andrew Evans,
Benjamin Allen, and Pulaski Poe) finds the defendant not guilty; County to pay
costs.
          William B. Gordon VS David Right (No. 1497).   Motion as Security. Came
the plantiff by his attorney and a jury (John Leuty, Barefoot Armstrong, Brutin
Peters, David Ragsdale, John Witt, John A. Smith, William Walker, William Swanny,
William Lauderdale, Pulaski Poe, William Walker, and Andrew Evans) which says that
the plaintiff (W.B. Gordon) was security for David Right and paid for him as such
security $14.97½. Plaintiff to recover sum and costs.

(p. 261)   Jesse Poe, Admr. of William Lewis VS William M. Smith & Jacob Slover,
his security (No. 1498).   Came the parties by attorney and a jury (Allen Kennedy,
Peter Daniel, James Price, Merideth Cox, Benjamin Bond, Charles Woodard, Kenedy
Cooper, James Taylor, Joseph Rice, William Lowry, John Parker, and Samuel McDaniel)
which finds a verdict in favor of the plaintiff and assesses his damage to $15.90.
          John Rice Successor &c for the use of Jane Lawson VS David Ragsdale.
Came the parties by attornies; Commission is awarded defendant to take the deposition de bene esse of William Carter; cause is continued until next term.
          William Featherstone VS Mark Massey (No. 1499).   Debt. Came plaintiff
by attorney and dismisses suit; defendant to recover his costs from plaintiff.
          Grand Jury returned a presentment: State against Isaac West as overseer
of the road.

(p. 262)   William Walker, Exr. of George Walker, dec'd VS Mary Walker. Appeal.
On motion of the plaintiff by attorney, ordered by Court that Zachariah Nelson
one of the plaintiffs securities for the appeal in this cause be released; whereupon came Daniel D. Armstrong and undertakes that if the plaintiff is cast in
this suit that execution may issue against him jointly with the plaintiff for the
condemnation of the Court.
          William Walker, Exr. VS Mary Walker (No. 1500). Appeal. Came the par-
ties by attornies and a jury (Allen Kennedy etc. same as above) which finds for
the defendant the sum of $5.00, the balance upon the set off of accounts due said
defendant.

(p. 263)   Justices on bench (9th February)— William Smith, Thomas Cox, Carson
Caldwell, John McClure, and James Wilson.
          John Love to John C. Dodd. Deed of Conveyance for 200 acres in Cald-
well County, Kentucky; acknowledged by Grantor; certified to Kentucky for registration.
          William L. Bradley et al VS William Lewis (No. 1501). Certiorari. Came
the parties by attornies and a jury (Allen Kennedy etc. same as above) which
finds for the defendant, who is to recover costs from plaintiff.
          Andrew Evans, Admr. of William Floyd, dec'd VS Elias Majors. Appeal.
Came the parties by attornies and a jury (David Day, Brinkley Hornsby, Robert
Montooth, William Runyon, James P. Miller, Peter Minnick, Rubin Freeman, William
Lewis, Miles Vernon, Jonathan F. Robinson, Robert Small, and Orville Paine) which
cannot agree; mistrial is entered; cause is continued until next Session.

(p. 264)   Andrew Evans, Admr of William Floyd, dec'd VS Jesse Reece. Appeal.
Came the parties by attornies; commission is awarded plaintiff to take the deposition of Elizabeth Floyd de bene esse at the house of Andrew Evans in Rhea County
to be read as evidence on the trial of this cause.
          John Parker VS John Rice (No. 1502). Debt. Plaintiff dismisses suit;
defendant to recover costs from plaintiff.

State VS John Laney (No. 1503). Affray. With consent of Thomas J. Campbell, Attorney General, and the Court a Nolle proseque is entered in this cause. County to pay costs.

State VS John Ball (No. 1504). Affray. Nolle proseque entered.

(p. 265) State VS Jacob Lawson (No. 1505). Bastardy. Nolle proseque entered.

State VS John Harrel (No. 1506). Scire Facias. Defendant made default; Conditional forfeiture entered against defendant at August Session for $500 is made absolute.

State VS William Harral (No. 1507). Scire Facias. Defendant made default; conditional forfeiture entered against him at August Session for $250 is made absolute.

(p. 266) State VS Samuel Harrel (No. 1508). Scire Facias. Defendant made default; conditional forfeiture entered at August Session for $250 is made absolute.

John Barnett for use of Love & Kennedy VS James C. Mitchell. Debt. Came parties by attornies and a jury (William Gordon, Jesse Day Sr., Peter Daniel, Merideth Cox, Benjamin Bond, Kennedy Cooper, James Taylor, Joseph Rice, William Lowrey, John Parker, Samuel McDaniel, and Lewis Wilkerson) which says the defendant has not paid the debt in the declaration, nor any part thereof. Damages assessed at $38.52 (debt of $107.45) plus costs.

William Johnson permitted to keep a house of Ordinary; bond with Henry Collins, Woodson Francis, and John Lewis.

(p. 267) William S. Leuty VS Jacob Slover (No. 1509). Debt. Came the parties by attornies and a jury (same as above) which says the defendant has not paid the sum of $152.65, the debt in the declaration, or any part thereof; damages assessed at $5.34 1/3. Plaintiff to recover debt, damages, and costs.

William S. Leuty VS Orville Paine (No. 1510). Came the parties by attornies and a jury (same as above) which says the defendant hath well and truly paid the debt in the plaintiffs declaration except the sum of $99.25; they assess the plaintiffs damage to $6.96. Plaintiff to recover the remaining portion of debt, damages, and costs.

(p. 268) William Runyon VS Woodson Francis. Upon affedavit of Defendant this cause is continued until next session of this Court.

Jesse Thompson VS Robert Brabson (No. 1511). Came the parties by attornies and a jury (William Gordon, Jesse Day Sr., Peter Daniel, Merideth Cox, Benjamin Bond, Kennedy Cooper, James Taylor, Joseph Rice, Allen Kennedy, Brinkley Stricklen, Samuel McDaniel, and Lewis Wilkerson) which says the defendant has not paid the sum of $95.00 the debt in the declaration, or any part thereof; damages assessed at $14.00.

Henry Welker VS Abraham Howard, Exr. of John Howard, dec'd. Covenant. Came the parties by their attorneys Elihu Barclay and Willis H. Chapman and the Defendants Demurrer to the plaintiffs declaration being solemnly argued and fully understood and because it seems to the Court that the plaintiffs declaration is good and sufficient in law, it is considered that the defendants demurrer be overruled; plaintiff is entitled to recover against the defendant the damages being uncertain, Sheriff is ordered to summon a jury to assess damages.

(p. 269) James Price released from further attendance as a Grand Juror; William Lowrey also released from further attendance as a Grand Juror at this Term.

Elijah Rice to William Johnson. Deed of Conveyance for a lot in Town of Washington; proven by Brinkley Hornsby and Robert Locke; certified for registration.

Upon affidavit of David Day, ordered that a duplicate Jury Ticket issue in favor of said Day if it can be assertained when he served as a juror and the number of days he served.

(p. 270) Justices on bench (10th February)— Carson Caldwell, John McClure, Thomas Cox, and William Smith.

Rezin Rawlings VS John McClenahan (No. 1512). Covenant. Came plaintiff by attorney Willis H. Chapman and dismisses this suit; defendant to recover his costs from plaintiff.

James P. Miller VS George W. Thompson (No. 1513). Debt. Came plaintiff by attorney Return J. Meigs and dismisses this suit; defendant to recover his costs from plaintiff.

Moses Thompson VS George Gordon. Certiorari. Came the parties by attornies; agree and with assent of Court the award heretofore returned in this cause is set aside; also the rule of referance set aside; cause is continued.

John Barnett for the use of Love & Kennedy VS James C. Mitchell (No. 1514). Demurrer. Ordered that the plaintiffs demurrer to the defendants several pleas be sustained. Considered by the Court that the plaintiff upon the finding of a jury sworn on yesterday recover from the defendant $107.45 debt and $38.52 plus costs.

(p. 271) George W. Thompson VS James P. Miller. Appeal. On motion of defendant by attorney, ordered that Joseph Rice, the defendants security for the appeal in this cause be released. Jacob Brown then undertakes for the defendant.

Same (No. 1515). Appeal. Came the parties by attornies and a jury (Allen Kennedy, Peter Daniel, Merideth Cox, Benjamin Bond, Charles Woodward, John Barnett, Kennedy Cooper, James Taylor, George Locke, William Walker, Samuel McDaniel, and Peter Minnick) which finds for the plaintiff the sum of 30¢. Plaintiff to recover 30¢ and costs from defendant. Defendant prays an appeal to the next Circuit Court; allowed upon the appellants giving bond and security.

Henry Henry VS John Parker (No. 1516). Appeal. Came the parties by attornies and a jury (same as above) which finds for the defendant the sum of $1.37½, the balance upon the set off of accounts due the defendant; also to recover costs.

(p. 272) William Hill VS Barefoot Armstrong. Appeal. Came the parties by attornies and a jury (same as above) which says they cannot agree; mistrial is entered; cause continued until next Session of this Court.

Samuel Hoskins VS John Rice. Rule is entered to shew cause why a new trial should be granted. Came the parties by attornies and the said rule being argued, considered by the Court that the said rule be discharged. Defendant excepts in law and prays writ of error to the next session of Circuit Court.

John Rice VS David Ragsdale. This cause is revived in the name of William Smith, Successor &c.

MAY TERM 1826

(p. 273) Court of Pleas and Quarter Sessions held at Courthouse in Washington on first Monday and first day of May 1826. Justices on bench— Daniel Walker, James McDonald, John Robinson, James A. Darwin, Thomas Cox, Peach Taylor, Jesse Thompson, Carson Caldwell, Azariah David, Samuel Gamble, and James Wilson.

William Walker released from further attendance as a Juror at this term.

John Burk ADS The State. "It having been certified to this Court from the Circuit Court . . . that a Nolle proseque had been entered in this cause in the Circuit Court and that the County should pay the cost on said suit. It is

84

therefore ordered that the County pay the sum of $9.05½ . . . ."
William S. Leuty & Polly Leuty ADS The State. Sum of $18.39 certified
from Circuit Court.
Adam W. Caldwell permitted to keep a house of entertainment in County.

(p. 274) John Foshee appointed overseer of road in place of Williamson Todd; to
have the same bounds and hands the said Todd had with the addition of the following hands: all the hands from Tennessee River at John Foshees Still House running
up the ridge to Snelsons Road along said road to Isaac Rush, then down the ridge
to the mouth of Wats Creek, thence to the beginning.
Elias Ferguson appointed overseer of road in place of Isaac West, dec'd.
Townley Rigg, Addison Rigg, David Mahan, Edward Templeton, and Gilbert
Kennedy appointed Jury of View to examine and report the propriety of turning the
road a short distance on the land of Alexander Philpot as he believes the same
may be done without injury to the public.
Thomas Price, James Price, Samuel Price, Jacob Price, William Allen,
John Randal, Daniel Brigs, and Philip D. Maroney appointed a Jury of View to turn
the road on Clayton Stocktons land.
Ordered that Samuel Looney, overseer of road from Kellys Ferry to Samuel
McDaniels have all the hands in the following bounds: beginning on Tennessee River
so as to include Sebert Martin, thence to include Thomas Eaves, thence a direct
line to include Meredith Cox and Nicholas Couch, thence to include Abraham Cox,
thence to include David Greer, thence to include Jacob Wammac, thence to William
Rivers, thence to Thomas Shaffers, thence down said river to the beginning.
Ordered that the road from Kellys Ferry to Rosses Ferry be discontinued.
Ordered that the land reported by the Sheriff for the taxes of 1825 be
set aside so far as it respects the land reported on the south side of Tennessee
River.

(p. 275) Ordered that the road as reported by the Jury of View be established as
follows: beginning at Rosses Ferry, thence to Townley Riggs, thence by David Mahans, thence by Gilbert Kennedys and Edward Templetons, thence by Gentrys leaving
John Knight on the left, thence to Benjamin McKenzies, thence to Thomas Kings
leaving him on the right, thence to Samuel McDaniels leaving Cyrus Quiett on the
left, said road to be of the 2nd Class. Thomas Harp appointed overseer of said
road and to have the following hands to work under him on said road: John McCormick, David Seybolt, Ansalom L. Dareing, Amos King, Abraham Massey, George Ramsey,
Benjamin McKinsey & hands, Isaac & Taverner Masoner, John Neawls, Anderson & William Fitzgerral, Samuel Fitzgerral & hands, Allen Gentry, John Knight, Jonathan
Owens, William Casey, Josiah Howser, James Lee, James Gothart, Barney Hicklan,
Edward Templeton, Gilbert Kennedy, and David Mahan.
James Coulter, Abraham Miller, John Lewis, Jackson Howerton, Joshua Tindle, Jesse Day Sr., and Willie Lewis appointed a Jury of View to turn that part
of the Valley Road from where John Bell now lives to Woodson Francis.
Absolam Barnes appointed overseer of road in place of Wright Smith.
Ordered that the Commissioners appointed to settle with the Collector
and Trustee of Rhea County, "Forthwith call on Col. William Johnson former Trustee
of said county and enter into and close a definetive settlement of all unsettled
accounts between him and said County and further to demand and receive from said
former Trustee all books papers and money of every name nature and description in
any wise appertaining to the county (if any there be) and said Commissioners are
hereby required to pass any residue that may come to their hands to the now Trustee charging him therewith for and in behalf of the county."

(p. 276) Ordered that the Commissioners appointed to settle with the Collector and Trustee, "call on William Kennedy former Trustee of said County and demand and receive from said former Trustee all the money in his hands of every name nature and description &c (same as above)"

Jurors appointed for next term of this Court:

Jasper Romines	Absolam Barnes	Peter Majors	Matthew English
Peter Daniel	Orville Paine	Edmund Howerton	William Woodward
Benjamin Marbury	Elijah Collins	Isaac Mahan	John Walker
Thornton Creed	Daniel D. Armstrong	George W. Mayo	David Leuty
Jesse Poe	Beriah Frazier	Edmund Bean	Jeremiah Washam
Cornelius Moyers	Lewis Knight	Miles Vernon	Robert Love
	John Hill	Mantion Howard	

Anson Dearmon, a Constable to attend

Jurors appointed for next term of Circuit Court:

William Hornsby	John Riggle	Jesse Roddy	Robert Walker
George Gillespie	Micajah Howerton	Jackson Howerton	John Wasson
Vaden H. Giles	Jesse Martin	Azariah David	Joseph Williams
David Caldwell	John McClure	Thomas Hunter	John Whaley
Leonard Brooks	James Kelly	John Taff	Robert Elder
John Cozby	William C. Wilson	Stephen Winton	Peach Taylor
Anson Dearmon, a Constable to attend Court			Joseph Love

State VS Addison Rigg. Bastardy. Came the defendant and his security Edward Templeton; indebted to State for $500 each; void on condition that defendant make his appearance on Wednesday of this Session.

(p. 277) Thomas Cox, Coroner, allowed $15.00 for holding three inquests over the bodies of Mary, a Black woman belonging to William S. Leuty; Isaac West and John Beason.

Azariah David appointed guardian for William Jenkins, an aged and infirm man; bond with Woodson Francis and Jesse Poe, his securities, for $1000.

Anson Dearmon, a Constable, allowed $9.00 for attending the Court.

John Love permitted to keep a house of entertainment in this County.

Ordered that the order made at last session appointing James Smith as overseer of the road in place of Leonard Brightwell be revived.

"A paper writing purporting to be the last Will and Testament of Isaac West deceased was exhibited to Court for probate, & thereupon William Kennedy one of the Witnesses thereto made oath that he heard the said Isaac West a short time before his death dispose of his estate by parol in manner and form as is set forth in said Writing, that said Isaac West departed this life on the 1st of April 1826 and that his Will was committed to Writing as in said paper purporting on the 6th day of April 1826. Whereupon It is ordered by the Court that said Will be continued for further probate."

"On application, John Locke is permitted to sware in as deputy Clerk of this Court and he took the oath accordingly."

(p. 278) Ordered that James Berry, Clerk of this Court, purchase one good sledge hammer and one good crow bar for the use of the several overseers of roads; to be paid for out of the County treasury. And that the said tools remain for the purposes aforesaid in the care of the said James Berry, who shall have power to require receipts for the redelivery of the same to his care.

Justices on bench (2nd May)— Daniel Walker, Jesse Thompson, and Samuel Gamble.

Woodson Francis, Sheriff, returned a list of Jurors summoned to appear for this Court (see list on page 75), out of whom the following were elected a

Grand Jury: Jesse Day Sr., Edward Templeton, Elijah Wyatt, Landon Rector, Palatiah Chilton, Charles Ryon, Bryan McDonald, John Smith, James Woodward, John Parker, Micajah Clack, James Carroll, and Edward Stokes. Jesse Day Sr. appointed foreman and David Shelton a Constable to attend the Grand Jury.

(p. 279) There remained of the original pannel: Abijah Harris, Charles Witt, James McCanse, Charles Reavely, Henry Walton, and John Chatten.

"John Parker, a Grand Juror at this Term, being solemnly called came not but made default. It is therefore considered by the Court that for such his contempt he make his fine with the people of this State by the payment of fifty cents for the better support of the Government."

"Anson Dearmon, a Constable summoned to attend the Court being Solemnly called came not but made default; fined 50¢ "for the better support of the Government."

A paper writing purporting to be the last Will and Testament of Isaac West dec'd was exhibited for further probate. Joseph Kelough, one of the witnesses thereto made oath that he heard the said Isaac West a short time before his death dispose of his estate by parol in manner and form as is set forth in said writing. Will was ordered to be recorded.

Andrew Evans, Admr. of William Floyd dec'd VS Elias Majors. From reasons appearing to the satisfaction of the Court, this cause is continued until next session of this Court.

(p. 280) Moses Thompson VS George Gordon. Cause is continued until next session.

Andrew Evans, Admr. of William Floyd, dec'd VS Jesse Reece (No. 1517). Appeal. Came the parties by their attornies and a jury (Abijah Harris, Charles Witt, James McCanse, Charles Reavely, Henry Walton, John Chatten, James P. Miller, William Runyon, William Lewis, Eli Ferguson, John McClenahan, and David Blevins) which finds for the defendant, who is to recover from the plaintiff and his security, Joseph Rice, his costs.

Henry Welker VS Abraham Howard, Admr. of John Howard, dec'd. (No. 1518). Came the parties by their attornies and a jury (Abijah Harris, Charles Witt, James McCanse, Charles Reavely, Henry Walton, John Chatten, William Runyon, David Blevins, John Hudson, Thomas McNutt, William Hill, and Daniel D. Armstrong) which assesses the plaintiffs damages at $428.45 "to be paid in Bank Notes at par with Specie. "

John O. Cannon produced his Licence as a practicing Attorney at law.

(p. 281) John McGhee, Matthew McGhee, and John L. McCarty VS Jacob Slover (No. 1519). On motion of the plaintiffs by attorney and it appearing to the satisfaction of the Court that the Sheriff has failed to pay over the costs on an execution duly issued in this cause as required by law, judgment is rendered against Woodson Francis, Sheriff, for the sum of $8.52½ the costs in this cause.

Rezin Rawlings VS Anson Dearmon. Cause is continued until next Session.

Robert Walker VS John Robinson et al. Cause is continued until next session of this Court for the want of a competant Court.

William Hill VS Barefoot Armstrong. Cause is continued until next Court.

(p. 282) Justices on bench (3rd May)— Samuel Gamble, Daniel Walker, Jesse Thompson, and Carson Caldwell.

Ordered that the fine of 50¢ assessed against John Parker juror on yesterday be set aside on payment of costs. (No. 1520)

Ordered that the fine of 50¢ assessed against Anson Dearmon be set aside on payment of costs. (No. 1521)

John Rice VS David Ragsdale (No. 1522). Came the parties by their attornies and for reasons disclosed to the Court on the affadavit of the Defendant
leave is given him to file the plea of Non est factum in this Cause upon the payment of all costs which have accrued therein since the issue term. Cause is continued until next Term of this Court.

State VS Isaac West (No. 1523). Overseer of road. With the assent of
the Court, this cause is dismissed; County to pay costs.

(p. 283) State VS Addison Rigg (No. 1524). Bastardy. Came the defendant and
Edward Templeton; acknowledged themselves indebted to State for $1000; void on
condition that the defendant "do save harmless the County of Rhea from any charge
in the support and maintainance of a bastard child begotten upon the body of Milly
Paine by the said Rigg . . ." Defendant confesses judgment for costs.

Richard G. Waterhouse for use of Elisha Kirklan VS John Robinson. Covenant. Defendant demurres to the plaintiffs declaration; seems to Court that plaintiffs declaration is good and sufficient; defendants demurrer is over ruled.
Ordered that the Sheriff summon a jury to assess the damages of the plaintiff.

William Runyon VS Woodson Francis. From affidavit of defendant, this
cause is continued until next session. Commission awarded defendant to take the
depositions of Anderson Vernon and Obediah Vernon of Bledsoe County.

(p. 284) William Runyon VS Woodson Francis. Commission awarded to plaintiff to
take deposition of Samuel Waggoner in Grainger County and John C. Wade in Bledsoe
County.

Stephen Plumley VS James P. Haynes (No. 1525). Guarnishment. Came the
defendant and being first dult sworn says he owes Thomas B. Swan nothing, that he
has nothing in his hands belonging to said Swan, that he knows of no person who
owes the said Swan or has any of his effects in their hands. Considered by the
Court that the said James P. Haynes be discharged from his guarnishment and that
Stephen Plumley pay the costs.

State VS Isaac Jones (No. 1526). Peace Warrant. It appearing to the
Court that this prosecution is frivilous, defendant is discharged. Thomas Blankenship, the prosecutor in this cause, to pay costs; Washington Weems security
for payment.

AUGUST TERM 1826

(p. 285) Court of Pleas and Quarter Sessions met at the Courthouse in Washington
on the first Monday and 7th day of August 1826. Justices on bench— John Cozby,
Peach Taylor, John McClure, James Wilson, George Gillespie, Crispeon E. Shelton,
William Smith, Carson Caldwell, Jesse Thompson, Daniel Walker, James A. Darwin,
Thomas Cox, and Azariah David.

Charles Rector appointed overseer of road in place of Rector Preston.
Dempsey Sulliven appointed overseer of road in place of John Able.
Abijah Bogas appointed overseer of road in place of Joseph Thompson.
William Greenfield appointed overseer in place of Patrick Martin.
Samuel Garwood appointed overseer of road in place of Joshua Hill.
William Runyon appointed overseer of road in place of John Benson.

(p. 286) William Lisenbay appointed overseer in place of Elijah Runnels.
John Pharis appointed overseer in place of Calvin Robinson.
Jasper Romines appointed overseer in place of William Smith.
Ustus Humphrey appointed overseer in place of Alexander Coulter.
Wilson Blevins appointed overseer in place of John Lillard.
John Igo appointed overseer in place of John D. Williams, from the 4-mile

88

post on the road from Kellys Ferry to Calhoun to the McMinn County line; to have
the following hands to work under him: Samuel McDaniel & hands, Irey(?) Haines,
Anson L. Dering, Samuel Stewart, David Sebolt, John McCormick, Alexander Underwood, John Underwood, William Knight, Robert Cooley, William Blevins, Allen Blevins, Joseph McCorkle, and David Lewis.

Thomas Harp appointed overseer of road from the 4 mile post (on road
from Kellys Ferry to Calhoun) to said Harps house and to have the following hands
to work under him: Isaac Masoner, Tavnor Masoner, Anthony King, Amos King, William
Hail, Able Massey, George Ramsey, Benjamin McKenzeys hands, Benjamin McKenzey Jr.,
Reuben McKenzey, John Fitzgerral, and Knives.

(p. 287)   John Knight appointed overseer of road from Thomas Harps to Rosses Ferry
and to have the following hands to work under him: (blank) Esserey, Jonathan Owin,
William Casey, Josiah Howser, James Lea, James Gothard, Barney Hicklan, Edward
Templeton, Gilbert Kennedy, David Mahan, West Runyon, William Fitzgerral, Anderson
Fitzgerral, Aron Fitzgerral, Samuel Fitzgerral & hands, and Allen Gentry.

William Lauderdale appointed overseer of road from Richland Creek at
Mrs. Lauderdales to the Grassy Branch and to have the following hands to work under him: James Lauderdale, Owin David, Samuel Casteel, John Woods, Andrew Casteel
and the sons of said Casteel.

Samuel Ferguson appointed overseer in place of William Ferguson.

Armstead Bridwell, Joshua Atchley, Thomas York, Matthias Shaver, George
W. Bridwell, John Lillard, and Harden Blevins appointed a Jury of View to lay off
and mark a road beginning at the cross roads at Bogis', thence to Yorks Mill,
thence to Joshua Atchleys, thence by Armstead Bridwells so as to intersect Kellys
Ferry Road at John Lillards.

Palatiah Chilton released from payment of Tax on 109½ acres, he being
charged with 160 acres in place of 50½ acres.

(p. 288)   Oliver Pike released from payment of poll tax, he being over age.

Thomas Kelly allowed to keep a gate across the road leading from his
ferry to Washington at the mouth of the lane next to the river.

James Walton allowed to keep a gate across the road at or near his ferry.

James Wilson allowed $74.25 for running the County line between Rhea and
Bledsoe counties.

Abraham Howard allowed $20.37½ for settling with the Collector and Trus-
tee of Rhea County for 1824 and 1825, and transcribing the record and furnishing
paper for the settlement.

Joseph Love allowed $12.00 for settling with William Johnson late Trus-
tee and Carson Caldwell the present Trustee of Rhea County.

William G. Welker produced his licence as a practicing attorney at law.

(p. 289)   William T. Gillenwaters allowed $8.00 for settling with William Johnson,
late Trustee of Rhea County.

Miles Vernon allowed $6.00 for settling with William Johnson.

James Wilson allowed $6.00 for settling with William Johnson.

Abraham Cox allowed $5.00 for attending this Court at last February Term.

David Shelton allowed $7.00 for attending this Court at May Sessions,
and for attending the Circuit Court at March Term.

Elijah Runnels allowed $45.00 for keeping Mary Owens for 12 months.

Ordered that Thomas Price, James McDonald, and James Walton may charge
$1.00 for ferrying a five horse Team across the River at each of their ferries.

(p. 290)   Richard G. Waterhouse & Enoch Parsons to Arthur Fulton. Deed of Conveyance for 200 acres; proven by Richard Waterhouse and Jeremiah Howerton, subscribing witnesses; certified for registration.

Woodson Francis, Sheriff to Thomas McCallie. Bill of Sale for Sundry property; acknowledged by Francis; certified for registration.

James C. Mitchell to Calvin Robinson. Deed of Conveyance for 60 acres; proven by William Piper and William Wann; certified for registration.

William Piper to Calvin Robinson. Deed of Conveyance for 40 acres; acknowledged by Grantor; certified for registration.

Armstead Bridwell appointed Admr. on estate of Elias Bridwell, dec'd; bond with Andrew Kincannon and Matthias Shaver for $400. Said administrator returned an Inventory of said estate; ordered to be recorded.

Abraham Hughes appointed overseer of road in place of William Johns.

(p. 291) Isaac Love appointed administrator on estate of William Love, dec'd; bond with Joseph Love and John Smith for $3000.

Thomas M. Kennon appointed administrator on estate of William Kilgore, dec'd; bond with James Wilson for $200.

Andrew Kincannon appointed a Constable in Capt. Wm Farmers Company; bond with Miles Vernon and James Lillard, his securities.

Micajah Howerton appointed a Constable in Capt. Willie Lewis' Company; bond with Miles Vernon and James A. Darwin, his securities.

James Swann undertakes to keep Mary Owens, a poor woman, for 12 months for $40.00.

Bremillion Holloway undertakes to keep Mrs. McKeel, a poor woman, for 12 months for $49.00.

(p. 292) On application of Isaac Braselton Senr., ordered that Harmon W. Braselton be bound to the said Isaac and live with him after the manner of a bound apprentice for the term of 16 years from this date, and at his freedom is to give him a horse saddle and bridle to be worth $75 and to give him two good suits of clothes one of which is to be out of the store and during said apprenticeship is to give said Boy two years schooling.

Jurors appointed for next term of this Court:

Patrick Martin	John Mahan	John Smith	Rector Preston
Jacob Wassom	Thomas McNutt	Audley P. Defriese	Allison Howard
Robert Bell Jun.	James Roddy	Robert Cooper	Moses Thompson
Archibald Paul	Elisha Parker	William Johns	Thomas Hunter
Abraham Miller	William Ingle	David Day	Martin Ferguson
David Campbell	David Maxfield	John Redmond	William Baldwin
David Shelton to attend as Constable			William Matlock

Miles Vernon, James Lillard, and Robert Elder, Commissioners for a School Section of land in the Hiwassee District in Range 3rd, Fractional Township 3rd.

Report of Jury of View (to turn part of Valley Road from where John Bell now lives to Woodson Francis) was quashed by Court.

Nancy Martin to Jasper Romines. Power of Attorney dated 7th August 1826; ordered to be certified.

(p. 293) William Smith, Chairman of this Court, reported in writing the sale of the old jail of Rhea County to Joseph Williams for the sum of $35.00 at six months credit.

On motion of Thomas J. Campbell, Attorney General, the children of Isaac Jones are ordered to be taken into the custody of the Sheriff and by said Sheriff placed in the care of their Mother until the next session of this Court, she giving (blank) Blankenship Security for their delivery in Court. The mother of said children having given her assent in open Court to this order. Ordered that a copy of this order be served upon Isaac Jones, the father, to appear at next Court to shew cause why the said children should not be bound out.

William Smith, George Gillespie, and Jesse Thompson, Commissioners to settle with William Johnson, late Trustee of Rhea County, with power to overhal the account of the County treasury from 1812 to the time of his going out of office inclusive, and to charge him with all sums which he was bound by law to collect and credit him with the amount of such Vouchers as he shall hand over to them though the same be uncollected and to adjust the account of the principles of equity.

Ordered that the precinct Elections on the South side of Tennessee River in Rhea County be held at the house of Robert Elder and William Miller, and that those heretofore held at the house of William Price be discontinued.

(p. 294)   Justices on bench (8th August) — John Cozby, Peach Taylor, and James McDonald.

Woodson Francis, Sheriff, returned a list of Jurors summoned to appear at this Court (see list on page 85), out of which a Grand Jury was appointed: Robert Love, Orville Paine, William Woodward, Benjamin Marbury, George W. Mayo, Thornton Creed, Daniel D. Armstrong, Mantion Howard, Jasper Romines, Jeremiah Washam, Peter Majors, Lewis Knight, and Beriah Frazier. Robert Love was appointed foreman and Anson Dearmon a Constable to serve the Grand Jury.

There remained of the original pannel: Elijah Collins, Peter Daniel, John Hill, Cornelius Myors, Miles Vernon, David Leuty, and Edmund Howerton.

Woodson Francis, Sheriff, to Orlando Bradley. Deed of Conveyance for Lot No. 27 in Town of Washington; acknowledged by Francis; certified for registration.

Grand Jury returned a Bill of Indictment against Orlando Bradley for an assault and battery.

(p. 295)   Thomas McCallie to Joseph C.S. Hood. Bill of Sale for sundry property dated 7th August 1826; acknowledged by McCallie; certified for registration.

John Thompson VS William Murphree (No. 1527). Motion as Security. Came the plaintiff by his attorney, William C. Dunlap, and a jury (Peter Daniel, John Hill, Cornelius Myors, Miles Vernon, Elijah Collins, Jacob Runnells, Levi Ferguson, Henry Beck, David Leuty, Avara Hannah, Mumford Smith, and Nathaniel Crenshaw), which says that the plaintiff was security for the defendant and paid $65.42½ as his security. Plaintiff to recover the $65.42½ plus $10.45 damages and his costs.

Samuel Murphey VS Major M. Gilliam (No. 1528). Motion as Security. Came the plaintiff by his attorney, Return J. Meigs, and a jury (same as above), which says that the plaintiff was security for the defendant and as such paid $71.82½. Plaintiff to recover the $71.82½ and his costs.

(p. 296)   James Lillard VS Jacob Slover (No. 1529). Motion. John Lea, Deputy Sheriff, returned an attachment issued by Thomas Cox, Justice of the Peace, for $32.54½; levied on a quarter section of land (the same quarter section that Jacob Slover entered where John Martin now lives). Ordered that the land be sold.

James Lillard VS Jacob Slover (No. 1530). Motion. John Lea returned into Court an attachment issued by Thomas Cox for $40.50; levied on a quarter section of land (same as above). Ordered that the land be sold.

Andrew Evans, Admr. of William Floyd, dec'd VS Elias Majors. Appeal. Came the parties by attornies and a jury (William Lewis, William Sullivan, John Hill, Cornelius Myors, Elijah Collins, Jacob Runnels, Levi Ferguson, Henry Beck, David Leuty, Avara Hannah, Mumford Smith, and Nathaniel Crenshaw) which says it cannot agree; mistrial is entered and cause is continued until next Term.

(p. 297)   Richard G. Waterhouse for the use of Elisha Kirklan VS John Robinson (No. 1531). Came the plaintiff by his Agent William C. Dunlap and dismisses this suit; defendant to recover costs from plaintiff.

Samuel E. Rowdan VS Eli Brocke for the use of Richard Manley (No. 1532). Certiorari. Came the plaintiff by his Attorney, W.H. Chapman, and dismisses this suit; defendant to recover his costs from plaintiff.

Thomas M. Kennon to Willie Redwine. A plat and Certificate of survey for 50 acres of land; the transfer thereon was dule acknowledged in Court by T.M. Kennon; ordered to be certified.

William Murphree to John Thompson. Power of Attorney dated 7th August 1826 was acknowledged by Murphree; ordered to be certified.

William S. Leuty VS Roger Reece (No. 1533). Came the plaintiff by his attorney and dismisses this suit; defendant confesses judgment for the cost.

(p. 298) The order made on yesterday concerning the children of Isaac Jones is suspended.

Isaac Love, Admr. on estate of William Love, dec'd, returned an Inventory of the property of said estate.

William Ferguson & Margaret Ferguson, his wife to John Day. Deed of Conveyance for an undivided moiety or one childs part of 210 acres of land; acknowledged by William Ferguson and his wife, who was examined separately; certified for registration.

Moses Thompson VS George Gordon (No. 1534). Came the parties by their attornies; upon affedavit of John Madden, Agent for the defendant, this cause is continued until the next session of this Court upon the defendants paying the costs of this Term.

William P. Hackett to Daniel Rawlings. Deed of Conveyance for Lot No. 44 in Southern Liberties; proven by Woodson Francis, one of the subscribing witnesses, who swears that James C. Francis, his son, the other subscribing witness is not in this State and that he believes the signature of James C. Francis to be written by him; certified for registration.

(p. 299) Thomas M. Kennon VS James Kelly. On motion of the Defendant by his attorney he is allowed a rule in these causes to shew cause why the Warrant and proceedings before the Justice of the Peace should be quashed.

Justices on bench (9th August)— James McDonald, John Cozby, and Peach Taylor.

State VS Orlando Bradley (No. 1535). Assault and Battery. Came Thomas J. Campbell, Attorney General, and the defendant who says he is not guilty as charged. The jury (William Locke, Michael Stoner, James McCallie, Miller Francis, John Barnett, William Runyon, Elijah Collins, Peter Daniel, John Hill, Cornelious Myors, Miles Vernon, and David Leuty) finds the defendant guilty; fined $5.00 and costs.

(p. 300) William Runyon VS Woodson Francis (No. 1536). Came the parties by their attornies and it appearing to the satisfaction of the Court from the affidavit of John Skilleran, this cause is continued until next session of this Court upon the defendants paying the cost of this Term.

Andrew Evans, Admr. of William Floyd, dec'd VS Elias Majors. Appeal. Came the parties and with the assent of the Court they submit all matters in dispute between them in this cause to the final determination of John Locke, Rezin Rawlings, and James Berry. The arbitration to be held in the Town of Washington at any time when it may be convenient for the parties to attend.

State VS John Day (No. 1537). Assault and Battery. Came Thomas J. Campbell, Attorney General, and the defendant who says he is not guilty as charged. The jury (William Hill, Thomas McNutt, George Locke, William Gwinn, Jacob Wassum,

Jonathan F. Robinson, James Kelley, Richard Manley, Charles Reevely, William Walton, Alexander Coulter, and Robert Cooley) finds the defendant guilty; fined $1.00 and costs.

(p. 301)   Luke Tiernan assignee VS William L. Bradley.   Debt.   Came the plaintiff by his attorney and the defendant in his proper person and agree in this cause to plead and try at the next term of this Court.

John Clack to Thomas Kelly.   A Certificate of No. 1223 for 160 acres in Hiwassee District; transfer thereof acknowledged by Clack; ordered to be certified.

Thomas Kelly to Robert Locke.   A Certificate of No. 1223 for 160 acres in Hiwassee District; transfer thereof acknowledged by Kelly; ordered to be certified.

State VS Addison Rigg (No. 1538).   Bastardy.   Ordered that Addison Rigg pay to Milly Paine the sum of $24 for the first year commencing on the 9th day of February 1826; $18 for the second year, and $12 for the third year; to be paid in equal quarterly payments.   Ordered that the said Milly Paine recover against the said Addison Rigg and his security, Edward Templeton the aforesaid sums and her costs in this behalf.

State VS John Witt (No. 1539).   Bastardy.   Ordered that John Witt pay to Dorcas Taylor the sum of $10.00 for the third year commencing on the 4th day of August 1826, to be paid in equal quarterly payment.   Dorcas Taylor to recover against the defendant and his securities Chispien E. Shelton and James Kelly the sum aforesaid and her costs.

(p. 302)   William Runyon VS Woodson Francis.   Commission is awarded the defendant to take the deposition of John Rice of Marion County to be read as evidence.

William Runyon VS Woodson Francis.   Commission is awarded the plaintiff to take the deposition of John C. Waade of Bledsoe County to be read as evidence.

Grand Jury returned a Bill of Indictment against James A. Vernon for an assault.

(p. 303)   Justices on bench (10th August) — James McDonald, John Cozby, and Peach Taylor.

State VS James A. Vernon (No. 1540).   Assault.   Came Thomas J. Campbell, Attorney General, and the defendant who says he is not guilty.   The jury (Miller Francis, James Kelley, David Caldwell, Orlando Bradley, William D. Collins, Alford Rockhold, James P. Miller, Jacob Brown, Peter Daniel, Elijah Collins, Cornelious Myors, and Miles Vernon) finds the defendant not guilty; County to pay costs.

State VS Thomas Blankenship.   Assault and Battery.   Came the Attorney General and defendant, who acknowledges himself indebted to State for $250, and James Kelly, his security, in sum of $250; void on condition Blankenship appears "from day to day and answer a charge of the State . . ."

Grand Jury returned a presentment against Thomas Blankenship for an assault and battery.

The Court nor Attorney General not requiring any further attendance from the Grand Jury they are discharged from further attendance at this term.

(p. 304)   William Hill VS Barefoot Armstrong (No. 1541).   Appeal.   Came the parties by their attornies and a jury (Miller Francis, William D. Collins, Edmund Howerton, Abraham Miller, Elijah Collins, Cornelious Myors, Miles Vernon, John Hill, James P. Miller, John Roper, David Caldwell, and William Fowler) which finds for the defendant, who is to recover his costs from plaintiff.   From which verdict and judgment, the plaintiff prays an appeal to the next Circuit Court; granted.

State VS Thomas Blankenship. Assault and Battery. Appearance bond for $250 (Blankenship) and his security, James Kelly, $250; void on condition Blankenship appears at next term of this Court.

Robert Walker VS John Robinson et al. Debt. Came the parties by their attornies and a jury (Miller Francis, Edmund Howerton, Abraham Miller, Miles Vernon, John Hill, John Roper, David Caldwell, William Fowler, Orlando Bradley, Richard Haslerig, Jacob Brown, and David Leuty) which was respited until tomorrow.

(p. 305) Justices on bench (11th August)— James McDonald, John Cozby, and Peach Taylor.

Woodson Francis, Sheriff to Thomas McCallie. Deed of Conveyance for Lot No. 37 in Town of Washington; acknowledged by Grantor; certified for registration.

Rezin Rawlings VS Anson Dearmon. Came the parties by their attornies and a jury (William Locke, William D. Collins, James Kelly, George Henry Sr., James C. Piper, Samuel Johnson, James Stewart, Cornelious Myors, Elijah W. Collins, Robert Bell Sr., and Isaac Crow). Jury was respited untill tomorrow.

Mordica Lewis VS William Gwin. Certiorari. Came plaintiff by attorney and upon his motion a rule is granted him to dismiss the petition for certiorari and supersedeas in this cause.

David Leuty & Jesse Poe VS Elijah Rice (No. 1542). Motion on Security. Came the plaintiffs by their attorney Thomas J. Campbell, and a jury (Hopkins L. Turney, William Locke, Hugh Crozier, William D. Collins, James P. Miller, Elijah W. Collins, Samuel Johnson, Kennedy Cooper, William L. Welker, Cornelious Myors, Wyllys H. Chapman, and Peter Daniel) which says that the plaintiffs were security for Rice. Whereupon the plaintiffs by attorney moved the Court for judgment against the said defendant for such sum as they were liable to pay as security. A Writ of Fieri facias issued from the Clerks office of Knox County directed to the Sheriff of Rhea County against the estate of the said plaintiffs as security aforesaid for said defendant to make the sum of $104.10 for debt & costs against the said plaintiffs as securities. Considered by the Court that the plaintiffs recover against the defendant the sum of $104.10 and costs.

(p. 306) Mordicai Lewis VS William Gwinn (No. 1543). Came the plaintiff by his attorney George W. Churchwell and discharges the rule to dismiss by petition and on his motion this charge is dismissed. Defendant to recover against Mordicai Lewis and Orville Paine the costs in this behalf expended.

Robert Walker VS John Robinson et al. The jury that was respited until this day "upon their oaths do say they cannot agree." Jury is discharged and cause is continued until next session of this Court.

Woodson Francis to Orlando Bradley. Deed of Conveyance for Lots No. 22, 23 & 47 in Southern Liberties of town of Washington; acknowledged by Grantor; certified for registration.

(p. 307) William B. Lewis, Atty in fact &c VS Joseph Williams. Cause is continued until next session of this Court.

Samuel Roberts & Thomas McCallie VS Edmund Bean (No. 1544). Came the parties by their attornies and a jury (Miller Francis, Edmund Howerton, Abraham Miller, Miles Vernon, John Hill, John Roper, David Caldwell, William Fowler, William Lewis, Jacob Brown, David Leuty, and Orlandy Bradley) which says the defendant has not paid the sum of $110.26½ the debt in the declaration, nor any part of it. Damages assessed to $3.63.

Samuel Roberts & Thomas McCallie VS Edmund Bean (No. 1545). Came the parties by their attornies and a jury (same as above) which says the defendant has paid the debt in the declaration except $71.06; jury assesses the plaintiffs

94

damage to $3.14. Plaintiffs to recover the debt, damages, and costs.

(p. 308) William E. Anderson for the use of Roberts & McCallie VS Alexander Coulter and Robert Parks (No. 1546). Appeal. Came the parties and a jury (same as above) which finds for the plaintiff; damages assessed at $27.00. Whereupon on motion of the plaintiff by his attorney for judgment against James Woodward, the security for the prosecution of the appeal. Plaintiff to recover $27.00 and costs from Woodward.

(p. 309) Justices on bench— (12th August)— John Cozby, Peach Taylor, and Carson Caldwell.
    John Dudley for the use of James King VS Miller Francis (No. 1547). Came the plaintiff by his attorney George W. Churchwell and dismisses his Scire facias. Case is dismissed and defendant recover his costs from plaintiff.
    John Rice Successor &c for Jane Lawson VS David Ragsdale. Demurrer. Came the parties by their attornies and the plaintiffs demurrer to the defendants plea of non ert factum being solemnly argued and because it seems to the Court that the defendants plea is not good and sufficient in law, it is considered by the Court that the plaintiffs demurrer to the defendants plea be sustained. And because it appears to the Court that the plaintiff is entitled to a recovery against the defendant and the damages being uncertain, ordered that the Sheriff summon a jury at next session to enquire of the plaintiffs damages.
    Thomas M. Kennon VS James Kelley. Appeal. In these three causes came the defendant by his attorney and pray a rule to shew cause why the proceedings had therein should be quashed, and on Solemn argument had thereon and considered by the Court here not setting. Whereupon it is ordered that said rule be discharged.

(p. 310) Rezin Rawlings VS Anson Dearmon (No. 1548). The jury that had been respited in this cause came into Court and said they could not agree. Jury is discharged and the cause is transferred to Circuit Court.
    Nathaniel Smith assignee of James & Aron Haynes VS George Gordon. Came the parties by their attornies; with assent of Court time is given the defendant to file his pleas on or before first Wednesday after the third Monday of September next at the Clerks office of this Court.
    Byrum Breeding VS Woodson Francis (No. 1549). Motion. Came the defendant by attorney and the plaintiff came not, making default. Therefore on motion of the defendant by his attorney, Wyllys H. Chapman, it is considered by the Court that the defendant go hence and recover against the plaintiff his costs.

(p. 311) John Dudley for the use of James King VS James G. Martin & Frederick Fulkerson (No. 1550). Motion. Woodson Francis, Sheriff, returned a bond signed and sealed by the defendants dated 15th June 1825, in and by which the defendant James G. Martin had undertaken to appear at the present session of this Court, and abide by perform and satisfy such judgment as this Court Might render against him in behalf of the plaintiff, in and about a judgment rendered on behalf of the plaintiff at November Session 1825 of this Court for the sum of $107 debt & damages. And the said Martin failing to appear here at this Court according to the tenor and effect of his said undertaking, it is considered that the said plaintiff recover against the defendant (Martin) and his security, Frdderick Fulkerson the aforesaid sum and damages, plus the costs in this behalf.
    All cases not decided at this Term are continued until next Court.

NOVEMBER TERM 1826

(p. 312)   Court of Pleas and Quarter Sessions met at the Courthouse in Washington on the first Monday and sixth day of November 1826. Justices on bench— William Smith, Daniel Walker, Azariah David, George Gillespie, Jesse Thompson, John McClure, John Cozby, Peach Taylor, Carson Caldwell, Samuel Gamble, and Crispeon E. Shelton.

William James appointed overseer of road in place of Benjamin F. Jones.

Farley Brady appointed overseer of road in place of Thomas Breeding.

Robert Love appointed overseer of road in place of Abraham Miller.

Allison Howard appointed overseer of road in place of William Howard; to have same hands and all the hands on the land of Azariah David, Henry Airhart, Samuel Howard, Asahel Johnson, William Howard, John Jack, and David Day.

Robert Montooth appointed overseer of road in place of Samuel Minnick.

Merideth Cox appointed overseer of road in place of Samuel Looney.

James Paul appointed overseer of road in place of John Alexander.

William McHenry appointed overseer of road in place of Robert Hagen.

Daniel D. Armstrong released from payment of poll tax for present year.

(p. 313)   James Lillard & Polly Lillard, his wife to John Gorman. Deed of Conveyance for two tracts of land in Cock County, Tennessee dated 6th November 1826; acknowledged by James Lillard and Polly (after being examined separately); certified for registration to Cock County.

James Wilson (Yellow Creek), James Montgomery, and Raleigh Clack appointed Commissioners to settle with Joseph Harwood, Admr. on estate of John Chapman.

William Stewart appointed administrator on estate of John Stewart; bond with Reuben Jackson, his security, for $225.

Mariah Howard appointed administratrix on estate of Mantion Howard, dec'd; bond with James Coulter and Robert Parks, her securities, for $500.

Willie Lewis, Abraham Miller, and James Coulter appointed Commissioners to lay off a years provisions for the widow and children of Mantion Howard.

(p. 314)   William Howard and Allison Howard are appointed administrators on estate of Abraham Howard, dec'd; bond with Samuel Howard, James Stewart, and George Manas, their securities, in the sum of $1200.

Henry Airhart, Joshua Tindle, and Abraham Miller appointed Commissioners to lay off a years provisions for the widow and children of Abraham Howard.

Jesse Poe appointed administrator on estate of Burley Godsey; bond with Richard Manley, his security, for $300.

Thomas Little, Thomas Hunter, and James Taylor appointed Commissioners to lay off a years provisions for the widow and children of Burley Godsey, dec'd.

Jesse Poe returned an inventory of the property of Burley Godsey.

Armsted Bridwell, Admr. of Elias Bridwell, returned an inventory and account of sales of said estate.

Spencer Benson allowed $30.00 for keeping Mary David part of one year.

William Lauderdale, overseer of road, to have the following hands to work under him in addition to his former hands: William Alexander & sons, John Bolin & son, sons of John Casteel and William Kelly; and said road is to be continued to where it intersects the Washington Road.

(p. 315)   John Day allowed $12.75 for a sledge and crowbar furnished the County for working on the road.

David Shelton is permitted to keep a house of entertainment.

Abijah Boggess permitted to keep a house of entertainment.

Thomas J. Campbell, Solicitor, allowed $25.00 for exofficio services.
Woodson Francis, Sheriff, allowed $25.00 for exofficio services.
James Berry, Clerk of this Court, allowed $25.00 for exofficio services for 1826 and $12.50 for making out the Tax Lists for the same year; also $6.00 for making out tax lists and recording the land on the south side of Tennessee River as per surveyor Generals returns.
Robert H. Jordan appointed a Constable in Capt. Sharp's Company; bond with Abijah Boggess, his security.

(p. 316) Anson Dearmon allowed $5.00 for attending this Court five days.
David Shelton allowed $6.00 for attending Circuit Court.
Nancy Peck undertakes to keep Mary David for 12 months for $50.00.
David Day allowed a duplicate Jury ticket for four days attendance as a Juror at November Sessions 1820.
Ruben Freeman, overseer of road, to have in addition to his former hands, Samuel R. Hackett to work under him.
Kennedy Cooper, overseer of road, to have Joseph Loves hands, Audley P. Defriese & hands, and Jacob Runnels as hands to work under him in addition to his former hands.
John H. Henderson, overseer of road, to have in addition to his former hands to work under him all Edward Stokes sons.
Jeremiah Howerton, Eli Ferguson, Samuel Holloway, Moses Paul, Bruton Peters, Elijah Runnels, George W. Riggle, James Swan, and Edmund Bean appointed a Jury of View to lay off and mark a road from Waltons Ferry to intersect a road at or near Jeremiah Howertons.
John Pharis, William Piper, Rolly Miller, John Miller, Calvin Robinson, Mark Johnson, and William Wann appointed a Jury of View to turn the road from Waltons Ferry so as to run up the north side of Big Sowee Creek commencing at the point of a large ridge about three miles from Waltons Ferry then the nearest and best way to Ten Mile Creek at the mouth, then to intersect said Waltons Road at the most convenient place.

(p. 317) John Redmon, Benjamin Maxfield, James Blackwell, John Bennett, Abraham Davis, David Hounshell, and John Davis appointed a Jury of View to lay off and mark a road from George Gillespies Ferry on Tennessee River to Cazeys Mill.
John Lea allowed $5.00 for bringing Isaac Jones children to Court.
Abijah Boggess appointed a Constable in Capt. Keeton's Company for two years; bond with Miles Vernon and Hiram Gibson, his securities.
John Igou appointed a Constable in Capt. White's Company for two years; bond with Miles Vernon and William Runyon, his securities.
David Shelton appointed a Constable in Capt. Howard's Company for two years; bond with John Witt and James Stewart, his securities.
Jurors appointed for next term of this Court:

Bryant McDonald	Alexander Coulter	John Gray	Moses Thompson
Archabald Paul	Joseph Martin	Robert Cooper	Abraham Wright
Charles Ryan	Elisha Parker	Jacob Reynolds	Pulaski Poe
William Tillary	John Miller	Thomas Caffy	William Fowler
Robert Bell Jr.	Allen Gentry	Robert Ray	Cumberland Rector
Jesse Atwood	John Riggle	Bruten Peters	Charles Witt
William Russell, Constable to attend Court			William Hill

Jurors appointed for next term of Circuit Court:

William Lauderdale	James Stewart	William Buice	Benjamin Jones
John Day	Beriah Frazier	Grief Howerton	Richard A. McCandless
John Lewis	William Ferguson	James Coulter	Ezekiel Bates
William Wright	John Lillard	Samuel McDaniel	William Smith Y.C.

Jonathan Fine	Daniel Walker	Thomas Anderson	George Gillespie
Jesse Thompson	John Cozby	Col. William Johnson	

William Russell, a Constable to attend said Court.

(p. 318) Elihu S. Barclay appointed Attorney General protem for the present session of this Court.

The following Justices were appointed to take the lists of taxables for 1827:

William Smith	in Captain Howard's Company
James A. Darwin	in Captain Lewis' Company
Jonathan Fine	in Captain Swann's Company
John McClure	in Captain Hill's Company
Daniel Walker	in Captain Rowden's Company
Stephen Winton	in Captain Baker's Company
Samuel Gamble	in Captain Russell's Company
ditto	in Captain White's Company
Peach Taylor	in Captain Farmer's Company
James Wilson	in Captain Stockton's Company
ditto	in Captain Keeton's Company
Thomas Cox	in Captain Lusk's Company
William C. Wilson	in Captain Sharp's Company

John Mullins released from the payment of a poll tax for present year.

Joseph Kilough released from the payment of a poll tax for 1826.

Rezin Rawlings presented in open Court a petition for the emancipation of his Slave Primus which is as follows: "The Worshipfull Court of pleas and quarter sessions for Rhea County now in Session. Your petitioner would respectfully represent to your Worships that he is vested with the legal title to a certain black man by the name of Primas a slave for life that has for many years past has demeaned himself as a faithfull servant to your petitioner and his progenitors there with many other considerations your petitioner thereunto moving he prays your worships to extend him the previledge contemplated in the statutes in such case made and provided of emancipating his your petitioners said black man Primus, And your petitioner as in duty &c. 6th Augst. 1826. Rezin Rawlings "

A majority of Court present the prayer of this petition is granted. (signed) William Smith, Chairman.

(p. 319) Upon said petition being granted, Rezin Rawlings entered into bond: "Know all men by these presents that we Rezin Rawlings and Allen Kennedy all of the County of Rhea . . . are held and firmly bound unto William Smith, Chairman of the Court of pleas and quarter sessions . . . and his successors in office in the sum of one thousand dollars . . . 6th November 1826.

"The condition of the above obligation is such that whereas the above bound Rezin Rawlings hath this day presented his petition . . . praying that the said court would emancipate and set free his slave Primus and the court . . . have granted the said petition and liberated the said Primus. Now if the said Rezin Rawlings and Allen Kennedy shall indemnify and save harmless the County of Rhea from any charge that may acrue against the said County by the said Primus becoming chargable upon said county then the said bond to be void and of no effect otherwise to be and remain in full force and virtue.

". . . therefore considered by the Court that the said Primus be hereby released from his bonds of Slavery and be forever emancipated liberated and set free and be allowed all the privaleges and immunities of other free people of colour within this State."

Joseph Love, Robert Locke, and James Wilson appointed to settle with the Collector of Taxes and Trustee of Rhea County.

Armstead Bridwell, Joshua Atchley, Thomas York, Battheas [sic] Shaver, George W. Bridwell, John Lillard, Hardin Blevins, Abijah Boggess, and William H. West appointed a Jury of View to lay off and mark a road beginning at the cross roads at Boggess', then to Thomas Yorks Mill, thence to Joshua Atchleys, thence by Armstead Bridwells so as to intersect Kellys Ferry Road at John Lillards.

(p. 320) Justices on bench (7th November)— Daniel Walker, Arthur Fulton, and Azariah David.

Woodson Francis, Sheriff, returned a list of Jurors summoned to appear at this session of Court (see list on page 89), out of which a Grand Jury was elected: Robert Bell Jr., William Johns, Allison Howard, John Mahan, Patrick Martin, Rector Preston, Archibald Paul, Thomas Hunter, Martin Ferguson, John Smith, Audley P. Defriece, John Redmond, and Abraham Miller. Patrick Martin appointed foreman and Anson Dearmon a Constable to attend the Grand Jury.

There remained of the original pannel: Jacob Wassom, William Ingle, James Roddy, Robert Cooper, Thomas McNutt, and David Day.

Richard G. Waterhouse to William Johnson. Deed of Conveyance for 1025 acres dated 18th April 1825; proven in part by oath of Richard Waterhouse; certified for further probate.

(p. 321) Sally Buster appointed administratrix on estate of William Buster, dec'd; bond with Miles Vernon and Leonard Brooks, her securities, for $400.

James Lillard, Leonard Brooks, and Andrew Kincannon appointed commissioners to lay off a years provisions for the widow and children of William Buster.

Moses Thompson VS George Gordon. Came the parties and with assent of the Court all matters in dispute between them is submitted to the final determination of George Gillespie, William T. Gillenwaters, and Arthur Fulton whose award will be the judgment of this Court.

William Kennedy VS Richard Walker (No. 1551). Motion. Woodson Francis, Sheriff, by his deputy Henry Collins, returned a fieri facias issued by James A. Darwin, Justice, for $25.04; levied on a tract on Clear Creek adjoining the lands of John Condley, Isaac Wests heirs, and Richard G. Waterhouse. Upon motion of plaintiff by his attorney Elihu S. Barclay, ordered that the land be sold.

William Kennedy VS Richard Walker (No. 1552). Motion. Woodson Francis by his deputy Henry Collins returned

(p. 322) a fieri facias issued by James A. Darwin, Justice, for 80¢ and costs; levied on tract of land on Clear Creek (same as above).

McGhees & McCarty VS Jacob Slover (No. 1553). Motion. John Lea, deputy Sheriff, returned an attachment issued by Samuel Gamble, a Justice, for $66.39½ besides costs; levied on a quarter section of land whereon John Martin now lives as the property of Jacob Slover. Ordered that the land be sold.

William Noblett VS John Knight (No. 1554). Debt. Came the plaintiff and dismisses this suit; defendant came and confessed judgment for the costs.

(p. 323) Robert Walker VS John Robinson, Joseph Williams, Daniel Walker, and Henry Collins (No. 1555). Debt. Came the plaintiff by attorney and the defendant (Robinson) and his securities (Williams, Walker, & Collins) who confess judgment jointly for the plaintiffs demand. Ordered that the plaintiff recover the sum of $274.56 3/4 debt and $58.54 damages.

State VS Townly Rigg. Assault and Battery. Defendant acknowledges himself indebted to the State for $250; Robert Bell Jr., his security, indebted for $250; void on condition Rigg makes his appearance from day to day to answer a charge exhibited against him.

Grand Jury returned Bill of Indictment against Townly Rigg for assault and battery; another against Mark Hardin for assault and battery.

Moses Thompson released from further attendance as a Juror this Term.

(p. 324)   Justices on bench (8th November)— Azariah David, Daniel Walker, Carson Caldwell.

John Lea VS Malachia Howard (No. 1556). Came the plaintiff by attorney and dismisses this suit; defendant to recover his costs from plaintiff.

Patrick Martin VS Hiram A. Defriese & William L. Bradley (No. 1557). Came the plaintiff by attorney and dismisses this suit; Hiram A. Defriese confesses judgment for costs.

Thomas M. Kennon, Admr. on estate of William Kilgore, dec'd, returned an inventory of estate and account of sales of said estate.

State VS Townley Rigg. Appearance bond for $250 each entered into by Townley Rigg and Wyllye H. Chapman; to appear at February session.

(p. 325)   William Runyon VS Woodson Francis. Came the parties by attorney; on motion of defendant by attorney and by consent Commissions are awarded defendant to take deposition of John Roper of Cumberland County, Kentucky and John Rice of Marion County, Tennessee.

State VS Thomas Blankenship (No. 1558). Came the Solicitor General and the defendant who says he is guilty and puts himself on grace and mercy of the Court; fined $1.00 and "be in Custody untill the Fine and Costs are paid."

Ordered that all Causes that have not been Specially acted on at this present term in this Court Stand Continued until next Term of this Court.

FEBRUARY TERM 1827

(p. 326)   Court of Pleas and Quarter Sessions met at the Courthouse in Washington on the first Monday and fifth day of February 1827. Justices on the bench— George Gillespie, Azariah David, Jonathan Fine, William Smith, Peach Taylor, James A. Darwin, Carson Caldwell, Jesse Thompson, Crispein E. Shelton, James Wilson, William C. Wilson, John Cozby, John McClure, Daniel Walker, and John Robinson.

On application of Thomas J. Campbell, Solicitor, James Berry, Clerk of this Court, produced in open Court a Receipt from the Treasurer of East Tennessee (M. Nelson) for $108.21 3/4 the amount of State Tax.

Also a receipt from the Trustee of Rhea County for $12.43½ the amount of fines and forfeitures collected by Francis.

Matthew Hubbart, Joseph McCorkle, Beal Gaither, Josiah Fike, Isaac Roddy, Daniel M. Stockton, and Ezekiel Bates, having been appointed Justices of the Peace by the State Legislature, produced their Commissions and took oaths of office.

(p. 327)   William Seymore, William Moore, Thomas Piper, Thomas Little, and James Taylor appointed a Jury of View to lay off and mark a road the nearest and best way from James Taylors Landing on Tennessee River to intersect the valley road at Henry Collins house.

Armstead Bridwell, Thomas York, Joshua Atchley, Batthias [sic] Shaver, George W. Bredwell, John Lillard, Hardin Blevins, Abijah Bogges, and William H. West appointed a Jury of View to lay off and mark a road beginning at the cross roads at Boggess, thence to Thomas Yorks Mill, thence to Joshua Atchleys, thence by Armstead Bridwells so as to intersect Kellys Ferry Road at John Lillards.

John Redmond, Benjamin Maxfield, James Blackwell, John Bennett, Abraham Davis, David Hounshell, and John Davis appointed a Jury of View to lay off and mark a road from George Gillespies Ferry on Tennessee River to Cazeys Mill.

Ordered that Wright Smith's Landing on the north bank of Tennessee River at Braselton's Ferry be a public landing and that the said Smith be allowed the same rates of ferriage that the said Braselton is allowed.

Anderson Jones appointed overseer of road in place of William Greenfield, removed; to have all the hands on the plantation of Benjamin Jones to work under him.

Ordered that Patrick Martin and William Baker work on the road under William Jones, overseer of the Valley Road.

(p. 328)   Peter Daniel appointed overseer of road in place of James Walker.
Robert Cooper appointed overseer of road in place of John Rogers.
John Weese appointed overseer of road in place of John Blythe.
Asa Jackson appointed overseer of road in place of Samuel Besheers.
Jesse Martin appointed overseer of road in place of John Roddy.
Jesse Poe, Admr. of estate of Burley Godsey, dec'd, returned an account of the sales of said estate.

Matthew Hubbart, Exr. of last Will and Testament of John Woodward, returned an additional sale & inventory of the property of said estate.

Maria Howard, Admrx. of estate of Mantion Howard, returned an account of the sale of said estate.

William Howard and Allison Howard, Admrs. of estate of Abraham Howard, returned an inventory of the property of said estate; also an account of the sale of said property.

(p. 329)   John Pharis, William Piper, Rolly Miller, Calvin Robinson, Mark Johnson, and William Wann appointed a Jury of View to turn the road from Waltons Ferry so as to cross Sewee at or near James Wilsons commencing at the most convenient place near Waltons Ferry thence the nearest and best way to said place on Sewee, thence the nearest and best way so as to intersect the old Federal Road at or near Warren Sams.

Peter Fine appointed overseer of road in place of Samuel Price.
David B. Staples appointed overseer of road in place of James Stockton.
Allen Holland appointed overseer of road in place of John H. Henderson.
David Buster appointed overseer of road in place of Robert Hagan.
Sally Buster, Admrx. of estate of William Buster, returned an account of the sale of said estate.

Orville Paine to Alford Paine. Deed of Conveyance for an undivided sixth part of 309 acres; acknowledged by Grantor; certified for registration.

Ordered that the road from Waltons Ferry to intersect a road at or near Jeremiah Howertons be established as reported by the Jury of View.

(p. 330)   Ordered that the road through Clayton Stocktons land as turned by said Stockton and viewed by Daniel Briggs, John Randles, Jacob Price, Samuel Price, and William Miller be established as reported.

Certificate for $3.00 issued to James Preston for a Wolf scalp.
Certificate for $6.00 issued to Cumberland Rector for two Wolf scalps.
Henry Collins, James A. Darwin, and William Kennedy appointed Commissioners to settle with Matthew Hubbart, Exr. of last Will and Testament of John Woodward, dec'd.

Jurors appointed for next term of this Court:

Charles McDonald	William Gray	Allison Howard	Asahel Johnson
Samuel Logan	Elisha Parker	Rezin Rawlings	Daniel Holland
Robert Goad	Moses Ferguson	Soloman Vernon	James Coal
James McCanse	Thomas Breeden	Daniel D. Armstrong	Joseph Williams
Moses Thompson	Matthew Allen	Absolom Foshee	John Parker

William Matlock   John Randles   Robert Kerr   William Locke
David Shelton, Constable to attend Court   Pleasent Love

(p. 331) John A. Hooke produced his licence as a practicing attorney of law.
John Witt returned his road order appointing him overseer of the road which was received and no overseer appointed in his place.
Ordered that part of Tuesday next be set apart for the transaction of public business.
Thomas M. Kennon, Admr. of estate of William Kilgore, returned an additional inventory of the estate; also an additional account of the sale of said property.

(p. 332) Justices on the bench — George Gillespie, Azariah David, Jonathan Fine, Daniel Walker, William Smith, Peach Taylor, James A. Darwin, Carson Caldwell, Jesse Thompson, Crispien E. Shelton, James Wilson, William C. Wilson, John Cozby, John McClure, John Robinson, Samuel Gamble, Matthew Hubbart, Joseph McCorkle, Beal Gaither, Josiah Fike, Isaac Roddy, Daniel M. Stockton, Ezekiel Bates, Arthur Fulton, Stephen Winton, and Thomas Cox.
Woodson Francis, Sheriff, returned a list of Jurors summoned to appear at this session (see list on page 96), out of whom the following were elected a Grand Jury: Robert Bell Jr., Alexander Coulter, Charles Witt, Pulaski Poe, Abraham Wright, Jesse Atwood, Thomas Caffey, William Fowler, Elisha Parker, Robert Rhea, John Riggle, Allen Gentry, and Robert Cooper. Robert Bell Jr. was elected foreman and William S. Russell a Constable to attend the Grand Jury.
There remained of the original pannel "who did not answer to their names:" Bryant McDonald, John Gray, Moses Thompson, Joseph Martin, Charles Ryan, Jacob Runnels, William Tillary, John Miller, Cumberland Rector, Brutin Peters, and William Hill.

(p. 333) Jonathan Collins and Robert Cooley, having been appointed Justices of the Peace by the State Legislature, produced their Commissions and took the oaths of office.
The Court proceeded to a Classification of the Justices: Ezekiel Bates, Isaac Roddy, Daniel M. Stockton, Joseph McCorkle, Jesse Thompson, John Cozby, and Crispien E. Shelton were drawn on the first class for holding this Court for the trial of Causes.
Peach Taylor, Thomas Cox, Azariah David, William C. Wilson, William Smith, Samuel Gamble, and Matthew Hubbart on the Second Class.
Josiah Fike, Beal Gaither, John McClure, James Wilson, Stephen Winton, Robert Cooley, and Jonathan Collins on the Third Class.
Daniel Walker, James A. Darwin, Carson Caldwell, George Gillespie, Jonathan Fine, Arthur Fulton, and James McDonald in the Fourth Class.
Ordered that the County Tax for this year be as follows: on each 100 acres of land, 12½¢; on each white poll, 12½¢; on each Town lot, 12½¢; on each Black poll, 25¢.
And that the Jury Tax shall be as follows: on each 100 acres of land, 6¼¢; on each white poll, 6¼¢; on each Town lot, 6¼¢; on each Black poll, 12½¢.
And that the Poor Tax shall be as follows: on each 100 acres of land, 6¼¢; on each white poll, 6¼¢; on each Town lot, 6¼¢; on each Black poll, 12½¢.
And that the Jail Tax shall be as follows: on each 100 acres of land, 25¢; on each white poll, 25¢; on each Town lot, 25¢; on each Black poll, 50¢.
David Hounshell appointed overseer of road in place of William Matlock.

(p. 334) William Talley appointed overseer of road in place of Absolom Majors.
James Smith appointed a Constable in Capt. Swan's Company for two

years; bond with George Gillespie and Isaac Baker.

John Thompson Sr., William Day, William Matlock, Samuel Pharis, Abner Cazey, John Seaton, and William Harmon appointed a Jury of View to lay off and mark a road from Stephen Wintons by William Matlocks to Cazeys Mill to the McMinn County line.

Lewis Wilkerson to Thornton Creed. Deed of Conveyance for 150 acres dated 12th January 1827; proven by William Johnson and Anson Dearmon; certified for registration.

Allen Kennedy to George T. Gillespie. Deed of Conveyance for 100 acres in Greene County dated 19th January 1827; acknowledged by Grantor; certified for registration to Greene County.

Abraham Howard, Exr. of Will of John Howard to William Howard & Samuel Howard. Title Bond dated 13th July 1822 for 440 acres; proven by Woodson Francis and William Smith, they proving the hand writing of Wm Howard; certified for registration.

(p. 335) Samuel Montgomery appointed overseer of road in place of Benjamin F. Locke.

James Airhart appointed overseer of road from Morganton by Azariah Davids to where it intersects the Lauderdale Road; to have following hands to work under him: John Buckhannon, David Shelton, Charles Witt, John Witt, and Edward L. White.

William Smith appointed administrator on estate of Mary David, dec'd; bond with Woodson Francis, his security, for $40.00.

Abraham Howard to Asahel Johnson. Deed of Conveyance for 202 acres dated 18th July 1826; proven by John Jack and Hazard Bean; certified for registration.

Daniel D. Armstrong VS Joseph Rice (No. 1559). Motion on Security. Came the plaintiff by his attorney, Thomas J. Campbell, and a jury (Robert Bell Jr., Alexander Coulter, Charles Witt, Pulaskie Poe, Abraham Wright, Jesse Atwood, Thomas Caffey, William Fowler, Elisha Parker, Robert Rhea, John Riggle, and Allen Gentry) which says that the plaintiff was security for the said Rice, and as such had paid $6.83 3/4. Plaintiff to recover the sum plus 34¢ interest and his costs.

(p. 336) Thomas Price and Wyllys H. Chapman appointed Commissioners to settle with the Clerks of Circuit Court and County Court.

William Johnson, James Moore, and James Berry appointed Commissioners to settle with the Entry Taker of Rhea County.

The last Will and Testament of Richard Haslerig, dec'd was produced in Court and proven in part by oath of Woodson Francis, one of the subscribing witnesses, who says that the saw Richard Haslerig sign seal publish and declare the said instrument of writing to be his last Will and Testament and that he believed he was of perfect sense and memory at the time of his publishing the same and that he subscribed his name as a witness thereto in his presence and at his request; ordered to lay over for further probate.

Thomas Hamilton allowed $15.00 annually for support of his son Milton, a pauper.

John Lea appointed Sheriff of Rhea County for two years; bond with William S. Leuty, George Gillespie, and James Wilson for $5000.

(p. 337) Bond of John Lea as Sheriff.

(p. 338) Bond of John Lea as Tax Collector for $5000 (same securities).

Thomas Cox appointed Coroner for Rhea County for two years; bond with Abraham Cox and Andrew Kincannon for $1000.

(p. 339)   Bond of Thomas Cox.
        Jonathan Fine appointed Register for Rhea County; bond with George Gillespie, James Wilson, and John Lea for $3000.

(p. 340)   Bond of Jonathan Fine.
        Isaac Braselton Sr. VS William Murphree & William Lewis. It appearing to the Court from the return of the Sheriff of Weakly County on the fieri facias heretofore issued from the Clerks office of this Court, that no goods or chattles belonging to either of the defendants are to be found in his County and that on the 23rd day of December 1826 he levied said fieri facias on a tract of land containing 987½ acres granted by the State of Tennessee to William Murphree and Richard G. Waterhouse (Grant No. 24503), lying in the 13th District in Weakly County in the 2nd range and 7th Section. Beginning at a Black and white oak, the heirs of William Hill's north west corner of their 525 acre Survey running South 400 poles to a white & dogwood then West with Blakemore & Pattersons line 80 poles to a Post oak and dogwood, then North west corner, then South with their line 144 poles to a Spanish oak Henry Betors corner, then west with his line 23 poles to a stake, then north 544 poles to two

(p. 341)   white oaks, then east 310 poles to the beginning, and that he the said Sheriff has advertised said sale of land to be sold on 10th day of February 1827, the said levy being too late to sell the said land according to law before the present session of this Court. Therefore it is ordered that the Clerk issue a writ of venditori exponas to the Sheriff of Weakly County.

(p. 342)   Justices on bench (7th February)— Jesse Thompson, Isaac Roddy, Daniel M. Stockton, Ezekiel Bates, and Joseph McCorkle.
        On application of Thomas M. Kennon, Admr. on estate of William Kilgore, dec'd, James Wilson, William Smith, and Mumford Smith appointed Commissioners to settle with said administrator.
        On application of Thomas J. Campbell, ordered that John Locke and Thomas Kelly be appointed Commissioners to take an inventory of the property of John Hudson, deceased.
        State VS William S. Able & James J. Able (No. 1560). Assault. Came Thomas J. Campbell, Attorney General, and with the assent of the Court a Nolle proseque is entered in this cause; whereupon came Cain Able and confessed judgment for all costs.
        State VS Mark Harden (No. 1561). Assault and Battery. Defendant says he cannot gainsay the charges; fined $1.00 and costs.

(p. 343)   State VS Arnold Thomason (No. 1562). Peace Warrant. Came Thomas J. Campbell, Attorney General, and the defendant. The prosecutor, Elizabeth Thomason not further requiring sureties of the peace of the said defendant; defendant released upon payment of costs.
        Moses Thompson VS George Gordon (Nos. 1563 & 1564). Certiorari. Came the parties by their attornies and produced an agreement signed by the plaintiff and defendant by which the defendant agrees to pay the plaintiff $10.00 and half the costs of this suit; plaintiff agrees to pay the other half of costs.
        Woodson Francis VS William Howard and Allison Howard, Admrs. of Abraham Howard, dec'd (No. 1565). Came the plaintiff and dismisses his suit and confesses judgment for the costs.
        James Berry permitted to swear in as deputy Register of Rhea County.

(p. 344)   John Rice successor &c for use of Jane Lawson VS David Ragsdale. Covenant. Came the parties by their attornies and a jury (Bryan McDonald, John

Gray, Jonathan Richmond, Samuel Fry, James Dannel, James Howser, William Howard, Allison Howard, Cain Able, Gilbert Kennedy, William D. Collins, and Jonathan Fry) which says they cannot agree; mistrial is entered and this cause is continued until next sessions of this Court.

Thomas M. Kennon VS James Kelley (No. 1566). Appeal. Plaintiff dismisses suit; defendant confesses judgment for costs.

Thomas M. Kennon VS James Kelly (No. 1567). Appeal. Plaintiff dismisses suit; defendant confesses judgment for costs.

Thomas M. Kennon VS James Kelly (No. 1568). Appeal. Plaintiff dismisses suit; defendant confesses judgment for costs.

(p. 345) Richard G. Waterhouse & Enoch Parsons to Roger Reece. Deed of Conveyance for 200 acres dated 27th February 1819; proven in part by Isaac Rush (heretofore proven by Jeremiah Howerton at November Sessions 1825); certified for registration.

William Runyon VS Woodson Francis (No. 1569). Plaintiff dismisses suit; William Skilleran confesses judgment for costs.

State VS Townley Rigg. Defendant acknowledged himself indebted to State for $250 and John Martin for $250; void on condition that the defendant make his appearance on the first Wednesday after the first Monday of May next to answer a charge.

State VS Townley Rigg. Gilbert Kennedy indebted for $250 for his appearance to give evidence in this suit.

(p. 346) State VS Abner Triplet. Margaret Ransom indebted to State for $125 for appearance to give evidence in this suit.

William B. Lewis, atty in fact for Exrs. of William T. Lewis dec'd VS Joseph Williams. Came the plaintiff by his attorney and the defendant having withdrawn his defence to the plaintiffs declaration, judgment is entered against him for $1600, the debt in the declaration, and $296.00 damages. (No. 1570)

Michael W. Buster VS James Kelley. Came the parties by their attornies; on motion of plaintiff a commission is awarded him to take the deposition of John Clack at the house of Col. William Johnson in Washington to be read in evidence on the trial of the above cause, which is continued until next Court.

John Robinson resigned as a Justice of the Peace.

(p. 347) On John Lea's application, Nathaniel W. Wilson is permitted to swear in as Deputy Sheriff of Rhea County.

Orville Paine is also permitted to swear in as Deputy Sheriff of Rhea County.

John Jackson VS William Cannon (No. 1571). Plaintiff dismisses suit and confesses judgment for costs; defendant to recover his costs from plaintiff.

Ordered that the Indenture between the Chairman of this Court and John Robinson for binding George Chapman be dissolved.

Bryant McDonald and John Gray who belong to the original pannel and did not answer to their names on Tuesday appeared in Court this day and swore as Jurors.

(p. 348) Justices on bench— Jesse Thompson, Crispien E. Shelton, Joseph McCorkle, Daniel M. Stockton, Ezekiel Bates, and Isaac Roddy.

John Rice successor &c for Jane Lawson VS David Ragsdale. Covenant. Defendant is awarded a commission to take the deposition of David Henderson in Hamilton County to be read in evidence on the above trial.

State VS Abner Triplett. Assault. Defendant acknowledged himself indebted to State for $250; Thomas McNutt for $250; void on condition defendant appear at May Session of this Court.

McGhees & McCarty assignees &c VS Azariah David & John Brown. Covenant. Came the parties by their attornies; defendants demurrer to the plaintiffs declaration is overruled. Court finds that plaintiff is entitled to recover against the defendant and the damages being uncertain, the Sheriff is ordered to summon a jury at next session to inquire of the plaintiffs damages.

(p. 349)   John Cozby to John Bowlin. Deed of Conveyance for 75 acres dated 7th April 1826; acknowledged by Grantor; certified for registration.

Orville Paine VS John McClenahan, Jacob Gross and Mason McClenahan (No. 1572). Appeal. John McClanahan confesses judgment for $50.00 and costs. Execution is stayed two months.

Luke Tieru, assignee of Martin Beaty, surviving partner of Lilburn L. Henderson and Martin Beaty VS William L. Bradley (No. 1573). Came the plaintiff by attorney and entered a non suit in this cause; defendant to recover costs from plaintiff.

J. & J. Obrian VS Edmund Bean (No. 1574). Came the parties by their attornies and a jury: Bryant McDonald, John Gray, John Manley, Thomas McNutt, Robert Locke, Jesse Poe, William Lewis, William Hill, John McClanahan, Alexander Rice, Jonathan Richmond, and William Locke, and the said pannel containing two of the original pannel, Bryant McDonald and John Gray were

(p. 350)   challanged premptorily by the defendants council, who objected that a trial could not be gone into without two of the original panel being sworn on the Jury which objection after argument was over ruled by the Court and the deficiency ordered to be made up by summoning tallismen not of the original pannel and the cause tried without any of the said original pannel, to which opinion of the Court the defendant by his council excepts in law. Whereupon came a jury not of the original pannel: John Manley, Thomas McNutt, Robert Locke, Jesse Poe, William Lewis, John McClenahan, William Hill, Alexander Rice, Jonathan Richmond, William Locke, William D. Collins, and John Rawlings. Jurors say the defendant has not paid the debt of $152.87 mentioned in the declaration and assess the damages of the plaintiff to $14.01. Defendant also to pay costs. Defendant prays an appeal in the nature of a writ of errors to the next Circuit Court; entered into bond and security as the law directs and appeal is granted.

John Robinson VS Orlando Bradly (No. 1575). Plaintiff has departed this life; suit is abated and defendant dismissed and to recover his costs from plaintiffs securities.

(p. 351)   Richard G. Waterhouse, assignee of Alexander Ferguson VS John Ferguson Sr. (No. 1576). Appeal. Came the plaintiff by his attorney and enters a non suit in this cause; defendant to recover costs from plaintiff.

Same VS Same (No. 1577). Plaintiff enters a non suit; defendant to recover costs from plaintiff.

Ordered that all causes not tried at this term or otherwise disposed of be continued until the next Session of this Court.

MAY TERM 1827

(p. 352)   Court of Pleas and Quarter Sessions met at the Courthouse in Washington on the first Monday and Seventh day of May 1827. Justices on bench— Jesse Thompson, James McDonald, Daniel Walker, James Wilson, Stephen Winton, John Cozby, Jonathan Fine, Joseph McCorkle, Ezekiel Bates, Thomas Cox, Azariah David, John McClure, Josiah Fike, Beal Gaither, Peach Taylor, and William Smith.

Samuel Tillery to Leonard Brooks. Deed of Conveyance for 30 acres dated 15th February 1827; proven by Abraham Coleman and George Kincannon; certified for registration.

Matthew Hubbart, Exr. of last Will and Testament of John Woodward to William Woodward, Charles Woodward, & James Woodward. Deed of Conveyance for 80 acres dated 7th May 1827; acknowledged by Grantor; certified for registration.

Willie Lewis to James Stewart. Deed of Conveyance for 75 acres dated 14th April 1827; proven by William Lowry and John Day; certified for registration.

John Gamble to Isaac Mahan. Deed of Conveyance for 5 acres dated 12th April 1827; proven by Ezekiel Bates and Edward Templeton; certified for registration.

Thomas Hamelton to Robert Glenn. Deed of Conveyance for 80 3/8 acres dated 1st May 1827; proven by Josiah Fike and James Walton; certified for registration.

(p. 353) State VS John Lawrie. It having been certified to this Court from the Circuit Court that a Nolle proseque had been entered in this cause; County to pay costs of $28.46.

State VS Wright Hankins. Nolle proseque entered in Circuit Court; County to pay costs of $25.79.

The last Will and Testament of Samuel Tillery was produced and proven by oaths of Absalom Coleman and Leonard Brooks, the subscribing witnesses.

John Tillery and Thomas Bell, executors named in the Will of Samuel Tillery, dec'd; entered into bond with Joseph Love and John Stewart for $700.

James Moore appointed overseer of road in place of Jacob Garrison.

(p. 354) The last Will and Testament of Richard Haslerig was produced and proven by Miller Francis, it having been proven at the last February Session by the other subscribing witness Woodson Francis. Ordered to be recorded.

John Locke and James Berry, Executors named in the Will of Richard Haslerig, appeared and took oath prescribed by law; entered into bond with Joseph Love and Samuel McDaniel for $8000.

John Tillery and Thomas Bell, Exrs., returned an account of the sale of Samuel Tillerys estate.

William Kennedy, Henry Collins, and James A. Darwin, Commissioners appointed to settle with Matthew Hubbart, Exr. of last Will and Testament of John Woodward, returned their settlement.

Richard G. Waterhouse to Asahel Rawlings. Deed of Conveyance for 632 acres in Hamilton County dated 2nd of January 1827; proven by Richard Waterhouse, one of the subscribing witnesses; certified for further probate.

Samuel Looney released from payment of a poll tax for present year, he being over age.

(p. 355) Robert Elder, James Lillard, Pulaski Poe, Jesse Poe, Robert Locke, William S. Leuty, William Johnson, John Day, Robert Parks, Woodson Francis, Henry Collins, and James Stewart appointed a Jury of View to lay off and mark a road from the Town of Washington to cross the Tennessee River at Haslerigs Landing or any place more suitable in a direction leading to Athens in McMinn County, and from the Town of Washington passing up the Mountain at James Stewarts or any other place more suitable leading to Pikeville in Bledsoe County.

James Bailey, Cumberland Rector, Matthew Allen, Robert Miller, John Smith, John Clary, and Jadire Brezeal appointed a Jury of View to lay off and mark a road from James Baileys to George Gillespies Ferry on Tennessee River, and from said ferry to Walter Edwards old plantation or to what is called the river road leading to the town of Washington.

James Blevins appointed overseer of road from forks of the Athens Road past John McDaniels to Samuel Igos; to have the following hands to work under him: Miles B. Davis, John Davis, William Davis, John McKinley, Malcom Stephens, Hugh

Blevins, David Blevins, Archibald Taylor, and (blank) Hickmon.

Samuel Igo appointed overseer of road from his house to where said road intersects the Kingston Road that passes by Miles Vernons and to have the following hands to work under him: Joseph Lusk, Jacob Slover, George Kerruns, Miles Vernon & hands, Joseph Wheeler, and John Runyon.

William B. Russell appointed a Constable in Capt. Russell's Company; bond with James McDonald and Ezekiel Bates, his securities.

(p. 356) Pleasant M. Miller appointed a Constable in Capt. Stockton's Company; bond with Miles Vernon and James Wilson, his securities.

Jesse Martin, overseer of road from John Roddys to Kellys Road have the following hands: John Roddys hands, Jesse Martins hands, Pleasant Lea, John Philpot, Samuel Martin, Thomas Johns, John Martin, and Jesse Craft.

Addison Rigg appointed overseer of road in place of Isaac Mahan.

Seaton Taylor appointed overseer of road in place of Elias Ferguson.

Thomas Cox, Coroner, allowed $5.00 for holding an inquest over the body of Jane McDowells infant child.

Certificate for $3.00 issued to Charles McDaniel for a Wolf scalp.

(p. 357) Nathaniel Smith to James Rodgers. Deed of Conveyance for 80 acres dated 27th February 1827; proven in part by Isaac Baker; certified for further probate.

Miller Francis to Michael W. Buster. Deed of Release acknowledged by Miller Francis; certified for registration.

Joseph Chastain released from payment of tax on 18½ acres of land, he having been charged with that amount more than he ought to be.

Isaac Love, Admr. on estate of William Love, dec'd, returned an account of sale of said estate.

James Wilson and Daniel M. Stockton appointed to lay off the hands to work under David Buster, overseer of the road.

John S. Richmond appointed overseer of road in place of John Foshee.

James Stewart appointed overseer of road from Washington to where the road intersects the Valley Road near Caswell Johnsons.

James P. Miller & Robert Bell to Crispien E. Shelton. Bill of Sale for a Negro girl dated 11th May 1826; acknowledged by Miller; certified for further probate.

(p. 358) Ordered that the road from Stephen Wintons passing by Cazeys Mill to the McMinn County line be established. Samuel Pharis appointed overseer of said road; to have all hands on William Matlocks plantation, all hands on Samuel Pharis plantation, all hands on Lewis Brannons plantation, all hands on Amelia Jacksons plantation, and William Seers to work under him on road.

Samuel Ferguson appointed overseer of road from Jacob Becks to William Lisenbys; to have Isaac Moore, James Beck, William McArthur, Aron Ferguson, John Miller, John Ferguson, Preston Knight, and Edward Wasson to work under him.

Thomas Anderson appointed overseer of road from William Lisenbys to Waltons Ferry on Tennessee River; to have George W. Riggle, Archabald Rhea, John Riggle, and George Stephens hand to work under him on road.

James Bailey & others to James Berry. Power of Attorney dated 6th May 1827 authorizing James Berry to sign their names; proven by James Rodgers and Brinkley Hornsby; certified for registration.

Joshua Tindle to James Stewart. Deed of Conveyance dated 14th April 1827 for 18 acres; acknowledged by Grantor; certified for registration.

Ordered that the Jurors be allowed 50¢ a day for each day served for the present year.

108

(p. 359) Jurors appointed for next term of this Court:

John Mahan	Abraham Brison	Lewis Morgan	Edward Stewart
Moses Thompson	James Stockton	Jacob Price	James Lillard
Isaac Rush	John A. Foshee	Roger Reese	Samuel Holloway
James Kelly	Martin Smiley	Jacob Beck	Abraham Hughs
Henry Johns	John Walker	Matthias Hines	Henry Davis
Silas F. Barnes	William Hill	Pleasant Love	Thomas Eaves
Anson Dearmon, Constable to attend Court			Samuel Frazier

Jurors appointed for next term of Circuit Court:

Edward Gray	Cain Able	Thornton Creed	James Rodgers
Robert Kerr	William Miller	Miles B. Davis	William Rice
Jeremiah Chapman	John Miller	Eli Ferguson	Frederick Fulkerson
James Cowan	John Smith	William Alexander	Joseph Love
John Hill	Joseph Williams	Daniel D. Armstrong	John Miller
John Jack	Jesse Witt	Samuel Igo	David Roper
Andrew Kincannon, Constable to attend Court			Townley Rigg

Andrew Kincannon released from payment of tax on 160 acres, be being charged with that amount of land more than he owes.

Brinkley Hornsby released from payment of 90¢ of his tax for present year.

Samuel Minnick to work on road under John Weese, overseer.

Spillsby Dyer appointed overseer of road in place of Jacob Garrison.

(p. 360) "In conformity with the usages in such case and the laws of the land, Carson Caldwell, John Cozby, and John McClure is appointed by the Court inspectors of the election at Washington on the first Thursday and Friday of August next to elect a Governor, a member to Congress &c."

Joseph McCorkle, Ezekiel Bates, and Thomas Cox appointed inspectors of election presinct at Robert Elders for the said purpose.

James Wilson, Josiah Fike, and Daniel M. Stockton appointed inspectors of election at the upper presinct on South side of Tennessee River.

George Gillespie, Jesse Thompson, and Matthew Hubbart appointed inspectors of election at presinct on Piney for the said purpose.

Joseph Love allowed $8.18 3/4 for settling four days with the Sheriff and Trustee of Rhea County for 1826; also a quire of paper used by the commission.

Robert Locke allowed $8.00 for settling four days with the Sheriff and Trustee of Rhea County.

James Wilson allowed $8.00 for settling with Sheriff and Trustee.

Ordered that part of Tuesday of this present term be set apart for the further transaction of County business.

Ordered that the road from Taylors Ferry to Henry Collins as reported by the Jury of View at this term be disaffirmed.

(p. 361) The last Will and Testament of Richard G. Waterhouse was produced and proven by oaths of William Kennedy, Arthur Fulton, Allen Kennedy, Brinkley Hornsby, and Matthew Hubbart, the subscribing witnesses. Ordered that the Will except the Codicil be recorded; the Codicil contained no devises and was no part of the Will of Richard G. Waterhouse.

Richard Waterhouse and Blackstone Waterhouse, executors named in the Will, appeared and took oaths; entered into bond with William Kennedy, Allen Kennedy, Matthew Hubbart, Brinkley Hornsby, Arthur Fulton, James Bailey, Charles Mitchell, Thomas McKedy, Jesse Atwood, Archibald D. Paul, John Wasson, Aron Ferguson, William Johnson, James McCanse, William Noblett, Thomas Price, Rezin Rawlings, John McClure, John Hill, Daniel Walker, Robert Parks, William Smith, Miles Vernon, Bruten Peters, Moses Ferguson, John Condley, James Stewart, Matthew English, William T. Gillenwaters, Samuel R. Hackett, James Wilson, and James A. Darwin, their securities for $80,000.

Woodson Francis, Sheriff and Collector of Public Taxes, allowed $8.50 on account of delinquent taxes for the years 1825 and 1826 on the following polls: Randolph Harwood, Joseph Leverett, William Preswood, Archabald Rhea, William Rader, Mark Stacy, Joseph Smith, William Shingleton, Thomas Breeden, James Bynum, Aaron Rhea, Thomas Pollard Sr., Thomas Pollard Jr., John Robinson, William Huffman, John Mullins, and John Henderson.

(p. 362) Ordered "that $25.30 3/4 in par money and $24.69½ in Nashville Money now in the hands of the Trustee of Rhea County be paid over to the Commissioners appointed by law to Superintend the building of a new jail in Washington and that the said Money be appropriated for the use of building said jail and that the said Commissioners make the best use they can of the Nashville money and account for the same accordingly and the receipt of the said Commissioners shall be a good voucher in the settlement of said Trustee with Commissioners appointed to settle with him."

Carson Caldwell, Trustee, returned a report of all the monies that have come into his hands for and during the preceding year, and likewise the amount by him paid out for the use of said County shewing particularly for what the same was disbursed.

Ordered that an account of William Johnson for keeping a Jury and an officer in the case of the State against Richard Waterhouse as certified by the Circuit Court for $78.00 be allowed.

Ordered that an account of William Johnson for keeping a Jury and an officer in the case of the State against William S. Leuty as certified by the Circuit Court for $9.75 be allowed.

Ordered that the road from Waltons Ferry to cross Sewee at or near James Wilsons &c as reported by the Jury of View be disaffirmed.

Ordered that the road from George Gillespies Ferry on Tennessee River to Abner Caseys Mill be established as reported by a Jury of View.

(p. 363) Daniel Rawlings & John Rodgers, Admrs. on estate of Alexander Ferguson for the use of Richard G. Waterhouse VS John Ferguson (No. 1578). Appeal. Came the parties and John Ferguson the appellant in this cause dismisses his appeal and confesses judgment for the costs.

(p. 364) Justices on bench (8th May)— William Smith, Azariah David, Samuel Gamble, Thomas Cox, and Peach Taylor.

William Carter appointed overseer of road in place of Dempsey Sulliven.

William Smith Jr. appointed overseer of road in place of Jasper Romines; to have additional hands of James McCanse and William Scruchfield [sic].

Robert Love VS Solomon Vernon (No. 1579). Came the plaintiff by his attorney, Thomas J. Campbell, and the defendant who dismisses his appeal and confesses judgment for $1.00 and costs.

Richard G. Waterhouse to Rezin Rawlings. Deed of Conveyance dated 6th June 1826 for 167 acres; proven in part by Richard Waterhouse; a subpoena awarded Rezin Rawlings to Hamilton County to compell S.R. Russell, the other witness, to come and prove the execution of said deed.

On Thomas C. Wroes petition, Mark Johnson, Adam Cole, William Wann, Robert Pharis, John Pharis, and Bijah Boggess are appointed a Jury of View to turn the Walton Ferry Road at or near where it intersects the Kingston Road on Thomas C. Wroes land.

(p. 365) John Lea, Sheriff, returned a list of Jurors summoned to appear at this Term of Court (see list on page 100), out of which a Grand Jury was elected: Elisha Parker, William Matlock, Moses Ferguson, Absolam Foshee, James McCanse, Moses Thompson, Joseph Williams, Matthew Allen, Pleasant Love, Robert Goad, William Locke, Allison Howard, and Daniel Holland. Elisha Parker was appointed foreman and David Shelton a Constable to attend the Grand Jury.

There remained of the original pannel: Solomon Vernon, William Gray, Charles McDonald, Daniel D. Armstrong, John Randle, Robert Kerr, Rezin Rawlings, and Thomas Breeding.

Michael W. Buster VS James Kelley. Cause is continued until next Term.

(p. 366) Jacob Slover VS William M. Smith (No. 1580). Motion as Security. Came the plaintiff by his attorney, William C. Dunlap and a jury (Solomon Vernon, William Gray, Charles McDonald, Daniel D. Armstrong, Robert Kerr, Rezin Rawlings, Thomas Breeden, Charles Witt, Alexander Coulter, Samuel Johnson, John Walker, and Cain Able) which says that Jacob Slover was security for Smith and paid for him $49.74. Plaintiff to recover from defendant $49.74 debt and $3.26 damages plus costs.

Andrew Evans, Admr. on estate of William Floyd, dec'd VS Elias Majors (No. 1531). Appeal. John Locke, Rezin Rawlings, and James Berry returned their judgment: ". . . are of opinion the aforesaid plaintiff has no good cause for this his action against the defendant. . . . considered by the Court that this suit be dismissed . . ."

Nathaniel Smith assignee of James & Aron Haynes VS George Gordon. Covenant. Came the parties by their attornies and a jury (same as above) which says the defendant has not well and truly kept and performed his said covenant as the plaintiff hath complained against him but has broken the same and they do assess the plaintiffs damage to $410.72.

(p. 367) Thomas Cox VS Abednego Hail. Petition for Certiorari and supersedias. Awarded to defendant to bring this cause from the justice into Court on his entering into bond and security.

Samuel Fry VS James Daniel & James Howser (No. 1532). Came the parties by their attornies and a jury (same as above) which says the defendants are guilty of the trespass in manner and form as declared by the plaintiff; damages set at $7.00, plus costs.

James C. Greer VS Daniel D. Stockton. Rule is allowed the plaintiff to dismiss the petition for Certiorari and supersedeas in this cause.

(p. 368) John Locke and Thomas J. Campbell appointed Administrators on the estate of John Hudson, dec'd; entered into bond with Edward Scott, Charles A. Scott, William T. Henderson, and John H. Henderson, their securities, for $40,000.

Report of James Montgomery and Rolly Clack, Commissioners appointed to settle with Joseph Harwood, Admr. on estate of John Chapman, dec'd, was returned.

Sebert Marten VS Joseph McDaniel (No. 1533). Appeal. Came the parties by their attornies and a jury (John Randle, Elisha Parker, William Matlock, Moses Ferguson, Matthew Allen, Pleasant Love, Robert Goad, William Locke, Absolam Foshee, James McCanse, Moses Thompson, and Daniel Holland) which finds for the plaintiff and assesses his damage to $14.37½. Considered that the plaintiff recover from the defendant and John Parker, his security for the appeal the sum of $14.37½ and $1.34 3/4 damages and his costs.

Roberts & McCallie VS Edmund Bean. Cause is continued until next Term.

(p. 369) Richard G. Waterhouse for the use of Elisha Kirkland VS Rezin Rawlings

(No. 1534). Covenant. Came the parties by their attornies and a jury (same as above) which says the defendant has not kept and performed his covenant, but has broken the same; plaintiffs damages assessed at $152.40. Plaintiff to recover the said sum and the costs in this behalf.

Rezin Rawlings VS John Robinson (No. 1535). Motion as Security. Came the plaintiff by his attorney, Thomas J. Campbell, and a jury (same as above) which says that Rezin Rawlings was security for the said Robinson and paid as such $140.82. Plaintiff to recover said sum plus costs.

McGhees & McCarty VS Azariah David & John Brown. Covenant. Came the parties by their attornies and with assent of Court this cause is continued until next session of this Court.

(p. 370) Woodson Francis VS William Howard & Allison Howard, Admrs. of Abraham Howard, dec'd (No. 1536). Came the parties by their attornies and a jury (same as above) which says that the defendants have well and truly administered all and singular the goods and chattles rights and credits of Abraham Howard, dec'd which came to their hands to be administered and the jury further say that the said Abraham Howard in his life time did not pay the debt in the plaintiffs declaration and they assess the plaintiffs damage to $63.87½.

Palatiah Shelton VS William Howard & Allison Howard, Admrs &c (No. 1537). Leave is given defendants to amend their pleadings upon payment of the costs of this Term. Plaintiff to recover against defendants the costs in said cause at present term.

(p. 371) Arthur Smith VS William Snelson. Cause is continued until next Term.

John Rice, successor &c for use of Jane Lawson VS David Ragsdale. Cause is continued until next session of this Court.

(p. 372) Justices on bench (9th May)— Azariah David, Matthew Hubbart, Samuel Gamble, Peach Taylor, and William Smith.

State VS Washington Morgan (No. 1538). Overseer. Defendant says he cannot gainsay the charge; fined 6¼¢ and costs. James Stewart security for the payment of fine and costs.

State VS Townley Rigg (No. 1539). Assault and Battery. Defendant says he is not guilty; a jury (Robert Kerr, Elisha Parker, William Matlock, Moses Ferguson, Absolom Foshee, James McCanse, Joseph Williams, Matthew Allen, Pleasant Love, Robert Goad, William Locke, and Daniel Holland) finds the defendant guilty as charged; fined $3.00 plus costs; Wyllys H. Chapman security for payment.

(p. 373) State VS James C. Mitchell (No. 1590). Overseer. Defendant says he cannot gainsay the charge; fined 25¢ and costs.

State VS Abner Triplet (No. 1591). Assault and Battery. Defendant says he cannot gainsay the charges; fined $1.00 and costs.

Joseph Martin to John Mahan. Deed of Conveyance for 60 acres dated 13th March 1827; proven in part by William Smith; certified for further probate.

Nathaniel Smith assignee of James & Aron Haynes VS George Gordon (No. 1592). Covenant. Came the parties by attornies; ordered by Court that the plaintiffs demurrer to the defendants second plea is sustained; considered that the plaintiff (upon the findings of a jury on yesterday in this cause) recover against the defendant the sum of $410.72 damages and the costs.

(p. 374) McGhees & McCarty VS Jacob Slover. Time is given to declare plead and try so as not to delay the trial of said cause.

Rezin Rawlings VS William Johnson (No. 1593). Defendant says he cannot gainsay the plaintiffs demand against him for $212.00 debt and damages. Plaintiff to recover debt, damages, and costs.

112

John A. Smith VS Daniel D. Stockton (No. 1594). Appeal. Came the parties by their attornies and a jury (William Locke, Rezin Rawlings, James Stewart, William Lowrey, John Wammac, George Maner, Thomas Henry, David Leuty, Samuel Johnson, Anson Dearmon, Giles S. Bogges, and William Howard) that finds for the plaintiff and assesses his damages to $50.00; plaintiff by attorney moves for judgment against Joseph C. Stockton, security for the prosecution of the appeal. Plaintiff to recover against defendant and his security the $50.00 plus $1.55 damages and the costs in this behalf.

John Love permitted to keep an ordinary for one year; entered into bond with George Gillespie, his security.

Samuel Fry VS James Daniel & James Howser. Came the defendants by their attorney and on their motion a rule is allowed them to shew cause why a new trial should be granted in this cause.

(p. 375) Abner Triplett VS George Ransom (No. 1595). Motion as Security. Came the plaintiff by his attorney Wyllys H. Chapman and a jury (same as above) which says that the plaintiff was security for Ransom and as such paid $14.55 3/5 . Plaintiff to recover the said sum plus 65¢ damages and costs.

David Ragsdale VS Samuel Beshars (No. 1596). Came the plaintiff by his attorney, William C. Dunlap, and the defendant not appearing to make defence, made default. On motion of plaintiffs attorney, considered that the plaintiff recover against the defendant $84.28 debt and $5.47 3/4 damages plus costs.

Adam W. Caldwell permitted to keep an ordinary for one year; bond with William Johnson and Matthew Hubbart, his securities.

Samuel Fry VS James Dannil & James Howser. Rule to shew cause why a new trial should be granted is discharged.

Ordered that all causes not tried at this term be continued until the next session of this Court.

AUGUST TERM 1827

(p. 376) Court of Pleas and Quarter Sessions met at the Courthouse in Washington on the first Monday and sixth day of August 1827. Justices on bench— Stephen Winton, Daniel M. Stockton, Jonathan Collins, Jonathan Fine, John Cozby, Josiah Fike, George Gillespie, James Wilson, Jesse Thompson, Thomas Cox, Isaac Roddy, William Smith, Peach Taylor, Matthew Hubbart, Joseph McCorkle, John McClure, Samuel Gamble, Carson Caldwell, Daniel Walker, Crispeon E. Shelton, James A. Darwin, Beal Gaither, and Ezekiel Bates.

Richard G. Waterhouse to Samuel F.D. Swan. Deed of Conveyance dated 29th October 1825 for 324 acres; proven by Joseph Garrison and Richard Waterhouse; certified for registration.

George Preston, David Hutson, Hiram Gibson, William Wann, Randolph Gibson, James Snelson, and Samuel Snelson appointed a Jury of View to lay off a road leading from Snelsons Ferry on Tennessee River to intersect the Federal Road at or near to Thomas C. Roes.

John B. Page appointed overseer of road from William Millers to Robert Pharis in place of John Pharis.

Jesse Roddy, Samuel Applegate, Joshua Kelly, James Bailey, James Roddy, Cumberland Rector, Robert Walker, and William Johnson appointed a Jury of View to lay off a road from or near Robert Walkers to Snelsons Ferry on Tennessee River with as little injury as possible to improvements.

George Maner appointed overseer of road in place of Washington Morgan.

(p. 377) James Roddy appointed overseer of road from the branch between William T. Gillenwaters and Robert Walkers to Whites Creek.

Peter Daniel appointed overseer of road from the dividing ridge between

Piney and Whites Creek to the branch between Gilleswaters and Walkers; to have hands on southwest side of branch to work under him.

Robert McClure appointed overseer of road from Kellys Ferry to where said road intersects the road leading from Washington to Richland Creek in place of Kennedy Cooper, resigned.

Charles Goaldsby appointed overseer of road from Fraziers Ferry on Tennessee River to Mud Creek in place of Abraham Hughes.

James Blevins to have following hands to work under him in addition to former hands: Pulaskie Poe, Thompson Merriott, William Long, Benjamin Looney, Isaac Matlock, and Benjamin Johnson.

Samuel Howard, George Maner, William Howard, Alexander Coulter, and Allison Howard appointed a Jury of View to turn the road from Washington to Pikeville so as to leave the old road at the corner of John Jacks field and run on the line between said Jacks and Asahel Johnsons to fall into the old road near George Maners, a distance of about a half a mile.

(p. 378) Cornelious Myors and Alta M. Myors to Orville Paine. Deed of Conveyance dated 13th May 1826 for an undivided sixth part of a tract of land; acknowledged by Cornelious and Alta M., after being privately examined apart from her husband; certified for registration.

Jurors appointed for next term of this Court.

Asahel Johnson	Elijah Blythe	David Clinghan	John Davis
James Pharis	Thomas Noblet	John Clarey	Jesse Martin
Robert Gamble	John McClanahan	Edward Templeton	Isaac Rush
Samuel Baker	William England	Volentine Houpt	William Hill
George Barnet	William M. Rogers	John Carrol	John Lillard
David Roper	Daniel D. Armstrong	Wright Smith	James Montgomery

James Walker to attend as Constable.

Robert Locke, Carson Caldwell, and William Johnson appointed commissioners to settle with Jesse Poe, Admr. on estate of William Lewis, dec'd.

Ally Runnels allowed $30.00 for keeping Mary Owens, a pauper, for part of a year, said Mary Owens having been heretofore (at August Sessions 1826) let out to James Swan but not kept by him.

Joshua Richards released from payment of poll tax for 1825, he being under age.

(p. 379) Isaac Baker appointed overseer of road from George Gillespies Ferry on Tennessee River to Ten Mile Creek; to have the following hands to work under him: John Bennet, Henry Nelson, John Nelson, Nathaniel Blackwell, James Blackwell, William White, Kiah Bennet, John Dannel, Alexander H. McCall, Mark Massey Jr., Plummer Dannel, Robert Rhea, Squire Burton, Jacob Oldham, Linton Hatchcock, and Adam Nelson.

Turner Casey appointed overseer of road leading from Gillespies Ferry to the McMinn County line from Ten Mile Creek to said McMinn County line passing John Redmonds near Caseys Mill and to have the following hands: Samuel Montooth, all the hands that live on the plantations of Samuel G. Davis, John Redmond, and William Harmen, Abner Casey, (blank) McCully, all the Greens(?) and the hands of John Arington.

Matthew Allen appointed overseer of road from Gillespies Ferry on Tennessee River to the great road leading to Washington at or near to James Baileys and to have the following hands: John Clerey, John Smith, Thomas Whitmore, and all George Gillespies hands.

James Smith appointed overseer of road from Gillespies Ferry to the great road leading to Washington at or near Walter Edwards old plantation and to have the following hands: Robert Miller, Henry Newman, James Carter, Joseph Perry, Jodire Brazeal, Joseph McCall, Moses Looney, and all George Gillespies hands.

Martin Ferguson appointed overseer of road from James A. Darwins to Clear Creek in place of James C. Mitchell.

Jonathan Collins resigned as a Justice of the Peace.

(p. 380) John Parker allowed $16.00 for keeping a Jury over night and breakfast on the trial of Arnold; and for keeping said Arnold and Blackwell in Jail 10 days.

John Parker allowed $3.50 for keeping John Harrel in Jail 8 days.

David Shelton allowed pay for attending two days as a Constable at February Sessions 1827 and five days as Constable at March Term of Circuit Court.

Rezin Rawlings and William S. Leuty appointed Trustees of Tennessee Academy.

Alvah Quiet, Admr. on estate of William Quiet, dec'd, returned an inventory of said estate.

Isaac Roddy to Jesse Martin. Deed of Conveyance dated 6th August 1827 for one rood and 13 poles of land; acknowledged by bargoner; certified for resistration.

Jesse Martin to Isaac Roddy. Deed of Conveyance for 12 acres (same date as above); acknowledged by bargoner; certified for registration.

(p. 381) Robert W. Caldwell appointed a Constable in Captain William Hill's Company; bond with Joseph Love, Thomas Kelly, and David Caldwell, his securities.

State VS Abner Triplet. James Stewart acknowledged himself the defendants security for the fine and all costs of said suit, and the said Abner Triplet was discharged from the custody of the Sheriff.

Samuel Gamble, John Masoner, Edward Templeton, Samuel Fitzgerald, Isaac Mahan, Allen Gentry, and Robert Gamble appointed a Jury of View to lay off a road from Bunkers Hill on Hiwassee to communicate with a road from Hamilton Courthouse through the Cherokee Nation to the said Bunkers Hill, thence the most direct way to the McMinn County line, leading to Athens.

Ordered that the road from Washington to the McMinn County line crossing Tennessee River at Haslerigs Landing be established as reported by a Jury of View as follows: beginning at the fork of Kellys Road near Washington, thence to Haslerigs landing leading from thence at or nearly at a right angle with the river' through the bottom lands of Robert Locke, thence passing William Ingles plantation thence through the gap of a ridge and intersecting a road leading from James Taylors to Athens, thence with said road continuing near to and generally on the direction of what is called the Pumpkin Town line passing James Lillards Mill, Aden Bridwells house &c to the McMinn County line; road to be of the first class.

Ordered that Col. William Johnson, late Trustee of Rhea County, be proceeded against as a delinquent according to law.

(p. 382) Robert Locke appointed overseer of road from Washington to Haslerigs landing; to have following hands: all the hands in the bounds of the Town of Washington that is subject to work on the road, all the hands on the plantation where Andrew Evans now lives, all the hands on the plantation of Conly F. Haslerig, and all the hands on the plantation of Robert Locke.

Pulaski Poe appointed overseer of road leading from Haslerigs landing to the McMinn County line, to the dividing ridge between the waters of Tennessee River and Goodfield; to have the following hands: all hands from mouth of Goodfield up the river to and including Daniel Stocktons, then running with the big ridge leading from Daniel Stocktons to and including David Blevins.

James Lillard appointed overseer of road leading from Haslerigs landing to the McMinn County line from the dividing ridge between the waters of Tennessee and Goodfield and to have the following hands: Henry Runals, Augustine Breedwell, Watson Breedwell, John Taylor, Leonard Brooks, Almond Gwin, John Howel, (blank)

Shaver, Armsted Breedwell, Aden Breedwell, William Galaway, and Abraham Gallaway.

Ordered that George Gillespies Ferry on Tennessee River be established.

Ordered that there be a ferry established on Tennessee River to cross at Haslerigs landing.

John Locke and Thomas J. Campbell, Admrs. on estate of John Hudson, returned an account of sales of said estate.

Ordered that the road from Yorks Mill to intersect the Athens road at or near John Lillards be disannuled.

(p. 383) John Locke and Thomas J. Campbell, Admrs. on estate of John Hudson, exhibited a bond from the Legatees of said John Hudson to refund.

Ordered that the rates of ferriage at all the ferries on Tennessee River in Rhea County be as follows: 4 horse team & over, $1.00; 3 horse team, 75¢; 2 horse, 50¢; 1 horse, 37½¢; Pleasure Carriage, $1.00; Gig, 50¢; Man and horse, 12½¢; foot men, 6¼¢; Loose horses, 6¼¢ each; Cattle, 3¢; Hogs & Sheep, 1¢ each.

Ordered that the hands that work on the road from Kelly's Ferry to Samuel Igos be exempt from working on said road for three months and help work the road from Haslerigs Landing under Pulaski Poe, overseer of said road.

(p. 384) Justices on bench (7th August)— James Wilson, John McClure, George Gillespie, Stephen Winton, Beal Gaither, Isaac Roddy, Josiah Fike, and Samuel Gamble.

John Lea, Sheriff, returned a list of Jurors summoned to attend at this session of Court (see list on page 108), of whom the following were elected a Grand Jury: James Lillard, Pleasant Love, Siles F. Barnes, Jacob Beck, Jacob Price, Abraham Hughes, John Walker, Samuel Holloway, William Hill, Henry Johns, Martin Smiley, James Kelly, and John Mahan. James Lillard appointed foreman and Anson Dearmon a Constable to attend the Grand Jury.

There remained of the original pannel who answered to their names James Stockton.

Ordered that the road leading from Washington to Pikeville be turned as reported by the Jury of View as follows: to leave the old road at the corner of John Jacks field and run on the line betweeen said Jack and Asahel Johnson to fall into the old road near George Maners a distance of about a half a mile; overseer of the road to work on the road as it is now turned.

(p. 385) Joseph Martin to John Mahan. Deed of Conveyance dated 13th March 1827 for 60 acres; proven by Milo Smith, one of the subscribing witnesses (heretofore proven by William Smith); certified for registration.

Thomas Eaves and Moses Thompson released from further attendance as Jurors at this Term.

State VS Henry Pearson. Recognizance. Defendant and his security, John A. Smith, acknowledged themselves indebted to State for $250 each; void on condition that Henry Pearson appear here from day to day to answer a charge of assault.

William Smith, Successor &c for the use of Jane Lawson VS David Ragsdale (No. 1597). Covenant. Came the parties by their attornies and a jury (James Stockton, Alexander Rice, Thomas Hunter, Reuben Freeman, James Robertson, Miles B. Davis, Isaac Braselton, John A. Smith, Caswell Johnson, John Smith, William Locke, and Jacob Brown) which assessed the plaintiffs damages at $10.00.

(p. 386) John McGhee, Matthew W. McGhee, & John L. McCarty VS Azariah David & John Brown (No. 1598). Came the parties by their attornies and a jury (Barefoot Armstrong, William Lewis, James Montgomery, John Able, Daniel D. Stockton, John McClenahan, Michael W. Buster, David Ragsdale, Charles Witt, and Charles Ryon)

116

which assesses the plaintiffs damages at $476.97½.

Michael W. Buster VS James Kelly. Cause is continued until next Session.

Arthur Smith VS William Snelson (No. 1599). Came the plaintiff by their attornies and a jury (Edmund Bean, John McDonnough, Barefoot Armstrong, William Lewis, James Montgomery, John Able, Daniel D. Stockton, John McClenahan, William Howard, David Ragsdale, Charles Witt, and Charles Ryon) which says the defendant is not guilty of the trover and conversion as the plaintiff in declaring hath complained. Defendant to recover his costs from plaintiff. From which verdict and judgment the plaintiff prayed an appeal to the next Circuit Court; granted.

(p. 387) Grand Jury returned the following Bills of Indictment: State against Thomas McNutt for an assault; State against Henry Pearson for an assault; also a presentment against David Clinghan.

Deed of Condition between Rezin Rawlings and Robert Locke dated 7th August 1827 was acknowledged by Rawlings and Locke; certified for registration.

John Locke and Thomas J. Campbell, Admrs. on estate of John Hudson, dec'd, exhibited a bond from the legatees of said John Hudson to refund, which bond is as follows: "Know all men by these presents that we Charles A. Scott Legatee in right of my wife Elizabeth of the estate of John Hudson Decd, Edward Scott guardian of Martha Ann Scott legatee of sd estate by my Attorney in fact Charles A. Scott, Robert W. Ashlin in right of my wife Sarah Ann legatee of sd estate, Columbus W. Kent in right of my wife Mary E. legatee of sd estate by my Attorney in fact Robert W. Ashlin, Robert W. Ashlin guardian of Rebecca Henderson legatee of said estate, John Henderson legatee of said estate in right of my wife, by my Attorney in fact John H. Henderson, Charles Hudson legatee of sd estate by my Attornies in fact Charles A. Scott & Edward Scott, Ann L. Cobs legatee of sd estate by my attorney in fact Charles A. Scott are Jointly Severally and firmly bound unto William Smith presiding Justice and Chairman of the Court of pleas and quarter Sessions in and for Rhea County or his successors in office in the Just and full sum of forty thousand dollars the which payment well and truly to be made and done we bind ourselves our several heirs &c Jointly Severally and firmly by these presents Sealed with our seals and dated as follows.— The condition of the above obligation is such that whereas we the above enumerated legatees of the estate of John Hudson late of Rhea County Decd have this day received and receipted for to John Locke and Thomas J. Campbell, Administrators of Said Estate Our respective dividends out of the disposable assets now in said Administrators hands of said Estate.—

"Now if any debt or debts truly owing by the deceased shall hereafter be sued for and recovered or otherwise be duly made appear to an amount that what may remain in the hands of said Administrators will not pay and satisfy, That then and in that case if the foregoing legatees shall well and truly satisfy and pay his and her ratable part of said debt or debts then the foregoing

(p. 388) obligation to be void as to them else to be and remain in full force and effect. Given under our hands and seals this 14th day of July 1827." (signed by the legatees listed above).

(p. 389) Justices on bench (8th August)— James Wilson, John McClure, Stephen Winton, Beal Gaither, and Josiah Fike.

State VS Henry Pearson (No. 1600). Assault and Battery. Defendant says he cannot gainsay the charges; fined $1.00 and costs; John A. Smith, security for payment.

State VS Henry Pearson (No. 1601). Peace Warrant. The prosecutor Daniel D. Stockton not further requiring sureties of the peace of the said defendant, it is considered that the defendant go hence upon the payment of the costs accrued upon said prosecution. Whereupon the defendant and John A. Smith confessed judgment for the costs.

State VS Thomas Farmer (No. 1602). Peace Warrant. A Nolle proseque is entered in this cause; County to pay costs.

(p. 390) State VS Randolph Harwood (No. 1603). Peace Warrant. Came Thomas J. Campbell, Attorney General and the defendant; the prosecutor Masey Powell not further requiring sureties of the peace of the defendant. Court considers that the defendant go hence upon the payment of the costs; defendant, Malakiah Harwood, and Jesse Harwood confess judgment for the costs.

State VS Thomas McNutt (No. 1604). Assault and Battery. Defendant says he cannot gainsay the charges; fined $1.00 and costs.

Roberts & McCallie assignees of Orville Paine VS Jacob Brown (No. 1605 & 1606). Appeal. Came the parties by their attornies and a jury (James Lillard, Pleasant Love, Siles F. Barnes, John Walker, Samuel Holloway, William Hill, Henry Johns, Martin Smiley, James Kelly, John Mahan, John Day, and Jacob Price) which finds for the plaintiff the sum of 24¢; Orville Paine confessed judgment for one third of the costs. Plaintiff to recover against the defendant the sum of 24¢ and two thirds of the costs.

(p. 391) Roberts & McCallie VS Edmund Bean. Came the parties by their attornies and a jury (Thomas Piper, Samuel Johnson, Henry Henry, Jacob Brown, William Seymore, Thomas McNutt, John Day, Rezin Rawlings, John A. Smith, John Starrett, James Montgomery, and Randolph Harwood) which says the defendant did assume and take upon himself in manner and form as the plaintiffs declaring hath complained against him and they assess the plaintiffs damage to the sum of $80.84 3/4.

James C. Grear VS Daniel D. Stockton (No. 1607). Certiorari. Came the plaintiffs by their attornies and a jury (Thomas Piper, Samuel Johnson, Edward Hide, Jacob Brown, William Seymore, Thomas McNutt, John Day, Rezin Rawlings, John Starrett, David Leuty, Randolph Harwood, and Alexander Rice) which finds for the plaintiff the sum of $28.00.

Roberts & McCallie VS Edmund Bean (No. 1608). Demurrer. Came the parties by their attornies; ordered that the plaintiffs demurrer to the defendants second and third pleas be sustained; considered that the plaintiff upon the finding of a jury recover of the defendant the sum of 80.84 3/4 and damages plus costs.

(p. 392) Palatiah Chilton VS William & Allison Howard, Admrs. of Abraham Howard dec'd (No. 1609). Came the parties by their attornies and a jury (Daniel D. Stockton, Thomas Piper, Samuel Johnson, Henry Henry, Jacob Brown, William Seymore, Thomas McNutt, John A. Smith, John Starrett, James Montgomery, Alexander Rice, and Randolph Harwood) which says the defendants have well and truly administered the estate of Abraham Howard; jury also says that Abraham Howard in his life time did not well and truly pay the debt in the plaintiffs declaration nor by the administrators since his death. They assess the plaintiffs damages to $123.70.

McGhees & McCarty VS Jacob Slover. Came the parties by their attornies and the defendants demurrer to the plaintiffs declaration being argued &c; seems to the court that the plaintiffs declaration is good and sufficient in law. The defendants demurrer is overruled. Plaintiff is entitled to recover against the defendant and the damages being uncertain, Sheriff is ordered to summon a jury at the next term to enquire of the plaintiffs damage.

Matthew Hubbart, James A. Darwin, and Henry Collins appointed Commissioners to settle with William Howard and Allison Howard, Admrs. of Abraham Howard.

(p. 393) John Locke and James Berry, Exrs. of last Will and Testament of Richard Haslerig, dec'd, exhibited a bond from the Legatees of said Richard Haslerig to refund, which bond is as follows: "We Condley F. Haslerig & Thomas J. Haslerig heirs and Devisees of the estate of Richard Haslerig late of said County Decd

118

this day have respectively Recd of James Berry & John Locke, Executors . . . the bequests and devises made to us and to our use by said Will so far as the same at this time can be administered and it is our Special request from feelings of respect to our aged and tender mother that the executors aforesaid shall refrain from the sale by public action of the household & kitchen furniture & her claim of cattle &c. For and in consideration of all the which we the said Condley & Thomas heirs as aforesaid acknowledge ourselves jointly and severally indebted to William Smith esquire Chairman & presiding Justice of the Court of pleas and quarter sessions in and for Rhea County in the Just and full sum of five thousand dollars the which payment well and truly to be made and done we bind ourselves our heirs &c. Jointly & firmly by these presents Sealed with our Seals and dated as follows.

"The condition of the above obligation is such that whereas the above bound Condley F. Haslerig & Thomas J. Haslerig having recd their respective devised dividents of the estate of Richard Haslerig decd from the hands of the executors thereof and further requested any further sale of the chattles of the said Estate to be discontinued— Now if the said Condley F. & Thomas J. in the event that any debt or debts truly owing by the deceased and shall at any time be sued for and recovered or otherwise duly made appear to stand against said estate, that then and in every such case they shall respectively refund and pay each his rateable share of said debt due or demand then and in that case the foregoing obligation to be void otherwise to be and remain in full force and effect—

"In witness whereof we have hereunto set our hands and Seals this 27th day of July 1827."   (Signed) C.F. Haslerig   Thos J. Haslerig
Test: Tho. McCallie & Robt N. Gillespie

John Locke and James Berry, Exrs. returned an Inventory and an account of the sale of said Haslerigs estate.

(p. 394)   John Hines VS Nathaniel W. Wilson. Came the parties and with the assent of the Court they submit all matters in dispute between them in this suit to the final determination of William Matlock and James Price and if they cannot agree they are to choose an umpire whose award is to be the Judgment of this Court.

Elizabeth Forbes VS John Lea. Cames the parties by their attornies; from affedavit of the defendant, a rule is granted him to cause the plaintiff to give security for the prosecution of this suit on or before the second day of the next session of this Court and before the trial of the cause.

Anthony Street VS David & Isaac Blevins. Came the parties by their attornies and agree and with the assent of the Court time is given the parties until the next term of this Court to plead and try so as not to delay.

(p. 395)   Justices on bench (9th August)— James Wilson, John McClure, Stephen Winton, and Beal Gaither.

State VS Isaac Jones (No. 1610). Peace Warrant. For reasons appearing to the satisfaction of the Court the defendant is discharged.

On application of Isaac Jones, ordered that the Sheriff take into his possession Elizabeth C. Jones, Rowland J. Jones, Martha M. Jones, and William G. Jones infant children of the said Isaac Jones and keep them until the next session of this Court at which time by request of the said Isaac Jones the said children above named are to be bound out by the Court.

Alexander Rice VS Thomas McCallie. Appeal. Came the parties by their attornies and a jury (William Hill, Pleasant Love, Woodson Francis, James Montgomery, John Barnett, George Henry Sr., Thomas Dickson, Jeremiah Washam, John A. Smith, Giles S. Bogges, Daniel D. Stockton, and William Poteat) to try the matter of controversy in this cause, say they cannot agree; mistrial is entered; cause is continued until next session of this Court.

Levi Griffett VS Thomas McNutt (No. 1611). Motion as Security. Came the plaintiff by attorney, George W. Churchwell, and a jury (Alexander Rice, Rezin Rawlings, John Haines, Thomas McCallie, John Locke, Isaac Braselton Jr., John Starrett,

(p. 396) Delmore Chapman, Abijah Bogges, Archabald McCallie, James Stewart, and Jacob Brown) which says that the plaintiff was security for the said McNutt and as such paid $8.65. Plaintiff to recover said sum and costs.

John McClenahan VS Thomas McCallie. Appeal. Came the parties by attornies and a jury (Abijah Bogges, Isaac Braselton Jr., Francis Reevely, William Lewis, John Starrett, William Gullion, Isaac Binyon, Samuel Johnson, William Johnson, William Howard, Robert Bell, and Willie Lewis) which says they cannot agree; mistrial is entered and cause is continued until next session.

John McClenahan & Alexander Rice VS Thomas McCallie. In these two cases it is agreed by the parties that George W. Churchwell of Knoxville, shall take the deposition of George Wells to be read in evidence.

NOVEMBER TERM 1827

(p. 397) Court of Pleas and Quarter Sessions met at the Courthouse in Washington on the first Monday and fifth day of November 1827. Justices on bench— James Wilson, Matthew Hubbart, William Smith, Peach Taylor, Jesse Thompson, Crispien E. Shelton, John McClure, James A. Darwin, Josiah Fike, Carson Caldwell, Daniel Walker, Arthur Fulton, John Cozby, Isaac Roddy, Azariah David, Robert Cooley, Daniel M. Stockton, Joseph McCorkle, and James McDonald.

James Bolen appointed overseer of road in place of William Lauderdale.

Matthew Hubbart, Henry Collins, and James A. Darwin, Commissioners appointed to settle with William & Allison Howard, Admrs. on estate of Abraham Howard, returned their settlement.

William Baker appointed overseer of road in place of William James (or Janus).

Robert Parks appointed overseer of Valley Road from James A. Darwins to the ford of the creek below James Coulters in place of Robert Love.

Anson Dearmon appointed a Constable in Captain William Hill's Company; bond with John McClure, James A. Darwin, and Jesse Poe, his securities.

(p. 398) Flemming H. Fulton appointed a Constable in Captain Thomas B. Swan's Company; bond with Daniel Walker and Arthur Fulton, his securities.

Anderson Smith appointed a Constable in Captain Samuel Rowden's Company; bond with Woodson Francis and Richard Waterhouse, his securities.

Isaac Baker appointed a Constable in Captain Isaac Baker's Company; bond with George W. Riggle and Woodson Francis, his securities.

John Parker permitted to keep an ordinary for one year; bond with James Montgomery and James Lillard, his securities.

David Shelton permitted to keep an ordinary for one year; bond with David Ragsdale, his security.

Abijah Boggess permitted to keep an ordinary for one year; bond with Daniel M. Stockton, his security.

(p. 399) Samuel Gamble, John Masoner, Edward Templeton, Samuel Fitzgerald, Isaac Mahan, Allen Gentry, and Robert Gamble appointed a Jury of View to lay off a road from Bunkers Hill on Hiwassee to communicate with a road from Hamilton Courthouse through the Cherokee Nation, thence the most direct way to the McMinn County line leading to Athens in said County.

A Commission issued and signed by Samuel Houston, Governor of Tennessee wherein James Piper Lowrey is appointed Attorney General for the 11th Solicitor-

ial District of said State was produced in Court, and took the oath to support the
constitution of the United States and the State of Tennessee, an oath to suppress
duelling and the oath of office of Attorney General.

Robert C. Crozier produced his Licence as a practicing attorney at law.

Robert Locke appointed a Commissioner in place of Wyllys H. Chapman to
settle with the Clerks of the Circuit and County Court of Rhea County.

William Lauderdale to Franklin Jones. Deed of Conveyance for 114 acres
dated 13th October 1822; proven by William Smith and William Rogers, subscribing
witnesses; certified for registration.

Thomas Shaffer appointed overseer of road in place of John Igo.

(p. 400) William Bryant appointed overseer of the Muddy Creek Road from the ford
of Piney River to the divide of the waters of Wolf and Yellow Creeks in place of
William Lisenby.

Benjamin C. Stout and Thomas J. Haslerig appointed administrators on
estate of Conly F. Haslerig, dec'd; bond with Miller Francis and Jesse Poe for
$6000.

James Swan appointed administrator on estate of William Randolph, dec'd;
bond with Richard Waterhouse, James C. Mitchell, Anderson Smith, and Thomas B. Swan
for $600.

Margaret Barnett appointed administratrix on estate of William Barnett;
bond with James Montgomery and John Barnett for $500.

(p. 401) Daniel Walker and John Locke appointed Commissioners to lay off a years
support for widow and children of William Barnett, dec'd.

Nathaniel Gillem appointed administrator on estate of John Davis, dec'd;
bond with Jesse Thompson and Arthur Fulton for $600.

James Dale, Charles Mitchell, Samuel Applegate, Thornton Creed, and
James Moore appointed a Jury of View to lay off the road on the land of Jesse
Thompson so as to let the old road continue in the Washington Road about half a
mile and then to intersect the old road as said Jury of View may think best.

Preston Knight appointed overseer of road from Jacob Becks to William
Lisenbys in place of Samuel Ferguson.

William B. Gordon appointed overseer of road from Edward Stewarts to
George Gordons Bridge in place of Robert Cooper.

Siles F. Barnes appointed overseer of road from Town of Washington to
Henry Collins house in place of William Cumpton.

(p. 402) James Lillard released from payment of Tax for 1827 on a quarter section
of land, it having been returned through a mistake.

John Parker allowed $27.00 for his account: keeping Isaac Jones in Jail
30 days & 4 Turnkeys; keeping Abner Triplett in Jail 5 days & 2 Turnkeys; keeping
Randolph Harwood in Jail 1 day & 1 Turnkey; keeping Thomas McNutt in Jail 1 day
& 2 Turnkeys; keeping James Cahell in Jail 19 days & 2 Turnkeys.

John S. Richmond appointed overseer of road in place of John Foshee.

Jesse Roddy, Samuel Applegate, Joshua Kelly, James Baily, James Roddy,
Cumberland Rector, Robert Walker, and William Johnson appointed a Jury of View to
lay off a road from or near Robert Walkers to Snelsons Ferry on Tennessee River
with as little injury as possible to improvements.

Alva Quiett, Admr. on estate of William Quiett, returned an account of
the sales of said estate.

Robert McClure, overseer of road from Kellys Ferry to where said road
intersects the Washington Road leading from Washington to Mrs. Lauderdales have
in addition to his former hands, all the hands on the plantation of John McCond-
leys to work under him.

(p. 403)   James Berry, Clerk of this Court, allowed $25.00 for exofficio services; $25.00 for making out the Tax lists for 1827; $6.00 for recording the land on the South side of Tennessee River as per Surveyor Generals return and making out the tax list for the same.

Thomas J. Campbell, Attorney General, allowed $20.00 for exofficio services for 1827.

John Lea, Sheriff, allowed $25.00 for exofficio services for 1827.

Samuel R. Hackett appointed overseer of road from the Town Spring to Grassy Branch on the road leading from Washington to Mrs. Lauderdales; to have the following hands to work under him: James P. Miller, Oliver Miller, Reuben Freeman, Jefferson B. Love, Kennedy Cooper, John McDonnough, John Stokes, Michael Stoner, and David H. Britton.

Asa Jackson appointed overseer of road from David Sheltons in Morganton to the four mile post on Blythes Ferry Road in place of John Benson.

(p. 404)   Jurors appointed for next Term of this Court:

William McDonald	Washington Morgan	William James	Rolly Clack
Wright Smith	Elisha Parker	John Day	David Caldwell
James Preston	Jesse Roddy	John Lewis	Lewis R. Collins
Joseph Lusk	Stephen Moore	Isaac Mason	Thomas Little
John Knight	William Rice	David Campbell	Vaden H. Giles
James Stockton	John Carrall	James Moore	Augustus Foshee
White Caldwell, a Constable to attend Court			William Hill

Jurors appointed for next term of Circuit Court:

Azariah David	Crispien E. Shelton	James McDonald	William Smith
Carson Caldwell	John Cozby	John McClure	Daniel Walker
Jonathan Fine	George Gillespie	Jesse Thompson	Arthur Fulton
Matthew Hubbart	James A. Darwin	Samuel Gamble	Ezekiel Bates
Thomas Cox	Joseph McCorkle	Peach Taylor	Robert Cooley
Daniel M. Stockton	James Wilson	William C. Wilson	Stephen Winton
Anson Dearmon, Constable to attend Court			Josiah Fike

The following Justices were appointed to take the list of Taxable property and polls for 1828:

James McDonald	in Captain Howard's Company
Daniel Walker	in Captain Rowdens Company
Carson Caldwell	in Captain Hill's Company
Beal Gaither	in Captain Baker's Company
Matthew Hubbart	in Captain Mitchell's Company
Robert Cooley	in Captain White's Company
Arthur Fulton	in Captain Swan's Company
Joseph McCorkle	in Captain Blevins' Company
Isaac Roddy	in Captain Rourak's Company
Peach Taylor	in Captain Farmer's Company
Daniel M. Stockton (p. 405)	in Caprain Stockton's Company
Hoyl Butram	in Captain Keeton's Company
Stephen Winton	in Captain Sharp's Company

Henry Roper (son of David Roper) is released from the payment of a poll tax for the present year.

Orville Paine, Deputy Sheriff, allowed $21.00 for taking into his possession and keeping Isaac Jones' three children for 12 weeks by order of the Court at August Session.

Ally Runnels undertakes to keep Mary Owens, a pauper, for one year from this day for $34.81¼.

Daniel Carmichael & James Carmichael, Admrs. of David B. Ayres, dec'd, assignee of Richard Taylor VS John Roddy & John Lea (No. 1612). Covenant. Came the plaintiffs by their attorney, James F. Bradford, and also John Roddy, who says he cannot gainsay the plaintiffs demand against him for $560.00.

Ordered that next Tuesday of this present term be set apart for the further transaction of County business.

(p. 406) William Renfro VS Isaac Blevins, William Blevins, & David Blevins (No. 1613). Came the plaintiff by his attorney, William L. Welker, and being unwilling further to prosecute this suit dismisses the same; defendants confess judgment for all the costs.

Anthony Street VS Isaac Blevins & David Blevins (No. 1614). Covenant. Came the plaintiff by his attorney, William C. Dunlap, and the defendants who say they cannot gainsay the plaintiffs demand against them for $47.37½. Caswell Hughes and Allen Blevins, securities for the appearance of Isaac Blevins, brings him into Court and surrenders him in discharge of themselves.

(p. 407) Justices on bench (6th November) — William Smith, Crispien E. Shelton, Daniel Walker, James A. Darwin, Arthur Fulton, John Cozby, Carson Caldwell, Jesse Thompson, and Daniel M. Stockton.

James Montgomery, William Locke, and Adam W. Caldwell appointed Commissioners to settle with Thomas M. Kennon, Admr. on estate of William Kilgore.

John Holland VS Elijah Tabor (No. 1615). Motion on Security. Came the plaintiff by his attorney, James P. Lowery, and a jury (Robert Gamble, James Montgomery, John Lillard, John McDunnah, William Hill, Brinkley Strickland, John Davis, William Noblett, John Buckhannon, Carson Caldwell, William Locke, and Cain Able) which says that John Holland was security for Elijah Tabor and paid as such $6.87½. Plaintiff to recover said sum and his costs.

Elisha Parker appointed administrator on estate of James Reece, dec'd; bond with John Cozby and William Smith, his securities, for $600.

David Shelton summoned to attend the Court as Constable, the Constable heretofore summoned failing to attend.

(p. 408) John McGhee, Matthew W. McGhee, & John L. McCarty VS Jacob Slover (No. 1616). Covenant. Came the parties by their attornies and a jury (John Davis, Robert Gamble, William Hill, John Lillard, Wright Smith, Woodson Francis, James Montgomery, Daniel D. Stockton, Cain Able, John Barnett, Brinkley Strickland, and Jeremiah Washam) which says the defendant has not well and truly kept and performed his covenant as the plaintiffs have complained against him and has broken the same; they assess the plaintiffs damage to $136.42.

Michael W. Buster VS James Kelly (No. 1617). Came the parties by attornies; from affidavit of defendant, this cause is continued until the next Term of this Court upon the defendants paying the cost of this Term.

John Haines VS Nathaniel Wilson. Came the parties by their attornies; by consent and assent of the Court, the rule of refference heretofore granted in this cause is set aside and the cause continued until next Term of this Court.

Alexander Rice VS Thomas McCallie. Cause is continued until next Term.

(p. 409) John Lea, Sheriff, by his deputy Orville Paine, returned into Court a list of "good and lawful men citizens of said County designated and appointed by the Justices . . . at the last Sessions of Said Court as Jurors to serve at this Term of said Court and that he had duly summoned and made known the Same to the following good and lawful men . . .: John Davis, Robert Gamble, John McClenahan, Edward Templeton, William England, Volentine Houpt, William Hill, George Barnett, William M. Rogers, Wright Smith, John Lillard, and James Montgomery, out of whom the following appeared in open Court: John Davis, Robert Gamble, William Hill,

John Lillard, Wright Smith, and James Montgomery. There not being a sufficient number of the original panel to make a Grand Jury, there was no Grand Jury empannelled for this Term"

John Ferrell & wife Priscilla to Matthew Stallons(?). Deed of Conveyance dated 9th August 1826 for 116 acres in Nash County, North Carolina; acknowledged by John and Priscilla (she having been examined separately); certified to North Carolina for registration.

Carson Caldwell appointed Trustee of Rhea County for two years; bond with James Stewart, John Holland, Thomas M. Kennon, David Ragsdale, Thomas Cox, and David Shelton for $5000.

Ordered that the order made at the last Term of this Court to proceed against William Johnson late Trustee of Rhea County as a delinquent be rescinded.

(p. 410) William Rogers VS William & Allison Howard, Admrs. &c. Petition for Certiorari and Superceedas. Came the plaintiffs by their attorney and on their petition a Certiorari and Supercedeas is awarded them to bring this cause into Court from before the Justice on their entering into bond and security.

Ordered that all cases not tried or otherwise disposed of at this present Term stand continued until the next Term of this Court.

FEBRUARY TERM 1828

(p. 411) Court of Pleas and Quarter Sessions met at the Courthouse in Washington on the first Monday and fourth day of February in 1828. Justices on bench— William Smith, George Gillespie, James McDonald, Josiah Fike, John Cozby, Crispien E. Shelton, James A. Darwin, Thomas Cox, Peach Taylor, Stephen Winton, Carson Caldwell, Isaac Roddy, Beal Gaither, Arthur Fulton, Samuel Gamble, James Wilson, Matthew Hubbart, Jonathan Fine, Daniel Walker, and Daniel M. Stockton.

Ezekiel Bates resigned as Justice of the Peace.

On application of James P. Lowry, Solicitor, James Berry, Clerk of this Court, produced a receipt from the Treasurer of East Tennessee (Miller Francis) for $150.40; also a receipt from the Trustee of Rhea County for $3.23.

Richard Waterhouse & Blackstone Waterhouse to Micajah Howerton. Deed of Conveyance for 15 acres; acknowledged by bargainers; certified for registration.

(p. 412) Richard & Blackstone Waterhouse to Benjamin F. Jones. Deed of Conveyance for 70½ acres; acknowledged by bargainers; certified for registration.

Richard & Blackstone Waterhouse to James Rogers. Deed of Conveyance for 240 acres; acknowledged by bargainers; certified for registration.

John Love to Rezin Rawlings. Deed of Conveyance for Lot No. 43 in the Southern Liberties of Town of Washington; proven by James Berry and Robert N. Gillespie; certified for registration.

Thomas Johns to John Bowles. Deed of Conveyance dated 5th September 1827 for 160 acres was proven in part by Joseph McDaniel; certified for further probate.

David Mahan to Townley Rigg. Deed of Conveyance for 1 acre; proven by Samuel Gamble and William B. Russell; certified for registration.

(p. 413) Hugh T. Blevins to Allen Blevins. Deed of Conveyance for 160 acres; acknowledged by bargainor; certified for registration.

Alexander Ish to John Parker. Deed of Conveyance dated 28th October 1827 for Lot No. 21 in Town of Washington; proven by Anson Dearmon and Jacob Brown; certified for registration.

John Locke & Rezin Rawlings, Exrs. of Daniel Rawlings, dec'd to John Whaley. Deed of Conveyance for 160 acres; acknowledged by Executors; certified for registration.

Grief Howerton to Edmund Howerton. Bill of Sale dated 1st October 1827 for Sundry property; proven by Henry Collins and Samuel Craig; certified for registration.

Thomas N. Clark to William Lawson. Deed of Conveyance dated 5th October 1811 for 200 acres; proven by William Smith and Rezin Rawlings, they proving the death and hand writing of William French and Daniel Rawlings, the subscribing witnesses to said deed. And the handwriting of Thomas N. Clark the bargoner therein named being proven by the oaths of Henry S. Purress and James McCampbell. Deed is ordered to be certified for registration.

(p. 414) Daniel Rawlings to John Merriott. Bill of Sale dated 19th January 1815 for a Negro Girl named Henrietta; proven by James Stewart, he proving the death and handwriting of Daniel Rawlings the bargoner, and also the death and hand writing of Andrew Wilhelm, the subscribing witness thereto; certified for registration.

John Buckhannon appointed overseer of road from Morganton by Azariah Davids to where it intersects the Lauderdale Road in place of James Airhart.

Hiel Butram and James Swan, having been appointed Justices of the Peace by the State Legislature, produced their Commissions and took oath of office.

Peggy Barnett, Admrx. on estate of William Barnett, dec'd, returned an account of sales of said estate.

Daniel Walker and John Locke, Commissioners to lay off a years support out of the crop &c on hand to the widow and relect of William Barnett, dec'd, returned their report.

Elisha Parker, Admr. on estate of James Reece, dec'd, returned an account of the sale of said estate.

(p. 415) John Locke allowed $29.75 for eight record books as Clerk of the Circuit Court.

James Berry allowed $62.71 3/4 for 23 record books as Clerk of this Court.

Bremillion Holloway allowed $49.00 for keeping Hannah McKeel, a pauper, for 12 months.

(p. 416) Ordered that William Johnson, late Trustee and Tax Collector, deliver to the Clerk of this Court all the official papers, Books, lists &c that he has in possession relative to his former office as Trustee and Tax Collector, including the abstract and settlement made by William Smith, George Gillespie, and Jesse Thompson signed by Smith on which after a deduction of $123.23½ in which he retains the interest, there remains a ballance in his favor of $371.67 3/4 to which he relinquishes all Interest title and claim and which the Court accepts and acknowledges to be payment in full for all dues and demands against him as former Trustee and Tax Collector. And the said William Johnson thereupon delivered the aforesaid papers, tax lists and books to the Clerk of this Court.

William Gibson appointed overseer of road from Town of Washington to the ford of Clear Creek in place of Samuel Montgomery.

Michael Kelly appointed overseer of road from Kellys Ferry to the Town of Washington in place of Allen Holland.

Frederick Fulkerson appointed overseer of road in place of James Paul.

Archabald D. Paul appointed overseer of road from ford of Piney River to said Pauls house in place of Farley Brady.

(p. 417) Thomas Griffen appointed overseer of road leading from Gillespies Ferry to the McMinn County line from Ten Mile Creek to County line in place of Turner Casey.

Micajah Clack appointed overseer in place of David B. Staples.

James Kelly appointed overseer of road in place of Merideth Cox.

Henry H. Beck appointed overseer in place of Abijah Bogges.

The order made at the August Sessions appointing Pulaski Poe overseer of the road be revived.

On application of Mary Clack, Robert Kerr is appointed her guardian; bond for $100 with Thomas Price, his security.

Margaret Lewis is appointed guardian to her infant children: Thomas Lewis, Elizabeth Lewis, and William H. Lewis; bond with James Taylor and Thomas Little for $500.

(p. 418) Benjamin C. Stout and Thomas J. Haslerig, Admrs. on estate of Conley F. Haslerig, returned an account of the sale of said estate.

Ordered that George W. Riggle be appointed public ferryman on the north bank of the Walton Ferry Road.

John Enmans appointed overseer of road in place of Larken Butram.

James Swan, Admr. on estate of William Randolph, dec'd, returned an inventory of said estate.

Joel Stanly, William Stanly, and George Lea to work on road under Vaden H. Giles, overseer.

Andrew Kincannon resigned as a Constable.

Micajah Howerton resigned as a Constable.

Commissioners (James Montgomery, Adam W. Caldwell, and William Locke) appointed to settle with Thomas M. Kennon, Admr. on estate of William Kilgore, dec'd, returned their settlement.

(p. 419) Thomas Cox, Thomas Kelly, and William S. Russell appointed Commissioners to settle with Armsted Bredwell, Admr. on estate of Elias Bredwell, dec'd.

Ordered that the Tax for this year be as follows: on each 100 acres of land, 18 3/4¢; on each white poll, 18 3/4¢; on each town lot, 18 3/4¢; on each Black poll, 31½¢. And the Jury, Poor, and Jail Tax be the same they were last year.

Jurors appointed for next term of this Court:

Charles McDonald	Tignal Wade	Washington Morgan	Alexander Coulter
John Wasson	Micajah Howerton	John Miller	Jeremiah Chapman
Leonard Brooks	Nicholas Fraley	John B. Page	James Keeton
John B. Hudson	James Roark	Charles McDaniel	Samuel P. Stewart
Jonathan Owens	George W. Riggle	John C. Ferguson	Abraham Hughes
John Parker	Absolom Colman	Nathaniel Britain	Edmund Bean
Anson Dearmon, Constable to attend Court			William Hill (Capt.)

Robert Locke, Samuel Looney, and Daniel Walker appointed Commissioners to settle with Jesse Poe, Admr. on estate of William Lewis, dec'd.

(p. 420) William Carter appointed overseer of Valley Road from Cain Ables to the creek at Mrs. Lauderdales; he is to apply to William Smith for a list of hands.

John Silkirk appointed overseer from David Sheltons in Morganton to the four mile post on Blythes Ferry Road; William Smith to furnish list of hands.

Ordered that the road leading from Snelsons Ferry on Tennessee River to intersect the Federal Road at or near Thomas C. Roes be established; George Preston appointed overseer of said road.

Ordered that the road from Bunkers Hill to the McMinn County line be established as reported by Jury of View, and all the hands in the bounds of said road are to keep open said road.

Robert Gamble appointed overseer of road from Bunkers Hill on Hiwassee River to where the path forks beyond James Cowens; to have following hands to work under him: James Cowen and all his hands, and all the hands west of the ridge from said Cowans.

Edward Templeton appointed overseer of road from the fork of the path near James Cowens to the top of the ridge beyond his house; to have the following hands: all the hands from his house to the ridge and all the hands from the old Agency up the river except the McClenahans and William Miller.

(p. 421) Samuel Fitzgerral appointed overseer of road from top of the ridge near Edward Templetons to the McMinn County line; to have following hands: all hands from his house to the County line and (blank) Ramsey and (blank) Massey.

Thornton J. Creed to Mumford Smith. Power of Attorney acknowledged by Creed; certified.

Joseph Love and Robert Locke appointed Revenue Commissioners to settle with the Clerks of Circuit and County Courts and the Trustee of Rhea County.

Abraham Cox was appointed a Constable in Captain Fitzgerrals Company; bond with Samuel R. Hackett and Daniel M. Stockton, his securities.

William S. Russell appointed a Constable in Captain Farmer's Company; bond with David Leuty and Thomas Cox, his securities.

Samuel Craig appointed Constable in Captain Mitchell's Company; bond with Henry Collins, Jackson Howerton, and James A. Darwin, his securities.

(p. 422) Jonathan Fry appointed a Constable in Captain Roark's Company; bond with Samuel Gamble and James Roark, his securities.

Ordered that the roads on the lands of Jesse Thompson be established as reported by the Jury of View: to leave the Washington Road near a half a mile from the old fork of the road, then along as marked by the Jury through the woods to intersect the old Valley Road near the corner of Arthur Fulton's fence.

In pursuance of an act of the General Assembly, the Court proceeded to appoint five Justices to be of the Quorum to hold the County Court for and during 1323,"and upon drawing lots for a choise thereof the worshipful James Wilson, James McDonald, Josiah Fike, Robert Cooley, and Crispein E. Shelton were chosen for the purpose aforesaid."

Richard G. Waterhouse to John Knight. Title Bond Plat and Certificate dated 20th August 1818 for 115 acres was proven by oath of Richard Waterhouse, he proving the death and hand writing of Richard G. Waterhouse; certified.

Ordered that part of Tuesday at this present term be set apart for the further transaction of County business.

(p. 423) Justices on bench— James Wilson, James McDonald, Josiah Fike, Robert Cooley, Crispien E. Shelton, George Gillespie, Isaac Roddy, Daniel Walker, and James A. Darwin.

John Whaley to Rezin Rawlings. Deed of Conveyance for 266½ acres; acknowledged by the bargainor; certified for registration.

Nathaniel Smith to James Rogers. Deed of Conveyance for 80 acres; proven by Return J. Meigs (proven at May Sessions 1827 by Isaac Baker) the other subscribing witness; certified for registration.

Elisha Blythe appointed overseer of road from the four mile post on Blythes Ferry Road to the Blythes Ferry in place of Samuel Garwood.

Henry Henry appointed overseer of road from Town of Washington to Henry Collins in place of Silas F. Barns.

Edmund Howerton appointed guardian to William Johnson and Lusinda Johnson, infant children of James Johnson, dec'd; bond with Henry Collins and James A. Darwin, his securities for $1000.

(p. 424) John Lea, Sheriff, returned a list of Jurors summoned to appear at this session of Court (see list on page 121), out of which a Grand Jury was elected: John Day, Rolly Clack, Wright Smith, William McDonald, Washington Morgan, Elisha

Parker, David Caldwell, John Lewis, Lewis R. Collins, Thomas Little, James Stockton, John Carroll, and William Hill. Rolly Clack appointed foreman and Anson Dearmon a Constable to attend the Grand Jury.

There remained of the original pannel who did not answer to their names: James Preston, Jesse Roddy, Joseph Lusk, James Moore, William Rice, John A. Foshee, Stephen Moore, Isaac Mason, and John Knight.

(p. 425)   Roberts & McCallie allowed $6.50 for a record book furnished the Clerk of this Court.

Thomas N. Clark to Asahel Johnson. Deed of Conveyance for 235 acres; proven by Henry S. Purris, one of the subscribing witnesses; certified for further probate.

Ordered that Hannah McKeel, a pauper, be set up to the lowest bidder, whereupon Anderson Smith undertook to keep her 12 months for $54.87¼.

Ordered that the road leading to Braselton's Ferry be discontinued as a public road from the forks of the road leading to Price's Ferry to said Braselton's Ferry.

Michael W. Buster VS James Kelly. Came the parties by their attornies and a jury (John Ferrell, Robert McCracan, Allison Howard, George Maner, William Gibson, Ruben Freeman, Franklin B. Locke, James Stewart, William Locke, Elijah W. Collins, Jeremiah Washam, and Willie Lewis) which was respited until tomorrow.

(p. 426)   John Lea, Sheriff and Collector of the public taxes, by his deputy Orville Paine, reported the following tracts of land and town lots as having been omitted to be returned for the public taxes for the year 1827; the same is liable to double tax and the double tax thereon remain due and unpaid; the respective owners or claimants thereof have no goods or chattles within this County on which he can distrain for said double taxes:

1618   1 tract belonging to Joseph Bishop on Waldens Ridge on waters of Richland Creek on Keadys Trace about a half mile from the fork of said road known by Entry No. 2 — 50

1619   1 tract in name of Richard G. Waterhouse heirs lying on the Mountain in the big fork of Whites Creek below David Knox's including Glazes Hickory flatt known by entry No. 7 — 165

1620   1 tract in name of R.G. Waterhouse heirs lying on waters of South fork of Whites Creek on both sides of trace leading from the Tennessee Valley to Willie Redwines known as Entry No. 8 — 50

1621   1 tract in name of R.G. Waterhouse heirs included in a square lying on the Mountain on the South fork of Whites Creek between the South and Middle Fork of said Creek below Willie Redwines known by Entry No. 9 — 50

1622   1 tract in name of R.G. Waterhouse heirs in an oblong square on the Mountain on waters of Middle Fork of Whites Creek between David Knox's Spring Branch and the Middle Fork of Whites Creek; known by Entry No. 10 — 52

(p. 427)
1623   1 tract in name of R.G. Waterhouse heirs on Mountain in Devils Fork of Piney River, on fork of path leading to Swaggerty's Cove and the Grassy Cove; known by Entry No. 11 — 53

1624   1 tract in name of R.G. Waterhouse heirs on Mountain on both sides of Girtmans Trace on waters of Piney River and Clear Creek, including a Cave Spring nearly opposite Oliver Pikes; Entry No. 12 — 62½

1625   1 tract in name of R.G. Waterhouse heirs on North Fork of Clear Creek on the Mountain on both sides of Girtmans Creek; Entry No. 14 — 65

1526   1 tract in name of Joel Lowry on Waldens Ridge on waters of

128

	Richland Creek; Entry No. 15	50
1627	1 tract in name of R.G. Waterhouse heirs on big fork of Whites Creek adjoining his former entry No. 70; known by Entry No. 16	54
1628	1 tract in name of Richard Waterhouse on the Mountain on both sides of Sandy Creek, a tributary of Whites Creek; Entry No. 17	84
1629	1 tract in name of R.G. Waterhouse heirs on Mountain on both sides of Devils Fork of Piney River adjoining his other entry No. 11; known by Entry No. 18	53

(p. 428)

1630	1 tract in name of Blackstone Waterhouse on Mountain and dividing the waters of Richland and Piney, including Bowins improvement; known by Entry No. 20	55
1631	1 tract in name of Myra Waterhouse on the Mountain including the Chinquepin Plain on the South side of the waggon road leading from Jacob Becks in Rhea County to Hugh Beattys in Bledsoe County; known by Entry No. 23	142½
1632	1 tract in name of Cyrus Waterhouse on or near the Rhea County line, on both sides of Sandy Creek, a tributary of Whites Creek on the Mountain and on both sides of Gordons Turnpike Road and part of an improvement made by William McClendan; Entry No. 24	80
1633	1 tract in name of Richard Richards on waters of Piney or Whites Creek; known by Entry No. 25	50
1634	1 tract in name of Darius Waterhouse on Mountain and East side main Richland Creek; known by Entry No. 26	640
1635	1 tract in name of Euclid Waterhouse on Mountain and East side of Richland Creek; known as Entry No. 27	520

(p. 429)

1636	1 tract in name of Blackstone Waterhouse on Mountain on dividing waters of Richland and Piney adjoining with his 55-acre tract (No. 10601) and Euclid Waterhouses 520-acre tract (No. 27); known by Entry No. 28	580
1637	1 tract in name of Joel Lowry on side of Waldens Ridge; Entry No. 29	200
1638	1 tract in name of John Garrison on the Mountain on both sides of Bumblebee Fork of Piney Creek; known by Entry No. 32	125
1639	1 tract in name of Joseph Garrison on Mountain and both sides of Bumblebee Fork of Piney; known by Entry No. 33	640
1640	1 tract in name of George Ransom on Waldens Ridge on both sides of Beattys Turnpike Road on waters of Piney River; Entry No. 35	400
1641	1 tract in name of Jonathan Denton on Waldens Ridge on waters of Piney River known by Entry No. 38	100
1642	1 tract in name of Henry Smith on Waldens Ridge on waters of Piney River on Moccasin Creek; known by Entry No. 39	50

(p. 430)

1643	1 tract in name of Henry Smith on Waldens Ridge on waters of Piney River; known by Entry No. 40	50
1644	1 tract in name of Cyrus Waterhouse on Mountain and south side of Whites Creek; known by Entry No. 42	170
1645	1 tract in name of R.G. Waterhouse heirs on Mountain in big fork of Whites Creek including Glazes Hickory flatt and his two entries (No. 7 and No. 16); known by Entry No. 43	421
1646	1 tract in name of Elizabeth Roulston on Waldens Ridge on the waters of Richland Creek on east side of Joel Lowrys line; Entry No. 45	100
1647	1 tract in name of Thomas Nail and Aquilla Farmer on Waldens Ridge on the waters of Piney; known by Entry No. 48	300
1648	1 tract in name of John Jett, Jesse Lincoln, Joseph Thomas, John	

H. Derens (or Diver), and Thomas B. Eastland on Waldens Ridge
on a fork of Piney, supposed to be on Duskins Fork; Entry No. 49   640

(p. 431)

1649	1 tract in name of Robert Beard on Piney River	130
1050	1 tract in name of Walter Edwards	100
1051	1 tract in name of Peter Majors	165
1652	1 tract in name of Bruton Peters	43
1653	1 tract in name of Elijah Runnells	85
1654	1 tract in name of Edward Stewart on Camp Creek	266
1655	1 tract in name of Lewis Wilkerson	150
1656	1 tract in name of John McCandless(?)	64
1657	1 tract in name of Anthony Brown on the Mountain	100
1658	1 tract in name of Charles Gamble	50
1659	1 tract in name of Lewis Morgan	200
1660	1 tract in name of Nicholas Murry	100
1661	1 tract in name of Joshua Tindle	185
1662	1 Town Lot in name of Samuel Weir, No. 16	
1663	1 Town Lot in name of George Walker heirs; No. 58	

Judgment is entered against the above tracts and lots; to be sold (or as much as necessary) to pay the taxes.

(p. 432) John Lea, Sheriff and Collector of Taxes, by his deputy Nathaniel W. Wilson, reported the following tracts of land as having been returned for Taxation for 1827, and that the Tax on the same is yet remaining due and unpaid:

		Acres	Quarter	Section	Township	Range
1664	John Brown	160	N.E.	22	F 3	4 W
1665	John Brown	160	S.E.	22	3	4 W
1666	John Brown	62½	N.W.	26	3	4 W
1667	Bowyer Bullard	160	N.W.	11	3	4 W
1663	Joseph Bird	160	N.E.	4	3	2 W
1669	Mike Sellers	160	S.W.	20	2	1 W
1670	John Crow	160	N.E.	29	2	1 W
1671	Christian Carrell	160	N.E.	34	2	3 W
1672	Andrew Crawford	160	N.E.	29	1	1 W
1673	Austin D. Dunn	160	N.W.	23	3	4 W
1674	John Darter	160	N.W.	32	2	1 W
1675	Austin Dunn	160	N.W.	32	3	3 W
1676	Miller Francis	160	N.E.	17	3	3 W
1677	John Hurt	160	S.E.	26	1	2 W
1678	John Hudson	160	N.W.	5	3	3 W
1679	Barnett Hicklin	160	S.W.	11	3	4 W
1630	John Hughes	160	S.W.	28	2	3
1631	William Sarew(?)	160	N.E.	32	2	1
1632	Charles McClung	160	N.E.	9	3	3

(p. 433)

1633	John Dellorsler(?)	160	S.E.	11	2	3
1634	Charles Matlock	160	N.E.	7	3	1
1635	Charles Matlock	160	S.W.	2	2(?)	2
1636	Jordan Morris	160	S.E.	27	3	3
1637	Charles Matlock	160	S.E.	7	3	1
1638	Henry Newkirk	160	N.W.	12	1	2
1639	Geo Actherton & Wm Anderson	160	N.E.	2	3	3
1690	Geo Actherton & Wm Anderson	160	N.E.	20	1	2
1691	Geo Actherton & Wm Anderson	160	S.E.	20	1	2
1692	Geo Actherton & Wm Anderson	160	S.E.	17	1	2

1693	Elendor C. Robison	160	N.W.	19	4	3
1694	Jacob Slover	160	N.W.	15	3	—
1695	Nathaniel Smith	160	N.E.	6	4	—
1696	Nathaniel Smith	160	N.E.	7	3	—
1697	Nathaniel Smith	160	S.W.	29	1	—
1698	Nathaniel Smith	160	S.E.	31	3	—
1699	Joseph Thompson	160	S.W.	11	1	2
1700	Robert Ursery	160	N.E.	18	4	3
1701	Hu A.M. White	89	N.E.	22	2	4
1702	John Ware	160	S.E.	14	3	4
1703	James Wood	160	N.E.	34	1	2
1704	Jeremiah Wright	160	S.E.	36	1	3
1705	James Wilson	160	N.E.	22	1	2
1706	Sampson Bridwell	160	S.W.	35	2	3

(p. 434)

1707	David Roper	160	S.W.	20	3	3
1708	Jacob Sharp	155	S.E.	25	3	4
1709	Jacob Sharp	36	N.E.	36	3	4
1710	Josua Atchley	40	S.E.	19	1	2
1711	Josua Atchley	40	S.E.	19	1	2
1712	Washington Bridwell	80	N.E.	36	2	3
1713	Washington Bridwell	80	S.W.	36	2	3
1714	Nathaniel Britton	40	S.E.	32	3	3
1715	Levi Combs	80	N.W.	30	2	1
1716	John Davis	80	N.W.	6	2	2
1717	Jamima Daniel	80	N.E.	17	3	2
1718	Edward Davis	80	N.W.	31	2	1
1719	Richard Greenway	40	N.E.	27	1	2
1720	Elijah Hurst	160	N.W.	20	1	2
1721	Henry Hackworth	80	S.W.	23	3	3
1722	John Hackworth	80	S.W.	35	3	3
1723	Caaty Hughs	80	S.E.	28	3	3
1724	Caty Hughes	80	S.E.	28	3	3
1725	Jacob Helms	80	N.W.	27	1	2
1726	David Hannah	40	N.E.	36	2	3
1727	Jesse Helms	40	S.E.	22	1	2
1728	Nathaniel Harwood	40	N.W.	1	2	3
1729	Isham Lackey	80	S.E.	22	2	2

(p. 435)

1730	William Marshall	80	S.E.	22	2	3
1731	Samuel Mooney	80	N.W.	34	3	3
1732	John Majors	80	N.E.	21	2	2
1733	John Moody	160	N.W.	14	1	2
1734	John Majors	40	N.E.	21	2	2
1735	Henry Nelson	80	S.W.	28	2	2
1736	John Nelson	80	S.W.	28	2	2
1737	John Peters	160	N.E.	21	3	4
1738	Eli Perry	40	N.E.	15	3	3
1739	James Rucker	80	S.E.	12	3	3
1740	Asa Rowden	80	S.W.	15	1	2
1741	Asa Rowden	80	N.W.	22	1	2
1742	John Rousey(?)	40	N.E.	33	2	3
1743	Micah Sellers	40	S.W.	21	2	1
1744	Julius Webb	40	S.E.	7	3	4
1745	Gideon Webb	40	S.E.	16	3	4

| 1746 | William Webb | 40 | S.E. | 7 | 2 | 1 |
| 1747 | Gideon Webb | 40 | S.E. | 16 | 3 | 4 |

Judgment was entered against the tracts of land and they were ordered sold to pay the taxes.

(p. 436) John Ferrell & Priscilla Ferrell, his wife, to Matthew Stallions. Deed of Conveyance for 116 acres in North Carolina; Priscilla examined separately by John Locke and Orville Paine; deed certified to North Carolina.

John A. Foshee who belonged to the original pannel and did not answer to his name when called appeared in open Court and answered to his name.

(p. 437) John Lea, Sheriff, to William Smith, Chairman. In pursuance of an Act of the General Assemble passed at Nashville 7th December 1827, John Lea executed a bond for the collection and paying over of the County Taxes for 1828. George Gillespie, James Wilson, and William S. Leuty were securities; bond for $3000.

(p. 438) Justices on bench (6th February)— James Wilson, James McDonald, Josiah Fike, Robert Cooley, and Crispien E. Shelton.

David Leuty VS Elijah C. Rice (No. 1748). Motion as Security. Came the plaintiff by his attorney, Thomas J. Campbell, and a jury (Rolly Clack, Washington Morgan, William McDonald, Wright Smith, Elisha Parker, David Caldwell, John Lewis, Lewis R. Collins, Thomas Little, James Stockton, John Carroll, and William Hill) which says the plaintiff was security for the said Rice and as such paid $52.05. Plaintiff to recover said sum plus $4.50 damages and costs.

Michael W. Buster VS James Kelly (No. 1749). The jury that was respited until today returned and said the Defendant did assume and undertake in manner and form as the plaintiff declared in his complaint; they assess the plaintiffs damage to $87.00; also to recover costs. From which verdict and judgment the defendant prayed an appeal to the Circuit Court; granted.

(p. 439) Woodson Francis VS Joseph McDaniel & Thomas Cox (No. 1750). Came the plaintiff by attorney and the defendants not appearing made default; plaintif to recover $1000 debt and the costs in this behalf expended.

Thomas Cox VS Abednigo Hale (No. 1751). Certiorari. Came the parties by their attornies and a jury (John Day, William Hill, John Carroll, James Stockton, Thomas Little, Lewis R. Collins, John Lewis, Elisha Parker, Wright Smith, William McDonald, Washington Morgan, and Rolly Clack) which finds for the defendant, who is to recover his costs from the plaintiff.

Thomas Cox VS Abednigo Hale. Rule for New Trial. Came the plaintiff by his attornry and on his motion a rule is granted him to shew cause why a new trial should be had in the above cause.

William Johnson permitted to keep an ordinary for one year; bond with Woodson Francis, Robert Parks, and David Caldwell, his securities.

State VS David Clinghan. On motion of James P. Lowry, Attorney General, ordered that a Plurias Capias issue to Warren County in this cause.

(p. 440) Roberts & McCallie VS Orlando Bradley (No. 1752). Came the plaintiffs by their attorney and being unwilling further to prosecute their suit in this behalf dismisses the same. Thereupon came Frederick Fulkerson and confesses judgment for all costs.

The Court nor attorney General not having any further business for the Grand Jury, ordered that Rolly Clack, Washington Morgan, William McDonald, Wright Smith, Elisha Parker, David Caldwell, John Lewis, Lewis R. Collins, and Thomas Little be discharged from further attendance as jurors at this term.

(p. 441) Justices on bench (7th February)— James Wilson, James McDonald, Josiah Fike, Robert Cooley, and Crispien E. Shelton.

Ordered that the following tracts of land reported for the Taxes of 1827 by Nathaniel W. Wilson, Deputy Sheriff, be Stricken out of said report and returned to the Sheriff for Collection. It appearing to the satisfaction of the Court that the claimants thereof have goods and chattels in Rhea County sufficient to pay the Tax due on Said land:

	Acres	Quarter	Section	Township	Range
Isaac Bullard					
Isaac Bullard	160	S.E.	22	3	4 W
Volentine Houpt	160	N.E.	28	2	3
Volentine Houpt	160	N.E.	25	1	3
Thomas Johns	160	N.W.	24	2	4
James McDaniel	29	S.W.	25	1	5
John Ross	100	N.E.	27	3	4
John Ross	42	N.W.	27	3	4
Lewis Ross	640	Reservation			
Palatiah Shelton [Chilton]	49	N.W.	F 14	2	4
Edward Templeton	160	N.E.	14	3	4
Robert Bell	15	N.E.	24	1	5
Robert Bell	22½	N.W.	24	1	5
Robert Bell	123	S.W.	24	1	5
Robert Bell	116½	N.W.	25	1	5
Beriah Frazier	160	S.W.	33	2	4
Joseph McDaniel	160	S.E.	14	2	4
Joseph McDaniel	149½	N.W.	F 13	2	4
Joseph McDaniel	160	S.E.	23	2	4
Joseph McDaniel	160	N.E.	23	2	4
James Preston	129	S.W.	36	1	3
James Preston	159	N.W.	1	1	3
John Parker	160	S.E.	25	1	4
Gideon Ragland	160	S.W.	10	1	2
Jesse Reece Sr.	160	N.E.	26	1	3
Robert Bell	123	S.W.	24	1	5
Plummer Daniel	80	N.W.	9	3	2
Robert Elder	40	S.E.	32	3	3
William Keaton	80	N.W.	13	1	2
Abner Casey	40	N.E.	19	2	1
(p. 442) Abner Casey	40	N.W.	18	2	1 W
Jesse Matthews	40	N.E.	25	3	4
Willie Murphy	40	S.W.	17	2	2
Solomon Nidever	40	S.E.	21	3	3
Archibald D. Paul	160	N.W.	27	2	2
Archibald D. Paul	160	S.W.	27	2	2
Roger Reece	80	N.E.	24	1	3
Joseph C. Stockton	160	S.E.	29	2	3
Archibald Taylor	80	N.E.	5	3	3
Hugh Blevins	160	S.W.	32	1	3
Hugh Blevins	160	N.W.	7	3	3

Alexander Rice VS Thomas McCallie (No. 1753). Appeal. Came the parties by their attornies and a jury (James P. Miller, John McCarroll, Thomas Henry, Lewis R. Collins, Ralph B. Locke, John Carroll, James Stockton, Willie Lewis, Allison Howard, Henry Davis, John Day, and Jesse Poe) which finds for the plaintiff the sum of $3.50, and the costs expended in this behalf.

David Leuty VS Jesse Poe (No. 1754). Came the plaintiff in proper person and being unwilling further to prosecute his suit in this half, dismisses the same. On motion of the defendant, this suit is dismissed and the defendant to recover costs from plaintiff.

Thomas C. Wroe VS Mark Johnson. Petition. Came the plaintiff by his attorney and on his petition a Certoriari and supercedeas is awarded him to bring this cause into Court from before the Justice on his entering into bond and security as the law directs.

(p. 443) Woodson Francis, Sheriff by his deputy Henry Collins to John P. Long. Bill of Sale for two Negroes named Clary and Fanny; acknowledged by Collins; certified for registration.

John McClenahan VS Thomas McCallie (No. 1755). Appeal. Came the parties by their attornies and a jury (John A. Foshee, Edmond Howerton, Martin Ferguson, George Locke, Abijah Bogges, William Locke, James C. Mitchell, Reuben Freeman, John Walker, David Leuty, Thomas C. Wroe, and Robert Small) which finds for the plaintiff the sum of $4.66 2/3 and the costs.

On application of Richard Waterhouse, one of the executors of estate of Richard G. Waterhouse, dec'd; ordered that all the land reported by Orville Paine, deputy Sheriff, at the present term, reported in the name of the heirs of R.G. Waterhouse, Richard Waterhouse, Blackstone Waterhouse, Myra Waterhouse, Cyrus Waterhouse, Darius Waterhouse, and Euclid Waterhouse for double tax for 1827 be released from the payment of the double tax on said land. The said Richard Waterhouse having agreed to pay the cost and single tax due thereon; ordered that the Clerk enter the said land on the Tax Lists for 1828 for the single tax due for the year 1827.

Barton McPherson released from payment of tax due on 160 acres of land for 1826 and 1827.

(p. 444) John Ryan for use of Orville Paine VS Edmund Bean. Came the defendant by his attorney and craved copies of the Covenant in writing in the declaration mentioned, and likewise of the assignment in writing indorsed thereon; granted.

Roberts & McCallie VS William & Allison Howard, Admrs. of Abraham Howard, dec'd. Appeal. Cause is transferred to the Circuit Court.

Roberts & McCallie VS William & Allison Howard, Admrs. Cause is transferred to Circuit Court.

(p. 445) Justices on bench (8th February)— James Wilson, James McDonald, Josiah Fike, Crispien E. Shelton, and Robert Cooley.

Hopkins L. Turney VS Wyllys H. Chapman (No. 1756). Came the defendant by his attorney and the plaintiffs failing further to prosecute this suit; ordered that the plaintiff be Non Suited; defendant to recover costs from plaintiff.

Same VS Same (No. 1757). Same as above.

Abijah Bogges VS William H. West (No. 1758). Came the parties by their attornies and a jury (John A. Foshee, James Stockton, John Day, William Hill, John Carroll, Archibald McCallie, Martin Ferguson, Robert Small, Ralph B. Locke, John Dearmon, George Glaze, and Thomas C. Wroe) which says the defendant has not paid the sum of $191.00 debt nor any part of it; they assess the plaintiffs damage to $21.42½. Plaintiff to recover debt, damages, and costs.

(p. 446) Edward Morris VS James Mitchell (No. 1759). Came the parties by their attornies and a jury (same as above) which says the defendant has paid the debt in the declaration except the sum of $420.70; they assess the plaintiffs damage to $260.30; plaintiff to recover debt, damages, and costs.

George Gillespie et al VS James Smith (No. 1760). Came the plaintiffs by their attorney and the defendant not appearing made default; plaintiffs to recover costs from the defendant and his securities, Andrew Kincannon and Edmund Bean.

John McClenahan VS John Spears (No. 1761). Attachment. Came the defendant by attorney; defendant made default; plaintiff to recover $35.00 and costs from the defendant and his securities, James Cowan and James G. Williams.

(p. 447) Thomas Cox VS Abednigo Hale. Rule for New Trial. Came the parties by their attornies and the rule heretofore granted in this cause to shew reasons why a new trial should be granted therein; after arguments, the Court ordered that the rule be discharged.

William Rogers VS William & Allison Howard, Admrs. On motion of the defendants by attorney, ordered by Court that an alias writ of Certiorari and supercedeas issue in this cause returnable to next session of this Court, and that a Counter part of the supersedeas issue directed to the Sheriff of Hamilton County.

Elizabeth Forbes VS John Lea (No. 1762). The rule heretofore entered in this cause requiring the plaintiff to give additional Security came on to be heard; after argument and deliberation ordered that the rule be made absolute and that the plaintiffs cause be henceforth dismissed. Defendant to recover his costs from plantiff and her security, Gabrial Howel.

Ordered that all causes not tried at this Term stand continued until next Court.

MAY TERM 1828

(p. 448) Court of Pleas and Quarter Sessions met at the Courthouse in Washington on the first Monday and fifth day of May 1828. Justices on bench— Josiah Fike, Robert Cooley, Crispien E. Shelton, James Swan, Isaac Roddy, Samuel Gamble, John Cozby, Carson Caldwell, Jesse Thompson, John McClure, Joseph McCorkle, Peach Taylor, Beal Gaither, Arthur Fulton, Thomas Cox, and Daniel Walker.

Joseph McDaniel to Arnold Thomason. Deed of Conveyance dated 23rd December 1826 for 100 acres; acknowledged by bargonor; certified for registration.

William Byse released from payment of tax on 30 acres and one white poll for the present year.

Archabald D. Paul to Thomas Stephens. Deed of Conveyance for 320 acres; acknowledged by bargonor; certified for registration.

William Baker appointed overseer of road in place of William James.

James Nail appointed overseer of road from the ford of Piney River to the forks of the road at or near Jesse Thompsons in place of James Moore; to have the same hands said Moore had except Charles Mitchell and Thomas Mitchell who is to work under Peter Daniel overseer.

Jesse Thompson appointed Chairman protem of this Court for present Term.

(p. 449) George Syphers appointed overseer of road from William Lesenbys to Waltons Ferry on Tennessee River in place of Thomas Anderson.

Thomas Eaves appointed overseer of road from Kellys Ferry on Tennessee River to Ross Ferry on Hiwassee River; to have following hands: Samuel F. Martin, John Martin Jr., Benjamin Armstrong, John H. Lea, Pleasant Lea, Thomas Coffey, Amos King, and Charles McDaniel.

James Piper appointed overseer of road from ford of Clear Creek to Yellow Creek in place of John Weese.

Jeremiah Chapman appointed overseer from Snelsons Ferry on Tennessee River to where said road intersects the Federal Road at or near Thomas C. Wroes in place of Elijah Evans; to have same hands as Evans had with addition of Isaac Rush and all his hands and Lorenzo Rush to work under him on said road.

Thomas Haws appointed overseer of road from James A. Darwins to James Coulters in place of Robert Parks; to have all hands from the Luminary Meeting House to and including James A. Darwins plantation.

Samuel Applegate to Asa Glascock. Deed of Conveyance dated 17th December 1827 for 137 acres; proven by Jesse Thompson and Arthur Fulton; certified for registration.

(p. 450) David Shelton, having been appointed by the Governor as Surveyor for Rhea County until the next Session of the General Assembly of the State, his Commission was produced and he took the necessary oaths and entered into bond with Richard Waterhouse, Thomas McCallie, and Thomas Kelly, his securities.

William Lockmiller appointed overseer of road from Captain Daniel M. Stocktons Muster Ground to Isaiah Sellers; to have all hands on north side of branch at said Sellers to work under him.

Leander L. Goodson appointed overseer of road from Isaiah Sellers to the Federal Road; to have all hands on south side of road at said Sellers.

Richard Waterhouse, Peter Majors, Archabald D. Paul, Asa Glasscock, and Arthur Fulton appointed a Jury of View to turn the road as now cut out on the lands of Jesse Thompson and establish the same if they think it no injury to the old road or to the lands of Jesse Thompson.

Thomas Woodward to James Woodward. Deed of Conveyance for 120 acres; acknowledged by bargonor; certified for registration.

Miller Francis to Thomas Woodward. Deed of Conveyance dated July 1820 for 120 acres; proven by James C. Mitchell, one of the subscribing witnesses thereto he proving the hand writing and death of Richard Roseygrant, the other witness; certified for registration.

(p. 451) Thomas Hamilton allowed $15.00 for keeping his son, Milton 12 months.

The last Will and Testament of John Redmond, dec'd, was produced and proven by William Sears and Thomas Griffen, two of the subscribing witnesses. Ordered to be recorded.

Nancy Redmond, Executrix named in Will of John Redmond, took oath and entered into bond with Lewis Brandon, her security, for $1000.

Thomas Price appointed overseer of road from Prices Ferry on Tennessee River to the top of the ridge; to have all the hands between the ridge and the river that formerly belonged to Peter Fine, the former overseer.

Moses Wiatt appointed overseer of road from top of ridge on Prices Ferry Road to the east side of William Prices land; to have all the hands east of the ridge that belonged to Peter Fine, the former overseer.

On motion of Margaret Lewis, ordered that Daniel Walker, Robert Locke, and Palatiah Chilton be appointed Commissioners to settle with Jesse Poe, Admr. on estate of William Lewis, dec'd, the accounts of said estate.

(p. 452) John Lea, Sheriff, allowed $21.93 3/4 for erecting Stocks and repairing Courthouse.

William Gibson, overseer of road, allowed $7.00 for boering tools and powder for public roads.

Joseph Love allowed $14.50 for a blank book at $2.00 and five days settling with the Trustee of Rhea County at $2.50 per day.

(p. 453) Robert Locke allowed $12.50 for settling with the Trustee five days.

Thomas N. Clark to William Howard. Deed of Conveyance for 205 acres; proven by oath of Thomas N. Clark Jr.; certified for further probate.

Daniel Walker, Robert Locke, and Jacob Brown appointed Commissioners to settle with Jesse Poe, Admr. on estate of Burley Godsey, dec'd.

William B. Lauderdale appointed a Constable in Captain Howard's Company; bond with James Kelly, James Lauderdale, John Day, and William Howard.

Samuel Frazier released from payment of tax on 100 acres for 1827.

(p. 454) Jurors appointed for next term of this Court:

Jacob Garrison	Matthew English	Thomas Eaves	John Lillard
Isaac Masoner	John McClenahan	William Locke	John Parker
Daniel Cates	John Roddy	William Collins	John Miller
Samuel Baker	Isaac Rush	Mumford Smith	James Paul
George W. Mayo	Jefferson B. Love	Jacob Brown	Rezin Rawlings
James Roark	Woodson Francis	Jeremiah Washam	Cornelious Moyers
Robert W. Caldwell, Constable to attend Court			James Montgomery

Jurors appointed for next term of Circuit Court:

Peter Majors	James L. Cobb	Palatiah Chilton	Robert McClure
Crispien E. Shelton	Isaac Roddy	James A. Darwin	Robert Gamble
Anselin L. Dearing	Andrew Kincannon	Peach Taylor	Joseph Love
David Caldwell	Joshua Green	James Lillard	Arthur Fulton
Edmund Bean	John Day	David Leuty	William Lowry
Samuel Price	Jonathan Collins	John Stewart	Avary Hanna
Anson Dearmon, Constable to attend Court			James McCanse

Ordered that the County Trustee pay to Woodson Francis claims of the following numbers: No. 57, No. 59, No. 60, & No. 58 agreeable to the dates of their filing (6th May 1825).

It appearing to the Court that the bond entered into by Azariah David with Woodson Francis and Jesse Poe his securities for the faithful guardianship of William Jenkins, an aged and infirm man, should be cancelled and held for nought. Ordered that said bond be cancelled. It also appeared to the Court on information of John McClure, an acting Justice, that the said William Jenkins is an idiot and requires the intervention and protection of the Court.

(p. 455) Court ordered Sheriff summon a jury of 12 freeholders to ascertain by inquisition the idiocy or lunacy of the said William Jenkins.

Justices on bench (6th May)— Josiah Fike, Crispien E. Shelton, Robert Cooley, James Wilson, and James McDonald.

John Lea, Sheriff, returned a list of jurors summoned to appear at this session of Court (see list on page 125), out of whom the following were elected a Grand Jury: John Wasson, John C. Ferguson, Abraham Hughes, Edmund Bean, Tignal Wade, Washington Morgan, John Parker, Micajah Howerton, Jeremiah Chapman, Leonard Brooks, Charles McDaniel, Samuel P. Stewart, and Jonathan Owens. John Wasson appointed foreman and Anson Dearmon a Constable to attend the Grand Jury.

(p. 456) There remained of the original pannel who did not answer to their names: George W. Riggle, Alexander Coulter, John Miller, Nicholas Fraley, and John B. Page.

Allen Kennedy permitted to keep an ordinary for one year; bond with Rezin Rawlings, his security.

Palatiah Chilton to Asahel Rawlings. Deed of Conveyance for an undivided half of 200 acres in Marion County, Tennessee; acknowledged by bargonor; certified to Marion County for registration.

David Johns by his next friend Jonathan Fry VS Anson Dearmon. Came the parties by their attornies and with assent of Court time is given to plead so as not to delay the trial at the next Term of this Court.

Simeon Jackson VS Micajah Howerton. Came parties by attornies; time is given to plead so as not to delay the trial of this cause at next term.

James P. Miller VS William Gibson (No. 1763). Appeal. Came the parties and James P. Miller the appellant in this cause dismisses his Appeal and confesses Judgment for all the costs.

(p. 457) Andrew Wells VS John Clack, John Parker, and Henry Collins (No. 1764). Came the defendants by attorney and the plaintiff failing further to prosecute this motion; Court ordered that the plaintiff be Non suited and the defendants recover their costs from plaintiff.

William Rogers VS William & Allison Howard, Admrs. (No. 1765). Came the defendants by their attorney and the plaintiff failing further to prosecute this suit; ordered that the plaintiff be Non suited and the defendants recover their costs.

John Able VS Joseph Williams, Rolly Clack, & Thomas Kelly (No. 1766). Covenant. Came the parties by their attornies and a jury (Allison Howard, William Hancock, George Hale, Joseph Harwood, William Howard, Robert Small, Zaph Jackson, David Ragsdale, James P. Miller, Drury Sykes, Thomas C. Wroe, and Charles McDonald) which says the defendant has not kept and performed their said Covenant as the plaintiff has complained, but has broken the same; they assess the plaintiffs damage to $218.56.

Thomas Kelly, Thomas Cox, and William S. Russell Commissioners appointed to settle with Armsted Bridwell, Admr. on estate of Elias Bridwell, returned their settlement.

(p. 458) John Ryon for use of Orville Paine VS Edmund Bean (No. 1767). Covenant. Came the plaintiff by his attorney; defendant says he cannot gainsay the plaintiffs demand fot $149.50 debt and damages.

William L. Brocksher VS Thomas Marshall (No. 1768). Certiorari. Came the defendant by his attorney and the Plaintiff failing further to prosecute this suit, he is Non suited by the Court. Defendant to recover costs from plaintiff.

Elijah W. Collins VS James McCarroll (No. 1769). Motion as Security. Came the plaintiff by his attorney, Thomas J. Campbell, and a jury (same as above) which says that Collins was security for McCarroll and as such paid $28.00. The plaintiff to recover said sum plus costs.

Peter Minnick VS William Hancock (No. 1770). Came the plaintiff and being unwilling further to prosecute his suit dismisses the same; defendant confesses judgment for the costs.

(p. 459) John Haines VS Nathaniel W. Wilson (Mo. 1771). Appeal. Came the parties by their attornies and a jury (James Kelly, Allison Howard, George Hale, William Hancock, William Howard, Robert Small, James P. Miller, Drury Sykes, Thomas C. Wroe, Zoph Jackson, David Ragsdale, and Charles McDonald) which finds for the plaintiff the sum of $7.00. From which verdict and judgment the defendant prayed an appeal to the Circuit Court; granted upon the appellant giving bond and security.

Samuel Roberts & Thomas McCallie VS William & Allison Howard, Admrs. Came the parties by their attornies and a jury (James Montgomery, George W. Riggle, John McDonough, John Moyers, Robert Small, Drury Sykes, Thomas C. Wroe, Zoph Jackson, Charles McDonald, William Ferguson, James Kelly, and Mumford Smith) which says the defendants do not owe the debt in the declaration. Defendants to recover costs from plaintiff. From which verdict and judgment the plaintiffs prayed an appeal to the next Circuit Court; granted.

George W. Riggle, one of the original pannel who did not answer to his name when called, appeared in open Court and answered to his name.

Thomas C. Wroe VS Mark Johnson. Certiorari. Came the defendant by his attorney and on his motion a rule is entered to dismiss the petition for Certiorari and supersedeas in this cause.

(p. 460) Grand Jury returned a Bill of Indictment, State against George Weaks, William Weaks, and Frederick Prysock for an assault and battery.

The Court nor Attorney General not having any further business for the Grand Jury; ordered that said Gtand Jury and those that remained of the original pannel except Tignal Wade, Edmund Bean, John Parker, and Abraham Hughes be discharged from further attendance at the present term.

John A. Rogers VS Volentine Houpt. Time is given to plead so as not to delay the trial of this cause at next term of this Court.

Orlando Bradley VS James Kelly & John Clack. Time is given to plead so as not to delay the trial of this cause at the next term of this Court.

(p. 461) Justices on bench (7th May)— James McDonald, Crispien E. Shelton, Robert Cooley, James Wilson, and Josiah Fike.

James Kelly VS Robert Bell. Time is given to plead so as not to delay the trial of this cause at next term of this Court.

Patrick Martin VS William & Allison Howard, Admrs. Time is given to plead so as not to delay the trial of this cause at next term of this Court.

State VS David Clinghan. Recognizance. Came James P. Lowry, Attorney General, and the defendant though solomnly called upon his recognizance to answer a charge of the State exhibited against him by a presentment of the Grand Jury for retailing Spirits came not but made default. Defendant to forfeit the $250 in the recognizance unless he shall show good cause to the contrary at the next session of this Court and that the State recover the costs.

State VS Thomas Lemons. Security for appearance of David Clinghan. Defendant made default by not bringing Clinghan into Court; to forfeit $250 in the recognizance bond and pay costs.

(p. 462) State VS George Weaks, William Weaks, and Frederick Prysock. Assault and battery. Defendants say the are not guilty; jury (Thomas C. Wroe, Robert Small, Simeon Jackson, Zoph Jackson, John Myors, William Locke, George W. Mayo, Cornileous Myors, William Howard, William Ferguson, Allison Howard, and Samuel Howard) says they cannot agree; mistrial entered and cause is continued until next session of this Court.

State VS Weaks & Prysock. William Long and William Gibson, bound for the appearance of the defendants in this cause, brings into Court the said defendants in discharge of themselves and the defendants are ordered into custody of the Sheriff.

Samuel Roberts & Thomas McCallie VS William & Allison Howard, Admrs. (No. 1772). Came the parties by their attornies; ordered that the plaintiffs demurrer to the defendants first plea be overruled, to which opinion the plaintiffs by their counsel excepts and prayed an appeal in the nature of a writ of error to the next Circuit Court; granted upon the appellants giving bond and security; whereupon the plaintiffs by their counsel replyed to the defendants plea of fully administered to which issue is Joined.

(p. 463) State VS Weaks & Prysock. Abraham Hughes, William Hughes, Isaac Geren, and Fletcher Edward endebted for $250 as securities for defendants; void on condition George Weaks, William Weaks, and Frederick Prysock appear at August Term of this Court.

John Love to Allen Kennedy. Deed of Conveyance for 2 lots in Southern Liberties; proven by James Berry and John Cozby; certified for registration.

Thomas N. Clark to Asahel Johnson. Deed of Conveyance for 235 acres; proven by Thomas N. Clark Jr. (previously proven by Henry S. Purris, the other witness); certified for registration.

Beriah Frazier VS George Barrett & Jeremiah Barrett. Came defendants by their attorney and the plaintiff failing further to prosecute this suit; on motion of the defendant, ordered that the plaintiff be Non suited and that the defendants recover their costs from plaintiff.

(p. 464) Samuel Roberts & Thomas McCallie VS William & Allison Howard, Admr. (No. 1774). Appeal. Came the parties by their attornies and a jury (John Moyers, Simeon Jackson, Cornileous Myors, William Ferguson, William Locke, Tegnal Wade, George W. Mayo, Thomas C. Wroe, Zoaph Jackson, Abraham Hughes, Samuel R. Hackett, and Charles Ryon) which finds for the defendants, who are to recover costs. From which verdict and judgment the plaintiffs prayed an appeal to the next Circuit Court; granted.

Samuel Roberts & Thomas McCallie, assignee of John W. Jones VS Richard McPherson & Crispien E. Shelton (No. 1775). Came the parties by their attornies and a jury (same as above) which says the defendant has not paid the sum of $80.00, the debt in the declaration; damages assessed at $1.60.

(p. 465) Thomas C. Wroe VS Mark Johnson. (No. 1776). Came the parties by their attornies and the rule heretofore granted in this cause to dismiss the petition for Certiorari and Supercedeas being argued, the Court ordered the rule be made absolute. Defendants to recover costs from plaintiff and his security, George Glaze.

Thomas Henry for use of Thomas McCallie VS James Kelly & Palatiah Chilton (No. 1777). Came the parties by their attornies and the defendants demurrer to the plaintiffs declaration being argued, seems to Court that the plaintiffs declaration is not good and sufficient in law. Considered by Court that defendants demurrer be sustained. On motion of plaintiff by attorney, leave is granted him to amend his declaration upon the payment of the cost at the present term.

All causes not otherwise disposed of are continued until next term.

AUGUST TERM 1828

(p. 466) Court of Pleas and Quarter Sessions met at Courthouse in Washington on the first Monday and fourth day of August 1828. Justices on bench— William Smith, John Cozby, Matthew Hubbart, James A. Darwin, Robert Cooley, James Swan, George Gillespie, Carson Caldwell, Crispien E. Shelton, John McClure, Beal Gaither, Azariah David, Jesse Thompson, Arthur Fulton, Heil Butram, Josiah Fike, Thomas Cox, and Peach Taylor.

Warren West appointed overseer of road from ford of Clear Creek to the forks of road at Lewis R. Collins in place of Seaton Taylor.

Robert Parks to William S. Leuty. Deed of Conveyance for 322 acres; proven by John Locke and William Johnson; certified for registration.

James Lewis to William S. Leuty. Deed of Conveyance for 1000 acres; proven by Orville Paine, Anderson Smith, and James Berry; certified for registration.

Lewis R. Collins to William S. Leuty. Deed of Conveyance for 125 acres; proven by James Berry and William Smith; certified for registration.

Caswell Johnson appointed overseer of road from Town of Washington to said Johnsons house in place of James Stewart.

(p. 467) James W. Cozby to John Cozby. Deed of Conveyance for 250 acres; proven by William Smith and Joshua S. Green; certified for registration.

John Bowls repeased from payment of tax on a quarter section of land, he having been charged for the same land on two tax lists.

Walter Edwards to Archaband D. Paul. Deed of Conveyance for 100 acres; acknowledged by Edwards; certified for registration.

Roberts & McCallie allowed $11.25 for Record Book furnished to Clerk of this Court.

Ordered that an orphan child named Wellington Chapman be bound to John Chastain to live with him as a bound apprentice for 13 years.

John Tillery appointed guardian to Thomas Tillery, Hugh Tillery, Samuel Tillery, Jane Tillery, Ellen Tillery, and Margaret Tillery, infant children of Samuel Tillery, dec'd; bond with Thomas Price and Joseph Love for $2000.

(p. 468) Jeremiah Chapman, overseer of road, is released from building a bridge across Ten Mile Creek.

Jurors appointed for next term of this Court:

Benjamin F. Jones	John Gray	John Able	Caswell Johnson
Ruben Jackson	James Nail	Jeremiah Howerton	Matthew English
John Rogers	Matthew Allen	Rector Preston	Meredith Cox
Anderson Fitzgerrel	James McCanse	Morris Putman	Thomas Majors
Thomas Carter	David Hudson	Edmund Bean	Jeremiah Barrett
John Parker M.C.	James Woodward	John Rawlings	Cornelious Myors

Anson Dearmon, Constable to attend Court

Woodson Francis, Sheriff to Cornelious Myors. Deed of Conveyance for Lot No. 7 in Town of Washington; acknowledged by Francis; certified for registration.

Nancy Redmond, Exrx. of last Will and Testament of John Redmond, dec'd, returned an inventory of the personal property belonging to estate.

Patrick Martin, guardian for Mary Jane Galbreath and John Galbreath, released from his said guardianship.

John Locke, William Johnson, and Joseph Love appointed Commissioners to settle with John Lea, Exr. of last Will and Testament of Lydia Roddy.

Carson Caldwell resigned as Trustee of Rhea County.

(p. 469) Elisha Parker appointed overseer of road from Mud Creek on Fraziers Ferry Road to where said road intersects with the road leading from Washington in place of James Smith.

Certificate for $3.00 issued to Peter Daniel for a Wolf scalp.

William Price to Samuel Price. Deed of Conveyance for 134 acres and 27 poles; proven by Henry Reynolds and Thomas Atchley; certified for registration.

William Price to James Price. Deed of Conveyance for 96 acres; proven by Henry Reynolds and Thomas Atchley; certified for registration.

Joshua Mosely to Byram Breeding. Deed of Conveyance for 40 acres; proven by Archabald D. Paul and Baty Breeding; certified for registration.

Henry Collins and Crispien E. Shelton appointed Commissioners to settle with Isaac Love, Admr. on estate of William Love, dec'd.

(p. 470) John Locke and William Johnson appointed to settle with John Tillery and Thomas Bell, Exrs. of last Will and Testament of Samuel Tillery, dec'd.

Isaac West to Commissioners of Concord Meeting House. Deed of Conveyance dated 23th July 1823 (number of acres not given); proven by Henry Walton, the subscribing witness, and by the oaths of Henry Collins and William Johnson, they proving the handwriting of Isaac West; certified for registration.

William Bryant appointed overseer of road from ford of Piney River on the Muddy Creek Road to the dividing ridge of Wolf and Clear creeks in place of William Lisenby.

Azariah David authorized to let out to the lowest bidder the flooring of the bridge across Richland Creek at or near Jesse Witts, the plank to be of oak or pine and to be two inches thick.

John Majors appointed overseer of road from Jacksons Ferry on Tennessee River to the first ridge north of Fords Spring Branch in place of William Tally.

James McCanse appointed overseer of road from ford of Piney at his house to Yellow Creek in place of William Smith.

(p. 471)   Hugh L. Brazeal produced his licence as a practicing attorney at law.

Byram Breeding, James Baily, Asa Glascock, Charles Mitchell, and Archibald D. Paul appointed a Jury of View to lay off and mark a road from Robert Walkers passing Bethel Meeting House to Snelsons Ferry on Tennessee River.

John Parker appointed overseer of road from Haslerigs Landing on Tennessee River to Town of Washington and overseer of Madison Street in said Town; to have all hands living on Madison Street and all hands living between Spring Creek and said road including the hands at William S. Leutys, George W. Mayos, and Mrs. Haslerigs to work under him.

Ordered that a public road leading from the lower end of Jefferson Street in Town of Washington be laid off and established by mutual consent as near as may be in a direct way with said street until it intersects the Valley Road and that William Gibson overseer is hereby ordered to work Jefferson Street and new road in addition to his former bounds; to have hands living on Jefferson Street and on west side of said street in addition to former hands.

Abraham Miller appointed overseer of road from Haslerigs Ferry landing on Tennessee River to the bank of Lick Branch; to have all hands from mouth of said branch up the branch crossing said road striking the river so as to include Thomas Hunters plantation.

(p. 472)   John Leuty appointed overseer of road from Lick Branch to the dividing ridge between the waters of Goodfield and Tennessee River; to have all the hands belonging to that part of the road that formerly was worked under Pulaski Poe.

Leonard Brooks appointed overseer of road from dividing ridge to James Lillards Mill; to have hands from Miles Vernons on by William Lillards passing said Mill with said ridge to George Marlows crossing the Valley to include Daniel Cates, John Rue, H. Runnels, John Runyon and so on to said Vernons making 17 hands.

Matthias Shaffer appointed overseer of road from James Lillards Mill to the McMinn County line; to have hands at said Mill and running to include John Walker, M. Norman, John Davis, crossing said road so as to include Adam Bredwell, Thomas Seay, and John Taylor, 17 hands.

Hatten Walker VS Nathaniel W. Wilson (No. 1778). Came the plaintiff and being unwilling further to prosecute his suit in this behalf dismisses the same. Defendant to recover costs from plaintiff.

This day came Coffield Tillery and presented his petition to the Court praying it to appoint Commissioners to divide and lay off to him his equal proportion of the real estate his father died possessed of between him and his three brothers, Thomas, Hugh, and Samuel Tillery, according to the last Will and Testament of his father, Samuel Tillery. Appears to the Court that Coffield Tillery has served 10 days notice in writing on Thomas Bell and
(p. 473)   John Tillery, Exrs. of Samuel Tillery, dec'd, and also on John Tillery, guardian of said Thomas, Hugh, and Samuel Tillery of his intention of petitioning this Court at the present Term for Commissioners to divide the said land.

Ordered by the Court that Thomas Price, James Lillard, Leonard Brooks, Absolum Coleman, and Miles Vernon be appointed Commissioners to divide the real estate of Samuel Tillery, dec'd.

142

(p. 474)   Justices on bench (5th August)— William Smith, George Gillespie, Josiah Fike, Crispien E. Shelton, John Cozby, John McClure, James Swan, Isaac Roddy, Robert Cooley, Carson Caldwell, Daniel Walker, Matthew Hubbart, James Wilson, and James McDonald.

John Lea, Sheriff, returned a list of Jurors summoned to attend this session of Court (see list on page 136), out of whom was elected a Grand Jury: Rezin Rawlings, Jefferson B. Love, Mumford Smith, John Parker, James Montgomery, Jacob Brown, Jeremiah Washam, James Roark, Isaac Mahan, Jacob Garrison, Matthew English, John Roddy, and William Locke. Rezin Rawlings appointed foreman and Anderson Smith a Constable to attend Grand Jury.

There remained of the original pannel who answered to their names: James Paul, George W. Mayo, Woodson Francis, William Collins, John Miller, and Cornelious Myors.

James Paul released from further attendance as a Juror at this Term.

(p. 475)   Crispien E. Shelton & Henry Collins, Commissioners appointed to settle with Isaac Love, Adm. of estate of William Love, returned the settlement made by them.

Adam Seabolt VS Jesse Matthews. Petition. Came the defendant by his attorney and on his petition a Certiorari is awarded him to bring this cause into Court from before the Justice on his entering into bond and security.

Richard Waldroft to Charles Kelly. Power of Attorney proven by James F. Bradford and Thomas W. Marston.

Court appointed a Trustee for Rhea County, John Cozby, who took necessary oaths and entered into bond with William Smith, Joseph Love, John McClure, and James A. Darwin, his securities, for $5000.

Daniel Walker & Robert Locke, Commissioners appointed to settle with Jesse Poe, Admr. on estate of Burley Godsey, dec'd, returned settlement.

Daniel Walker & Robert Locke, Commissioners appointed to settle with Jesse Poe, Admr. on estate of William Lewis, dec'd, returned settlement.

(p. 476)   John Locke and William Johnson, Commissioners appointed to settle with John Tillery and Thomas Bell, Exrs. on estate of Samuel Tillery, returned settlement.

Hugh Barton, Admr. on estate of Andrew Stewart, dec'd, for use of John Parks VS Edward Stewart. (No. 1779). Debt. Came the parties by their attornies and a jury (William Collins, George W. Mayo, Woodson Francis, John Miller, Cornelious Myors, Levi Griffitt, Thomas Godbehere, William Jackson, Simeon Jackson, Spillsbe Dyer, Robert Murphy, and Wright Smith) which says the defendant has paid the debt except for $227.00; they assess the damages to $197.48. Plaintiff to recover debt, damages, and costs.

Orlando Bradley VS James Kelly & John Clack (No. 1780). Came the parties by their attornies and a jury (William Cumpton, John McCarroll, Samuel Howard, Allison Howard, William Carter, Henry Johns, Drury Sykes, William Hill, Joshua Tindle, Asahel Johnson, Robert McCracken, and George Ransom) which says the defendant did not assume and undertake in manner and form as the plaintiff declares; defendants to recover against the plaintiff their costs. Plaintiff prayed an appeal to the next Circuit Court; granted.

(p. 477)   Calvin Morgan, Franklin H. Morgan, & Solomon D. Jacobs VS Benjamin C. Stout (No. 1731). Came the plaintiffs by their attorney and the defendant who says he cannot gainsay the plaintiffs demand against him for $183.85½ debt and damages for the detention of said debt. Plaintiffs to recover debt, damages, and costs. Execution stayed for three months.

David Johns by his next friend Jonathan Fry VS Anson Dearmon (No. 1782). Came the parties by their attornies and a jury (William Cumpton, John McCarroll, Samuel Howard, Allison Howard, William Carter, John Miller, Woodson Francis, William Hill, Joshua Tindle, Asahel Johnson, Robert McCracken, and George Ransom) which finds the defendant guilty of the trover and convertion as the plaintiff declares; they assess the plaintiffs damage to $23.00. From which verdict and judgment the defendant prayed an appeal to the next Circuit Court and entered into bond accordingly.

William Johnson and Joseph Love returned settlement made with John Lea, Exr. of last Will and Testament of Lydia Roddy, dec'd.

(p. 478) Anthony Street VS John W. Blevins & David Blevins. Came the parties by their attornies and it appearing to the satisfaction of the Court that a Writ of Capias ad Satisfaciendum issued from the Clerks office of this Court at the suit of the plaintiff against said defendants bearing date the 23rd May 1828 and returnable to the present August Session, and that the Sheriff in the execution of said Writ had taken bond from David Blevins, one of the Defendants, with Thomas Kelly as security under the provisions of an Act entitled "An Act to amend an Act entitled An Act for the relief of insolvent debtors with respect to the imprisonment of their persons passed October 29th 1811." And thereupon the said David Blevins appeared in Court in discharge of his said security Thomas Kelly, from his undertaking and liability in that behalf.

Roberts & McCallie VS Jesse Atwood (No. 1783). Came the parties by their attornies and Pharley Brady who was summoned by the Sheriff as a Garnishee in this cause on behalf of the plaintiff; upon his examination deluded upon oath that he was not indebted to Jesse Atwood at the service of the garnishment nor is he now indebted to him, but that he the said garnishee had at the date of the garnishment and now has in his possession a feather bed the property of the said Jesse Atwood and also some delph ware. The said Garnishee further declares that he was informed by the said Jesse Atwood that he held a note of hand for five dollars on William Archey. Court ordered that the bed in possession of the Garnishee be sold by the Sheriff for the satisfaction of the plaintiffs debt and costs.

(p. 479) The Grand Jury returned two Bills of Indictment: State against Nathaniel W. Wilson for an assault, and the State against Sarah Johnson for an assault.

(p. 480) Justices on bench (6th August)— Robert Cooley, Crispien E. Shelton, James Wilson, Josiah Fike, and Isaac Roddy.

State VS Sarah Johnson (No. 1734). Assault and Battery. Came James P. Lowry, Attorney General, and the defendant who says she cannot gainsay the charge; fined 6½¢ and costs.

State VS David Clinghan (No. 1735). Retailing Spirits. Defendant says he is not guilty; jury (George W. Mayo, Cornelius Myors, William Hill, Rolly Clack, William Collins, John Miller, Jackson Howerton, James P. Miller, William Carter, Robert Murphy, Woodson Francis, and William Ingle) finds the defendant not guilty; costs to be paid by County.

(p. 481) State VS George Weaks, William Weaks, & Frederick Prysock. Came Abraham Hughes, William Hughes, Isaac Geren, and Fletcher Edwards, who are bound here for the appearance of the defendants in this cause, and brings into Court the bodies of the said defendants and surrendered them in discharge of themselves and the said defendants are ordered into custody of the Sheriff.

State VS G. Weaks, W. Weaks, & F. Prysock (No. 1736). Assault and battery. Defendants say they are not guilty as charged; the jury (Woodson Francis, William Collins, John Miller, Joshua Hill, Elijah W. Collins, Jackson Howerton, William Woodward, William Ingle, William Carter, Joseph Stallion, Jesse Poe, and Thomas McNutt) finds the defendants not guilty; County to pay costs.

Robert H. Jordan VS George Glaze & Allen Webb (No. 1737). Motion as Security. Came the plaintiff by his attorney, Hugh L. Brazeal, and moved the Court for judgment against the defendants for $26.83½ paid by the said plaintiff as security for the defendants. Plaintiff to recover the sum plus costs.

(p. 482) State VS David Clingham (No. 1733). Sci Fa. Came Attorney General, James P. Lowry; on motion of defendant by attorney, Court sets aside forfeiture incurred by defendant. County to pay costs.

State VS Thomas Lemmons (No. 1739). Sci Fa. Ordered that the forfeiture incurred by the defendant as appearance bail of David Clinghan be set aside.

State VS Nathaniel W. Wilson. Assault and Battery. Defendant says he is not guilty; the jury (Peter Fine, Cornelius Myors, James P. Miller, William Cumpton, Robert Murphy, Thomas Piper, Spillsbe Dyer, James Kelly, Beriah Frazier, Henry Henry, Thomas Henry, and Daniel D. Armstrong) retired to consult their verdict and is respited until tomorrow morning under the care of an officer.

(p. 483) Grand Jury returned a Presentment: State against Edward Templeton for disturbing public worship.

The Court nor Attorney General not having any further business for the Grand Jury, ordered that the Grand Jury be discharged from further attendance at this Term.

Justices on bench (7th August)— Josiah Fike, Robert Cooley, Matthew Hubbart, Isaac Roddy, and Crispien E. Shelton.

Adam W. Caldwell permitted to keep an ordinary for one year; bond with James A. Darwin and William Lowry, his securities.

Edward Morris VS James C. Mitchell. Came the parties by their attornies; appearing to satisfaction of Court that a Writ of Capias ad Satisfactindum issued from the Clerks office at the suit of the plaintiff on 23rd May 1828 returnable to the present Court, that the Sheriff had taken bond from James C. Mitchell the defendant with Thomas McCallie, Allen Kennedy, and Edmund Bean as securities under the provisions of an act for the relief of insolvent debtors &c. Thereupon the said Mitchell appeared in open Court in discharge of his said securities McCallie, Kennedy, and Bean from their undertaking and liability in that behalf.

(p. 484) State VS Nathaniel W. Wilson (No. 1790 & 1791). Assault and Battery. The jury who was retired on yesterday to consult of their verdict, came into Court and on their oaths say they cannot agree; mistrial is entered. Defendant submits and confesses judgment for all the costs, except the cost of nine of the States witnesses. Came Calvin Robinson the prosecutor and confesses judgment for the balance of the costs. Considered by the Court that for his offence, the defendant is fined $1.00 and costs of this prosecution as above confessed.

John A. Rogers VS Volentine Houpt (No. 1792). Came the parties by their attornies and a jury (William Collins, William Carter, William Hill, Isaac Crow, William Fowler, Jesse Poe, Thomas Smith, Isaac Geren, William Howard, John McCarrol, Ralph B. Locke, and John Parker) which says that the defendant has paid the debt in the plaintiffs declaration by a set off of accounts due the said defendant; the jury further say that they find for defendant the sum of $19.00, the balance upon the set off of accounts. From which verdict and judgment the plaintiff prayed an appeal to the next Circuit Court; granted upon the appellant giving bond and security.

(p. 485)   Patrick Martin VS William & Allison Howard, Admrs. of Abraham Howard, dec'd (No. 1793). Came the parties by their attorneys and a jury (William Collins, Woodson Francis, George W. Mayo, William Hill, Isaac Crow, Jesse Poe, William Fowler, Thomas Smith, Isaac Geren, John McCarroll, Ralph B. Locke, and John Parker) which says the defendants have not well and truly administered all and singular the goods and chattles rights and credits of Abraham Howard deceased which came to their hands to be administered. The jury further say that the said Abraham Howard in his lifetime did assume and undertake within three years before the issuance of the original writ in this cause in manner and form as the plaintiff in declaring hath complained against him and they do assess the plaintiffs damage by reason thereof to $167.25.

On motion of the Attorney General it is ordered by the Court that an Alias Capias issue against Edward Templeton.

(p. 486)   Samuel Roberts & Thomas McCallie VS Jesse Atwood (No. 1794). Debt, Attachment. Came the plaintiffs by their attorney, John H. Hooke and the defendant not appearing to make defence, made default. Plaintiffs to recover against the defendant the sum of $78.13 debt in the declaration, and the further sum of $2.86½ damages plus costs.

James Kelly VS Robert Bell. Came the parties by their attornies and with assent of Court, a Commission is awarded plaintiff to take the deposition of Preston W. Davis; cause is continued until next term.

Roberts & McCallie VS Jesse Atwood. Attachment. Came the plaintiffs by their attorney, John H. Hooke, and the defendant not appearing to make defence came not and made default; plaintiff is entitled to recover against the defendant and the damages being uncertain, Sheriff to summon jury at next session to enquire of the plaintiffs damage.

(p. 487)   Semion Jackson VS Micajah Howerton (No. 1795). Came the parties by their attornies and agree and with assent of Court this cause is transferred to the Circuit Court.

Edward Morris VS James C. Mitchell. Came the parties by their attornies and it appearing that a Writ of Capias ad satisfacindum issued from the Clerks office at the suit of the plaintiff. The Sheriff took bond from Mitchell with Thomas McCallie, Allen Kennedy, and Edmund Bean, his securities under the provisions of an act for the relief of insolvent debtors. And it appearing to the Court that Mitchell has filed with the Clerks office a schedule of his property as required by law, and the said defendant now having applied to the Court to have administered to him the Oath of Insolvency, which was done.

(p. 488)   It is therefore considered by the Court that the defendant James C. Mitchell be discharged and his security aforesaid released and exhonorated from further liability in this behalf.

Jesse Poe, Admr of estate of William Lewis, dec'd VS William Lewis Sr. Motion. Cause is continued until next session of this Court.

(p. 489)   Justices on bench (8rd August)— Robert Cooley, Crispien E. Shelton, and Josiah Fike.

Richard Waterhouse VS Edward Stewart (No. 1796). Attachment. Came the plaintiff by his attorney and the defendant came not but made default; considered by Court that judgment final be entered against the defendant for $72.14 debt; upon motion of plaintiffs attorney and it apparing to the Court that the attachment had been levied on 200 acres of land, the property of the defendant; ordered that the land be sold for the satisfaction of the debt and costs.

Richard & Blackstone Waterhouse, Exrs. of R.G. Waterhouse VS Edward Stewart. Attachment. Came the plaintiffs by their attorney and defendant being called to defend this suit and replevy the property levied upon by attachment at the suit of the plaintiffs came not but made default. It appearing to the Court that the plaintiffs are entitled to a recovery against the defendant and the damages being uncertain, ordered that the Sheriff summon a jury at next session of this Court to inquire of the plaintiffs damage.

(p. 490) Anthony Street VS Isaac Blevins & David Blevins. Came the parties by their attornies; David Blevins, having heretofore on Tuesday of the present Term appeared in Court in discharge of his Security, Thomas Kelly, as required by the provisions of the Act for the relief of insolvent debtors. The defendant Blevins had filed with the Clerk a schedule of his property as required by law, and now applies to the Court to have administered to him the oath of insolvency; oath administered
(p. 491) and Blevins was discharged. Thomas Kelly, his security, was released and exhonorated from further liability in this behalf.
Court adjourned "untill Court in coarse."

NOVEMBER TERM 1828

(p. 492) Court of Pleas and Quarter Sessions met at the Courthouse in Washington on the first Monday and third day of November 1828. Justices on bench— Arthur Fulton, James A. Darwin, Daniel Walker, James Swan, Isaac Roddy, Stephen Winton, Daniel M. Stockton, Robert Cooley, Crispien E. Shelton, John McClure, Peach Taylor, John Cozby, Joseph McCorkle, Samuel Gamble, Josiah Fike, Hail Butram, James Wilson, Beal Gaither, James McDonald, Azariah David, Jesse Thompson, and Carson Caldwell.
Nathaniel Smith to James Keeton. Deed of Conveyance dated 19th April 1826 for 160 acres; proven by Benton Keeton and John Story; certified for registration.
John Hurt to John Story. Deed of Conveyance dated 10th September 1828 for 2 acres; proven by Joseph Hurt, James Keeton, and Beenton Keeton; certified for registration.
James Keeton to Benton Keeton. Deed of Conveyance dated 23rd May 1826 for 40 acres; acknowledged by James Keeton; certified for registration.
Robert Elder to James Lillard. Deed of Conveyance for 80 acres; acknowledged by Elder; certified for registration.

(p. 493) Leonard Brooks to James Lillard. Deed of Conveyance for 10 acres; acknowledged by Brooks; certified for registration.
David Mahan appointed overseer of road from Thomas Harps to Rosses Ferry in place of John Knight. 3rd Class Road.
Solomon Nideffer appointed overseer of road leading from Kellys Ferry to Athens from the forks of the road leading to Calhoun to the McMinn County line in place of Wilson Blevins. 1st Class Road.
Able Massey appointed overseer of road from 4-mile post on road from Kellys Ferry to Calhoun to Thomas Harps House in place of Thomas Harp. 2nd Class.
Samuel Fitzgerrall released from payment of Tax in 2 black polls and 1 white poll for 1828, he having been charged for the same on two lists.
Elijah W. Collins appointed overseer of road from James A. Darwins to the ford of Clear Creek in place of Martin Ferguson, resigned. 1st Class Road.
Sebert Martin released from payment of Tax on 480 acres for 1828, he having been charged with the same through mistake.

(p. 494) Samuel Richmond to William C. Wilson. Deed of Conveyance dated 2nd April 1828 for 7 acres; proven by Gideon Ragland and Elisha Sharp; certified for registration.

Lewis Morgan appointed overseer of road from fork of road at John Jacks to the house of John Witt in place of George Maner and to have James Lauderdale, Lewis Kelly, Charles Witt, Allen Danrimple, Walter R. Paine, and John Witt in addition to hands that formerly worked under Maner. 1st Class Road.

David George appointed overseer of road in place of James Bolin.

John Miller appointed overseer of road from Hornsbys Ferry on Tennessee River to where said road intersects the Federal Road at Thomas Rheas in place of John S. Richmond. 2nd Class Road.

Jeremiah Jack appointed overseer of road from Mrs. Lauderdales to the ford of creek at James Coulters in place of Allison Howard. 1st Class Road.

Barefoot Armstrong appointed overseer of road from four mile post on Kellys Ferry Road to the McMinn County line on the Calhoun Road in place of Thomas Shaffer. 1st Class Road.

(p. 495) Noah Butram appointed overseer of road from ford of Sowee at Philip Sebers to the McMinn County line in place of John Ginnans. 2nd Class Road.

John Mahan appointed overseer from Hamilton County line to Cain Ables in place of William Baker. 1st Class Road.

Samuel R. Hackett and all the hands that work under him & Thomas Haws and all the hands under him to work under Caswell Johnson, overseer, for two days at any time when said Johnson may call on them to work.

James P. Lowry, Attorney General, allowed $40.00 for exofficio services.

John Lea, Sheriff, allowed $40.00 for exofficio services.

(p. 496) James Berry, Clerk of this Court, allowed $40.00 for exofficio services and $25.00 for making out the Tax lists for 1828.

Rezin Rawlings to Abraham Bryson. Deed of Conveyance for 50 acres; acknowledged by Rawlings; certified for registration.

William Johnson, John Parker, George W. Mayo, Thomas Haws, James Berry, Adam W. Caldwell, and John Locke appointed Jury of View and John Locke is appointed a surveyor to lay off and mark the nearest practicable route on or as near as may be to a direct line between the seats of justice in Bledsoe and Rhea counties; John Locke to lay down and shew upon a plat said route with its relative position to other roads from the town of Washington to Pikeville. Said Jury is to correspond with a Jury of View to be appointed by Bledsoe County.

(p. 497) Samuel Igo, George Keenum, Thomas Lucas, Joseph Lusk, Daniel D. Stockton, John Taylor, and Thomas Seay to work under Robert Elder, overseer of road, in addition to his former hands.

Ordered that the road from Robert Walkers to Snelsons Ferry be established as follows: "Beginning at James Snelsons Ferry, thence with the road already cut to the top of the ridge above A.D. Pauls, thence down a left hand hollow intersecting the waggon road above the mouth of said hollow, thence with said road to Bethel Meeting House, thence up a hollow crossing the ridge at a gap where the path crosses with the road to Glasscocks upper field, then leaving the road at a large white oak marked "A" following a path leaving Glasscocks plantation to the left untill it intersects the road leading from Glasscocks to Robert Walkers leaving James Roddys old place to the right, then leaving the old road to the left, then coming in again at the School house at Robert Walkers." Said road to be 2nd Class. Farley Brady appointed overseer of road from Snelsons Ferry to Bethel Meeting house and to have the following hands: Aron Brady, Marrell Brady, John Marshall, Robert Stacy, William Snelson, William Johnson Jr., Jesse McFalls, and Richard McFalls.

Asa Glasscock appointed overseer of road from Bethel Meeting house to Robert Walkers; to have all the hands that work under the following overseers of other roads: James Roddy, Peter Daniel, Charles Rector, Archabald D. Paul, and James Moore.

(p. 498) Ordered that the road from George Gillespies Ferry to Bethel Meeting house be established as reported by Jury of View: "Beginning at said Gillespies Ferry thence with his Ferry road to the Stone Spring, thence a direct course through the woods to the path leading to the meeting house and with some small variations we followed said path to said meeting house; road to be 2nd Class. Matthew Allen appointed overseer of said road; hands to work under him: Robert Miller, James Smith, Richard Smith, Henry Newman, John Clary, (blank) Qualls, Moses Looney, and all George Gillespies hands.

Elisha Sharp, Gideon Ragland, Robert H. Jordon, Stephen Winton, and Levi H. Knight appointed a Jury of View to turn the road on the land of Robert S. Philips so as to run upon the east line of his land so as not to injure the land of any person.

Michail Arnold, George Arnold, Jonas R. Arnold, Absolam Foshee, and Polly Foshee to Matthias Flack. Power of Attorney acknowledged by Absolam and Polly Foshee; certified.

George Riggle, Baldwin H. Fine, Bruten Peters, Eli Ferguson, and John Riggle appointed Jury of View to lay off and mark a road from Piney Bridge to the top of the mountain where the Walton Ferry Road starts down the mountain.

Betsey S. Wilson appointed administratrix on estate of William C. Wilson, dec'd; bond with James Wilson, John Farmer, and Abijah Boggess, her securities, for $4000.

(p. 499) The last Will and Testament of Isaac Lewis, dec'd, was produced and proven in part by Joseph McCorkle, one of the subscribing witnesses; ordered that said will lay over for further probate.

Betsey S. Wilson, Admrx. returned an inventory of the estate of William C. Wilson, dec'd.

Allen Kennedy allowed $6.50 for furnishing Sheriff and Jury with supper and breakfast on the trial of State against Nathaniel W. Wilson.

Robert H. Jordan appointed a Constable in Captain Sharp's Company; bond with Abijah Boggess and John Miller, his securities.

(p. 500) Abijah Boggess appointed a Constable in Captain Keetons Company; bond with John Miller and John H. Beck, his securities.

John Igou appointed a Constable in Captain Blevins' Company; bond with Robert Cooley and Joseph McCorkle, his securities.

Allen Kennedy allowed $10.00 for furnishing a Jury on the trial of N.S. Cole with dinner, supper, room and breakfast.

John Parker allowed $15.00 for keeping N.S. Cole Cin Jail].

(p. 501) Court appointed the following Justices to take the lists of Taxables:

Crispien E. Shelton	in Captain Howard's Company
John McClure	in Captain Hill's Company
James A. Darwin	in Captain Mitchell's Company
James Swan	in Captain Rowden's Company
Jesse Thompson	in Captain Swan's Company
Samuel Gamble	in Captain Roark's Company
Daniel M. Stockton	in Captain Kimbrel's Company
Josiah Fike	in Captain Baker's Company
Thomas Cox	in Captain Blevins' Company
Hail Butram	in Captain Keeton's Company

Robert Cooley   in Captain Fitzgerrald's Company
Peach Taylor   in Captain Smith's Company
Stephen Winton   in Captain Sharp's Company

Jurors appointed for next session of this Court:

William Cumpton	Alexander Coulter	Joseph Thompson	Eli Ferguson
Ezekiel Bates	Benjamin McKenzie	Robert Robertson	Thomas Whitmore
Elijah Wyatt	Benjamin Putman	John Gray	Benjamin F. Jones
John Able	Levi H. Knight	Aden Humberd	Tavener Masoner
Abraham Hughes	Elisha Parker	Pulaski Poe	James Taylor
James Blevins	Hugh Blevins	George Frazier	Hazard Bean
	Allison Howard	John Whaley	

Anson Dearmon, a Constable to attend Court.

Jurors appointed for next Term of Circuit Court:

James Coulter	Jackson Howerton	Jacob Beck	Moses Thompson
Jesse Roddy	John Roddy	John Chatton	John Hill
(p. 502)	John Walker	Micajah Clack	John Randles
Elijah Blythe	Patrick Martin	Benjamin Jones Sr.	Robert Philips
Isaah R. Brown	James Montgomery	John Chattin	Archabald Fitzgerral
George Keenum	William Ingle	Bryant McDonald	Jesse Tyson
	Roger Reese Jr.	James Lauderdale	

Samuel Craig, a Constable to attend Court.

Samuel Roberts & Thomas McCallie VS William M. Rogers (No. 1797). Defendant says he cannot gainsay the plaintiffs demand for $108.05 and damages for detention of said debt. Plaintiffs to recover debt and costs.

Henry Henry VS Abraham Miller (No. 1798). Defendant confesses judgment for $9.00 and all costs.

Samuel Roberts & Thomas McCallie VS Benjamin McKenzie (No. 1799). Defendant says he cannot gainsay the plaintiffs demand for $81.74 debt and damages. Plaintiffs to recover debt and costs.

(p. 503) Robert H. Jordan, Gideon Ragland, Levi Knight, Stephen Winton, and Abijah Boggess appointed a Jury of View instanter to view and lay off a road leading from Robert Farris' to Kingston so as to change that part passing through the lands of Elisha Sharp so as to leave the old road at the creek thence south on the line of said Sharp about 100 yards thence the nearest and best way into the old road and make report to the present term.

Report of above Jury of View; the road to be established upon condition that said Sharp put the new road in as good order as the old road: "to leave the old road at the creek and run about 100 yards with E. Sharps south line and then about 100 yards further the nearest and best way to intersect the old road."

(p. 504) Report of Commissioners (Thomas Price, James Lillard, Leonard Brooks, Absolem Coleman, and Miles Vernon) appointed to divide the real estate that Samuel Tillery died possessed of between his four sons according to the last Will and Testament of said Samuel Tillery. Jury proceeded on the morning of 8th August 1828 to lay off and divide said real estate taking into view the (p. 505) quantity and quality so as the value may as nearly as possible be equal as follows: Lot No. 1— Beginning at the Southwest corner joining Robert Elder and Miles Vernons land, running east with the section line 42 poles to a stake, then north parallel with the section line 290 poles to Leonard Brooks land, then west 42 poles, then south 130 poles, west 97 poles, South 42 East 160 poles to a post oak tree, then with the section line south to the beginning, containing 115½ acres, which by lottery fell to Samuel Tillery. Lot No. 2— Beginning on Robert Elders line at the corner of Lot No. 1 and running east with said Elders land 40 poles, then north 290 poles to Leonard Brooks land, then west 40 poles, then with the line of Lot No. 1 290 poles to the beginning, containing 72½ acres, which lot fell to Coffield Tillery.

Lot No. 3— Adjoining the last mentioned lot on the east, having the same compliment of acres, by lottery fell to Thomas Tillery who is a minor.

Lot No. 4— Lying on east side of Lot No. 3 and containing 68 acres 3 roods and 20 poles is 38 poles wide and runs parallel to and adjoining Lot No. 3 and the land of Leonard Brooks; by lottery fell to Hugh Tillery.

Ordered to be recorded. Plat to right was reduced one half.

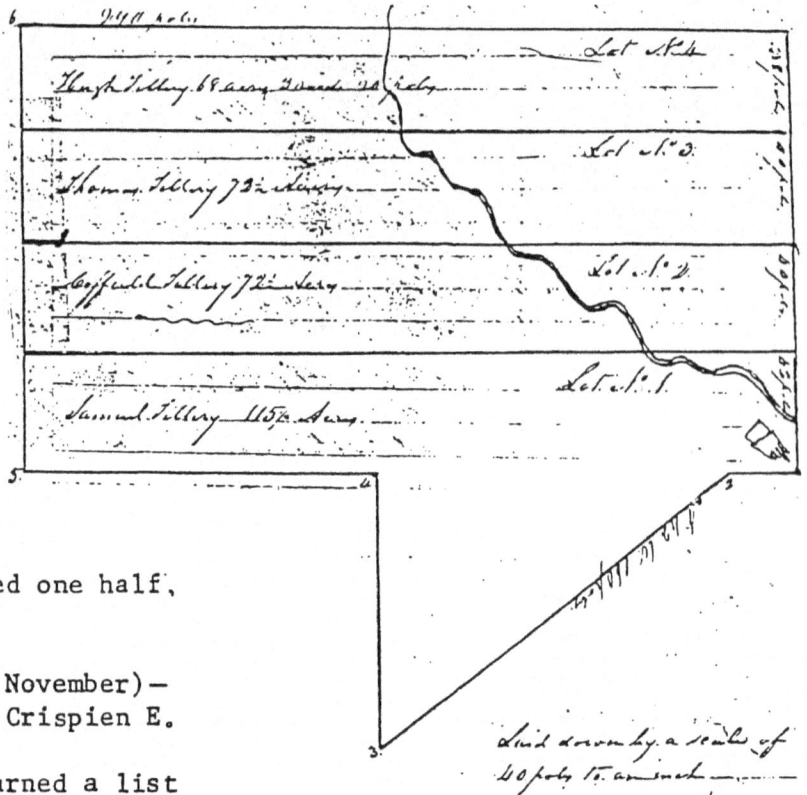

(p. 506) Justices on bench (4th November)— Josiah Fike, James McDonald, and Crispien E. Shelton.

John Lea, Sheriff, returned a list of jurors summoned to appear at this Session of Court (see list on page 140), out of whom the following were elected a Grand Jury: Matthew English, John Rawlings, Rector Preston, John Able, John Rogers, James Woodward, John Gray, Morris Putman, Meredith Cox, Benjamin F. Jones, Reuben Jackson, Jeremiah Howerton, and Thomas Majors. Matthew English appointed foreman and William B. Lauderdale a Constable to attend Jury.

There remained of the original pannel who answered to their names: Anderson Fitzgerral and Cornelious Myors.

For reasons appearing to the satisfaction of the Court, James McCanse, Caswell Johnson, Matthew Allen, and James Nail belonging to the original pannel are released from further attendance as Jurors at the present term.

(p. 507) Edmund Bean and Jeremiah Barrett, Jurors summoned on the original Venira being Solemnly called came not. Ordered that for their contempt they forfeit to the State the sum of $5.00 unless they shew good cause to the contrary at the next Sessions of this Court.

James Kelly VS Robert Bell. Commission is awarded the plaintiff to take the deposition of Preston W. Davis which is to be read as evidence; continued by consent until next term of this Court.

Thomas Henry for use of Thomas McCallie VS James Kelly & Palatiah Chilton (No. 1800). Came the parties by their attornies and a jury (Cornelius Myors, George W. Mayo, Anderson Fitzgerrald, John Miller, Alexander Galbreath, Joshua Tindle, Brinkley Hornsby, Alexander Coulter, William Locke, William Lewis, Baldwin H. Fine, and Allison Howard) which says the defendant has not paid the sum of $100 debt in the declaration nor any part of it. Plaintiffs damage assessed at $4.43 3/4; he is to recover debt, damages, and costs.

Miller Francis to William S. Leuty. Deed of Conveyance for 300 acres; proven by John Locke and Carson Caldwell; certified for registration.

(p. 508) William S. Leuty VS John Lea (No. 1801). Came the parties by their attornies and a jury (Cornelius Myors, Anderson Fitzgerrald, George W. Mayo, Brinkley Hornsby, Joshua Tindle, William Locke, William Lewis, Allison Howard, George Davis, James Stewart, John A. Foshee, and Alexander Coulter) which says the defendant has paid the debt in the declaration except the sum of $373.25; they access the plaintiffs damage to $16.30; also to recover costs.

Richard & Blackstone Waterhouse VS Edward Stewart (No. 1802). Writ of Inquiry. Came the parties by their attornies and a jury (same as above) which assesses the plaintiffs damages to 6½¢; also to recover costs.

Samuel Roberts & Thomas McCallie VS Jesse Atwood (No. 1303). Writ of Inquiry. Came the plaintiffs by their attorney and a jury (James Stewart, John A. Foshee, George Davis, Alexander Coulter, Allison Howard, William Lewis, William Locke, Joshua Tindle, Brinkley Hornsby, George W. Mayo, Cornelius Myors, and Anderson Fitzgerrald) which assesses the plaintiffs damages to $71.74; also to recover costs.

(p. 509) Abner Stults VS Gross Scrugs & Lewis Curton (No. 1804). Appeal. Came the plaintiff by attorney; also Gross Scruggs and John A. Foshee who confessed judgment for $15.75 debt. Plaintiff to recover against Scrugs and Foshee the debt and costs.

John Miller VS Baldwin H. Fine (No. 1805). Covenant. Came the parties by their attornies and a jury (same as above) which says the defendant did not deliver a lot of corn in accord and satisfaction of the said Covenant; they assess the plaintiffs damage to the sum of $121.87½. Upon solemn argument by council, Court ordered that the plaintiffs demurrer to the defendants first plea be sustained. Plaintiff to recover the damages and costs.

Grand Jury returned the following Bills of Indictment: State against John Miller for an assault and battery; State against James Stewart and John Stewart for an assault and battery; State against Edward Benum for as assault and battery.

(p. 510) Elizabeth Lewis appointed Administratrix on estate of Isaac Lewis, dec'd; bond with Meredith Cox and Samuel Craig, her securities, for $600.

James Swan, Admr. on estate of William Randolph, returned an additional inventory and an account of the sale of said estate.

Samuel Frazier produced his Licence as a practicing attorney at law.

Elias Majors VS Andrew Evans, Admr. of William Floyd, dec'd. On motion of Andrew Evans by his attorney to quash a Writ of Ca Sa heretofore issued, it is ordered that the same be quashed.

(p. 511) Justices on bench (5th November) – Crispien E. Shelton, James McDonald, and Josiah Fike.

State VS Edward Templeton (No. 1806). Disturbing Public Worship. Came James P. Lowry, Attorney General, and the defendant who says he is not guilty. The jury (Matthew English, John Rawlings, Rector Preston, John Able, John Rogers, James Woodward, John Gray, Morris Putman, Meredith Cox, Benjamin F. Jones, Reuben Jackson, and Jeremiah Howerton) finds the defendant guilty as charged; fined $1.00 and costs. From which verdict and judgment the defendant prays an appeal to the next Circuit Court; granted.

State VS Edward Bynum (No. 1807). Assault and Battery. Came the Attorney General and the defendant who says he is not guilty. The jury (Cornelious Myors, Anderson Fitzgerrald, Jefferson B. Love, Samuel M. Love, John Parker, Robert Small, Thomas Henry, John Dearmon, Benjamin F. Locke, William Moore, John Miller, and Isaac Mahan) finds the defendant not guilty; County to pay costs.

(p. 512) State VS John Miller (No. 1808). Assault and Battery. Came the Attorney General and the defendant who says he cannot gainsay the charges; fined $1.00 and costs.

State VS James & John Stewart (No. 1809 & 1810). Came Attorney General and the defendants who say they are not guilty as charged (assault and battery). The jury (William Runyon, Henry Henry, Joshua Tindle, Jesse Reece, William Ferguson, George Davis, John H. Beck, Beriah Frazier, Abraham Spurgeon, Caswell Johnson, Benjamin F. Locke, and Gilbert Kennedy) says the defendant John Stewart is not guilty and that the defendant James Stewart is guilty. John Stewart released; James Stewart fined $1.00 and costs; County to pay costs of John Stewart.

State VS George Davis (No. 1811). Came Attorney General and defendant in proper person. The witnesses in behalf of the State failing to appear, the defendant is discharged; County to pay costs.

(p. 513) Stephen Winton, John Baker, and Robert Farris appointed Commissioners to lay off a years maintainance for Betsy S. Wilson and children, widow of William C. Wilson, dec'd.

Grand Jury returned a Bill of Indictment, State against Berryman Kimbrel and John A. Foshee for an affray.

The Court nor Attorney General having no further business for the Grand Jury they are discharged from further attendance at this Term.

Jacob L. Wassum VS John Miller (No. 1812). Appeal. Came the plaintiff by his attorney and the defendant not appearing and his appeal not being further prosecuted; on motion of plaintiff, the appeal is dismissed; further considered that the judgment of the Justice in this cause be affirmed. Plaintiff to recover of defendant and his securities, Joseph Garrison and Lewis R. Collins, the sum of $8.04 and the further sum of 7¢ interest, plus costs.

Thomas Cate VS Joseph McDaniel & James Kelly. Petition of defendants praying Writs of Certiorari and Supercedeas is granted on said defendants giving bond and security.

(p. 514) Jesse Poe, Admr. of William Lewis VS William Lewis Sr., Samuel Craig, and Thomas Huddleston (No. 1813). Came the defendants by their attorney and the plaintiff not appearing and his motion not being further prosecuted, it is considered by the Court that the said plaintiff be Non suited. Defendants are released and to recover costs from plaintiff.

Ordered that the forfeiture heretofore entered against Edmund Bean and Jeremiah Barret for failing to attend this term as jurors be remitted.

Court adjourned till Court in Course.

#

INDEX

ABLE, Cain 2,11,21,38,42,43,46,56,57, 59,63,104,108,110,122,125,147; James J. 103; Jeremiah 62; John 6,11,21,28, 34,38,42,43,53,59,61,87,115,116,137, 140,149,150,151; William S. 103
ACRE, John 57; Polly 4; Washington 4
ACRED, John 46
ACTHERTON, Geo. 129
AINSWORTH, William 53
AIRHART, Henry 1,11,25,27,32,36,53,54, 66,95; James 102,124
ALDRIDGE, Henry 11,14
ALEXANDER, John 27,53,69,95; William 6, 18,21,57,95,108
ALLEN, Benjamin 63,71,72,73,81; Matthew 18,22,24,34,100,106,110,111,113,140, 148,150; William 84
ANDERSON, Thomas 14,55,63,97,107,134; Wm 18,129; William E. 94
ANGLAND, Celia 60,67; John 58,60,61,67
APPLEGATE, Samuel 6,11,25,34,112,120, 135
ARCHEY, William 143
ARINGTON/ARRINGTON, Abel 28; John 28, 37,38,113
ARMSTRONG, Barefoot 18,51,67,80,81,83, 86,92,115,116,147; Benjamin 134; D.D./ Daniel D. 18,23,43,48,81,85,86,90,95, 100,102,108,110,113,144; Elihu D. 13, 35,40
ARNOLD, George 148; Jonas R. 148; Michail 148
ARTHUR, Thomas 71
ASHLIN, Robert W. 116; Sarah Ann 116
ATCHLEY, Joseph 64; Joshua 32,41,46,56, 88,98,99,130; Moses 64; Therse 64; Thomas 42,46,62,140
ATWOOD, Jesse 96,101,102,108,143,145,151
AUSTIN, William 10
AXHLY, Joseph 64
AYRES, David B. 122
BABB, Joseph 25
BAILEY, James 13,106,108,112,113,120, 141; John 1,7,9,18,19,34,49,62,107
BAKER, Isaac 13,17,18,27,29,34,38,39, 40,41,42,49,63,69,70,102,107,113,119, 126; John 28,41,153; Samuel 40,49, 113,136; William 100,119,134,147
BALDWIN, William 42,45,89
BALL, John 30,82
BARCLAY/BARKLEY, David 30; Elihu 39,67, 73,82; Elihu S. 97,98

BARNES, Absolom 35,61,67,84,85; Silas F. 108,115,117,120,126
BARNETT/BARNET, George 113,122; John 12,18,40,70,74,80,82,83,91,118,120, 122; Margaret 120; P. 18; Peggy 124; William 120,124
BARNS, Catharine 53,78
BARR, Joseph 63; William McCamey 63
BARRETT, George 139; Jeremiah 139,140, 150,152
BARTON, Hugh 142; Roger 39
BATES, Ezekiel 96,99,101,103,104,105, 106,107,108,112,121,123,149
BEAN, Edmund 33,60,71,72,85,93,96,105, 110,116,117,125,133,134,136,137,138, 140,144,145,150,152; Hazard 102,149
BEARD, Robert 6,11,14,30,52,129
BEATY/BEATTY, Hugh 128; Martin 105
BECK, Henry 55,90,125; James 107; Jacob 2,10,11,14,16,46,55,57,58,61, 62,107,108,115,120,128,149; John H. 60,69,78,148,152
BEERMAN, William 14,63
BELL, John 84,89; Robert 6,18,45,50, 57,62,71,89,93,96,98,101,102,107,119, 132,138,145,150; Thomas 22,106,140, 141,142
BENNETT/BENNIT, George 22; John 12,17, 19,40,96,99,113; Kiah 113; William 59
BENSON, Benjamin 16,18,22,23,42; Isaac 16,18,29,57; John 1,2,20,56,85,87, 121; Matthias 45; Spencer 23,42,59, 69,95
BERRY, James 1,3,5,7,14,18,22,24,25, 26,39,40,43,44,45,59,64,69,74,76,78, 85,91,96,99,102,103,106,107,110,117, 118,121,123,124,138,139,147
BESHEER/BEERSHEARS/BESHARS, Samuel 56, 62,77,100,112
BETOR, Henry 103
BINNICH, S. 78
BINYON, Isaac 119
BIRD, Joseph 129
BIRDWELL, George 21
BISHOP, Joseph 127
BLACKBURN, Mary 42; Thomas 42
BLACKWELL, James 40,41,49,72,96,99,113; Nathan 72; Nathaniel 113
BLACKWOOD, William 20,63,70,71,72
BLAKELY/BLACKLEY, James 1,36
BLANKENSHIP, Thomas 87,92,93,99
BLEVINS, Allen 88,122,123; D./David 18,

156

CUNNINGHAM, Hugh 1; Samuel 14
CURTON, Lewis 151
DALE, James 120
DANIEL/DANNEL, James 30,37,38,104,110,
112; Jamima 130; John 113; Peter 11,
25,26,27,31,42,45,70,80,82,83,85,90,
91,92,93,100,112,134,140,148; Plummer
113,132
DANRIMPLE, Allen 147
DARTER, John 129
DARWIN, James 13,45,52; James A. 9,10,
19,21,23,25,31,33,34,39,44,46,54,61,
68,69,70,71,74,75,76,83,87,89,97,98,
99,100,101,106,109,112,114,117,119,
121,122,123,126,135,136,139,142,144,
146,148; William 8
DAVID, A./Azariah 1,7,19,25,31,36,42,
46,50,54,57,60,61,71,74,75,76,83,85,
87,95,98,99,101,102,105,109,111,115,
119,121,124,136,139,141,146; Mary 34,
40,46,69,95,96,102; Owin 88
DAVIDSON, George 15
DAVIS, Abraham 63,71,72,96,99; Edward
130; George 34,151,152; Henry 108,132;
John 96,99,106,113,120,122,130,141;
Miles B. 18,106,108,115; Preston W.
145,150; Robert H. 14; Samuel G. 113;
William 106
DAY, David 1,20,70,81,83,95,96,98;
Jesse 16,63,71,72,75,82,84,86; John
39,52,53,56,64,65,68,70,71,91,95,96,
106,117,121,126,131,132,133,136;
William 56,102
DEALE, William 59
DEAN, Archibald 9,10
DEARING/DAREING/DERING, Anson/Ansalom/
Anselin L. 84,88,136
DEARMON, Anson 42,54,69,71,73,75,80,85,
86,90,93,94,96,98,102,108,112,115,
119,121,123,125,127,136,140,143; John
133,151
DEFRIESE, Audley P. 19,27,37,45,89,96,
98; Huram A. 57,99
DELLORSLER(?), John 129
DENTON, Jonathan 128
DERENS, John H. 129
DEWITT, Washington J. 80
DICKSON, Thomas 118
DODD, John C. 81
DONELSON, Stokly 79
DOUGLAS/DUGLAS, William H. 14,16,43,52,
55,66
DOVER, John 15
DOWEL, Reuben 62

DRENNON, Robert 11
DUDLEY, John 61,72,94
DUNCAN/DUNKIN, Jeremiah 20,26,32,39,65;
Mary 32
DUNLAP, John 9,80; William C. 34,38,43,
58,90,110,112,122
DUNN, Austin 129; Austin D. 129; Austin
L. 79; Elizabeth 21; James 22,55;
John 64
DYER, Spillsbe/Spills B. 10,33,36,49,
60,69,108,142,144
EASTLAND, Thomas B. 129
EAVES, Thomas 20,23,29,52,84,108,115,
134,136
EDWARDS, Fletcher 138,143; Walter 13,18,
22,24,56,65,106,113,129,140
ELDER, Robert 2,45,55,85,89,90,106,132,
146,147,149
ENGLAND, William 113,122
ENGLISH/INGLISH, Matthew 56,77,85,108,
136,140,142,150,151
ENMANS, John 125
ERWIN, Benjamin 13,24,33
ESSEREY, — 88
EVANS/EVENS, Andrew 5,16,23,26,27,29,46,
59,71,80,81,86,90,91,110,114,151; Eli-
jah 2,21,34,45,135; Evan 7,16,17,19,
45,68,69,74; Jonathan 15; Joseph 27
FARMER, Aquilla 128; John 46,49,62,67,
148; Thomas 117; William 89
FARRIS/FERRIS, John 6,11,13,17,152
FEATHERSTONE, William 81
FERGUSON, Abigale 3,8,9,36,55,68; Alexander 63,80,105,109; Aron 28,37,38,107,
108; Betsy 9; Eli 8,9,10,40,43,60,69,
86,96,108,148,149; Elias 69,84,107;
James 3,10,30,34,42,43,44; John 3,9,
10,17,18,22,55,56,62,105,107,109; John
C. 125,136; John T. 8; Levi 90; Margaret 91; Martin 36,77,89,98,114,133,
146; Martin F. 8,10; Moses 3,18,20,
100,108,110,111; Robert 3,8,9,10,25,
28,30,36,37,38,45,55,68,77; Samuel
11,18,22,62,88,107,120; Samuel B. 33;
William 9,55,62,88,91,96,137,138,139,
152
FERRELL, John 123,127,131; Priscilla
123,131
FIKE, Josiah 63,79,99,101,105,106,108,
112,115,116,119,121,123,126,131,132,
133,134,136,138,139,142,143,144,145,
146,148,150,151
FINE, Baldwin H. 148,150,151; Boldin 69;
Bolin 39; Isaac 18; Jonathan 1,2,7,18,

158

John 42; Kitty 42; Robert C. 12,17,80;
  William 82; William B. 120
GORMAN, John 95
GORON, William B. 27
GOSSAGE, John 12,13,17,23; William 23
GOTHARD, George 3,12,14,18,55; James
  84,88
GOUGH, Elisha 9; James 14
GRAY, Edward 6,42,57,77,108; John 2,25,
  96,101,104,105,140,149,150,151; Sam-
  uel 59; William 39,45,68,100,110
GREEN, Joshua 28,34,37,38,42,44,136;
  Joshua S. 140; Phoebe 25
GREENFIELD, William 87,100
GREENWAY, George 18; Richard 130
GREENWOOD, John 41
GREER, David 84; James C. 110,117
GRIFFEN, Aron 44; John 44; Thomas 124,
  135
GRIFFET/GRIFFETT, Henry 38; Levi 119,
  142
GRIGSBY, James 7; Samuel 22,30,37,38
GROSS, Jacob 105
GRUBS, Ambler 25
GULLION, William 119
GWIN/GUINN, Almond 114; Bartholomew 3,
  46,57,58,61,62; D. 51; Susannah 3,4;
  William 21,33,35,36,38,48,49,60,30,
  91,93
HACKETT, John 79; Samuel 27,34,63,76;
  Samuel R. 34,38,42,43,44,71,72,73,96,
  109,121,126,139,147; William P. 91
HACKNEY, Aron 5; Hugh 5,6
HACKWORTH, Henry 1,46,57,130; John 45,
  130
HAGAN/HAGEN, Robert 56,95,100
HAINES, Irey 88; John 119,122,137
HALE/HAIL, Abednego 110,131,134; George
  137; William 38,88
HALL, John 56,65; Roswell 15,16
HAMILTON/HAMELTON, Milton 102,135; Tho-
  mas 5,35,36,38,60,73,74,102,106,135
HAMON/HAMEN, William 28,113
HANCOCK, William 137
HANKINS, Wright 106
HANLY, James D. 18
HANNAH, Avara/Avary 41,46,56,62,90,136;
  David 130; Joshua 52
HARDIN/HARDEN, Francis 11,14; Joseph
  63; Mark 63,99,103; Solomon 14
HARMON, Philip 69,75,79; William 78,102
HARP, Thomas 25,70,73,84,88,146; Thomas
  M. 69
HARPER, Thomas 1
HARREL/HARRAL/HARRALD, John 60,61,67,82,
  114; Samuel 61,67,82; William 61,67,82

HARRIS, Abijah 10,16,75,77,86
HARWOOD, Jesse 117; John 110; J./Joseph
  18,31,35,40,65,67,95,137; Malikiah
  35,117; Nathan 14; Nathaniel 130; Randolph 109,116,117,120; Zachariah 1,22,
  38,45
HASLERIG, Conly/Condley F. 114,117,118,
  120,125; Mrs. 141; Richard 23,29,46,
  50,59,93,102,106,117,118; Thomas J.
  117,118,120,125
HATCHCOCK, Linton 113
HAVENS, Charles 18
HAWS, Thomas 135,147
HAYNES, Aron 94,110,111; James 94,110,
  111; James P. 87; Jeremiah 6
HELM/HELMS, Jacob 46,130; Jesse 130;
  John 16; William 41
HENDERSON, Allen 14; Daniel 47; David
  71,104; John 13,14,51,55,109,116; John
  H. 7,42,75,96,100,110,116; Lilburn L.
  105; Rebecca 116; William T. 110
HENIGER/HENNEGER, Henry 50,51; Hiram 51;
  Jacob 51; John 51,71
HENRY, George 61,66,67,93,118; Henry 15,
  43,55,70,74,83,117,126,144,149,152;
  James 11,14,76; John 79; Thomas 6,11,
  28,66,112,132,139,144,150,151
HICKLAN/HICKLIN, Barnett 129; Barney
  84,88
HICKMON, — 107
HIDE, Edward 117
HILBURN/HILBOURN, Allen 4,5,14; John 5,
  14
HILL, David 49,63; James 49,63; John 11,
  18,22,23,24,63,71,72,73,85,90,91,92,
  93,108,149; Jonathan 10; Joshua 39,41,
  45,75,87,144; Melvina 49,63; Rebecca
  49,63; William 6,10,11,16,38,43,49,52,
  61,63,72,83,86,91,92,96,101,103,105,
  108,113,115,117,118,119,121,122,125,
  127,131,133,142,143,144,145
HINES, John 118; Matthias 108
HOLLAND, Allan 2,100,124; Daniel 61,100,
  110,111; Isaac 16; John 19,34,58,122,
  123; Orlando 53,60; Samuel 1,2,9,16,54
HOLLOWAY, Bremillion 89,124; Samuel 96,
  108,115,117
HOLT, Irby 29
HOMES, Jno 78
HOOD, John B. 43,61; Joseph C.S. 90; Ro-
  bert 2,64
HOOKE, John A. 101; John H. 145
HOOPHEY, John 22
HOPE, John 17
HOPKINS, Thomas 29,54,58
HORNSBY, Brinkley 63,71,72,73,81,82,107,

108,150,151; William 22,28,85
HOSKINS, Samuel 68,80,83
HOUNSHELL, David 66,72,96,99,101
HOUP, Jane 54
HOUPT, Volentine 113,122,132,138,144
HOUSTON, Samuel 119
HOWARD, Abraham 12,16,18,20,21,33,45,
  49,54,57,63,82,86,88,95,100,102,103,
  111,117,119,133,145; Allison 20,41,
  50,53,89,95,98,100,103,104,110,111,
  113,117,119,123,127,132,133,134,137,
  138,139,142,143,145,147,149,150,151;
  John 60,82,86,102; Malachia 99; Mantion 20,25,69,70,85,90,95,100; Mariah 95,100; Samuel 1,10,16,28,34,
  36,42,43,44,54,55,95,102,113,138,142,
  143; William 2,9,18,21,46,56,57,60,
  69,95,100,102,103,104,111,112,113,
  116,117,119,123,133,134,135,136,137,
  138,139,145
HOWEL/HOWELL, John 27,114; Thomas 57;
  William 21
HOWERTON, Edmund 1,42,45,63,71,72,85,
  90,92,93,124,126,133; Grief 45,55,
  96,124; Jackson 6,34,42,43,44,45,49,
  84,85,126,143,144,149; Jeremiah 69,
  70,88,96,100,104,140,150,151; Micajah 9,10,34,41,42,45,50,85,89,123,
  125,136,137,145
HOWSER/HOUSER, James 45,104,110,112;
  Josiah 25,84,88
HUBBART/HUBBERT, Matthew 3,8,9,10,27,
  28,30,32,33,36,55,56,62,67,68,69,71,
  99,100,101,106,108,111,112,117,119,
  121,123,139,142,144
HUDLESTON, Thomas 12,152
HUDSON/HUTSON, Charles 116; David 14,
  112; David S. 2,140; John 7,42,77,86,
  103,110,115,116,129; John B. 125
HUFF, John 63,78; William 3
HUFFMAN, William 109
HUGHES/HUGHS, Abraham 89,108,113,115,
  125,136,138,139,143,149; Caswell 25,
  28,122; John 6,11,34,45,129; Thomas
  11,14; William 138,143
HUMBERD/HUMBART, Aden 149; Samuel 41;
  William 7,63,71,72
HUMPHREY/HUMPHREYS, John 17; Ustus 87
HUNTER, Andrew 29,43; J. 78; Thomas 22,
  40,85,89,95,98,115,141
HURST, Elijah 130
HURT, John 78,129,146; Joseph 78,146
IGO/IGOU, John 41,55,87,96,120,148;
  Samuel 71,106,107,108,115,147
INGLE, William 22,41,49,50,89,98,114,
  143,144,149

IREDALE, William 14
ISH, Alexander 123
ISHAM, James 78
JACK, Jeremiah 147; John 1,2,53,54,95,
  102,108,113,115,147; Thomas 12
JACKSON, Amelia 107; Asa 100,121; John
  104; Reuben/Reubin 6,11,28,37,38,62,
  95,140,150,151; Semion 34,42,145;
  Simeon 43,44,137,138,139,142; William
  142; Zaph 137,138,139; Zoaf 55
JACOBS, James 20,29,46,55,75; Solomon
  D. 142
JAMES, Thomas 6,57; William 95,119,
  121,134
JENKINS, William 85,136
JENNINGS, John 16
JERNAGIN, Spencer 57
JETT, John 128
JEWELL, William 28,37,38
JOHNS, David 136,143; Henry 108,115,
  117,142; Thomas 107,123,132; William
  6,11,13,20,41,63,89,98
JOHNSTON/JOHNSON, Ann 55; Asahel 33,55,
  95,100,102,113,115,127,139,142,143;
  Asiel 79; Benjamin 63,113; Caswell
  79,107,115,139,140,147,150,152; Collier 38,63; Columbus 34,38,40; James
  55,126; John 3; Lucinda 55,126; Mark
  96,100,109,133,138,139; Polly 34,38,
  40; Samuel 93,110,112,117,119; Sarah
  143; William 3,8,9,10,13,16,22,33,34,
  39,43,47,50,55,62,68,71,74,76,80,82,
  84,88,90,97,98,102,104,106,108,109,
  111,112,113,114,119,120,123,124,126,
  131,139,140,142,143,147
JONES, Anderson 100; Benjamin 6,22,25,
  42,96,100,149; Benjamin F. 6,39,63,
  68,71,72,73,95,123,140,149,150,151;
  Elizabeth C. 118; Franklin 120;
  Isaac 87,89,91,96,118,120,121; John
  10,16,20,25,29,33,34; John W. 139;
  Martha M. 118; Richard 6,11; Rowland
  J. 118; Sebourn 29,54; William 100;
  William G. 118
JORDON, Robert H. 41,96,144,148,149
KEENUM, George 147,149
KEETON/KEATON, Benton 146; James 125,
  146; William 132
KELLY/KELLEY, Charles 142; James 6,18,
  23,24,28,37,38,52,66,68,70,72,73,85,
  91,92,93,94,104,108,110,115,116,117,
  122,125,127,131,136,137,138,139,142,
  144,145,150,152; John 25,45,63,71,72;
  Joshua 28,46,52,57,112,120; Lewis
  147; Michael 124; Robt 22; Stephen
  24,36,37; Thomas 4,6,25,60,88,92,103,

85,112,123,138; Joseph 3,18,28,31,42,
47,70,71,75,76,83,89,96,97,106,108,
114,126,135,136,140,142,143; Pleasant
101,108,110,111,115,117,118; Robert
14,41,43,50,52,85,90,95,109,119; Samuel M. 151; William 89,91,107,140,142
LOWRY/LOWREY/LOWRIE, James Piper 119,
122,123,131,138,143,144,147,151; Joel
127,128; John 106; William 29,61,71,
80,82,106,112,136,144
LOYCE, Cameral 32
LUCUS, Thomas 46,55,62,147
LUSK, Joseph 107,121,127,147
LYON, William 57
McARTHUR, William 107
McCALL, Alexander 34,52,56,61,65,66;
Alexander H. 113; Joseph 16,20,29,45,
61,113
McCALLIE, Archabald 119,133; James 91;
Thomas 89,90,93,118,119,122,132,133,
135,137,138,139,144,145,149,150,151
McCAMPBELL, James 57,124
McCANDLESS/McCANLESS, John 31,47,129;
Richard 11,34; Richard A. 6,11,43,96
McCANSE, James 3,22,28,39,41,46,50,53,
75,86,100,108,109,110,111,136,140,
141,150
McCARROLL, James 137; John 132,142,143,
144,145
McCARRY/McCRARY/McCRORY, Joal 14,21,36
McCARTER, Thomas 28
McCARTY, —— 98; Benjamin 34,46,57,63,
70; John L. 44,86,115,122; Thomas 13,
20,34,37,63,70; William 34,46,57,63,
70
McCLANAHAN/McCLENAHAN, —— 126; Elenor
17; John 17,49,67,83,86,105,113,115,
116,119,122,133,134,136; Mason 105
McCLENDON/McCLENDAN, John 17; William
128
McCLUNG, Charles 21,25,31,77,129
McCLURE, John 25,28,31,34,39,41,44,46,
49,61,68,71,72,74,76,80,81,83,85,87,
95,97,99,101,105,103,112,115,116,118,
119,121,134,136,139,142,146,148; Margaret 28; Robert 113,120,136; Sashwell 38,52,60
McCONDLEY, John 120
McCORD, Joseph 78
McCORKLE, Joseph 88,99,101,103,104,105,
108,112,119,121,134,146,148
McCORMACK/McCORMICK, John 84,88; William 38,44,52,53,54,70
McCOY, James 77
McCRACAN, Robert 127,142,143

McCULLY, —— 113
McDANIEL, Charles 125,134,136,137;
James 25,79,132; John 25,68,106; Joseph 3,12,13,18,36,37,56,61,65,66,
70,75,110,123,131,132,134,152; Samuel 1,2,17,18,19,25,45,46,56,63,71,
73,80,82,83,84,88,96,106,107
McDONAL/McDONEL, James 3; S. 79
McDONALD, Bryan 56,65,75,86,103; Bryant
96,101,104,105,149; Charles 100,110,
125; James 5,7,13,18,19,25,31,44,46,
63,70,71,72,74,76,83,88,90,91,92,93,
101,105,107,119,121,123,126,131,132,
133,136,138,142,146,150,151; William
17,28,41,50,56,65,66,67,121,126,131
McDONNAH/McDONNOUGH/McDONNAH, John 43,
116,121,122,137
McDOWELL, Jane 107
McFARLAND, Charles 17
McFALLS, Jesse 147; Richard 147
McGEE, David 14; Riley 34
McGHEE, —— 98; George 23; John 44,86,
115,122; Matthew 86; Matthew W. 44,
115,122
McGILL, Mary 51
McHENRY, William 95
McINTOSH, John 25
McKEDY, Thomas 3,108
McKEEL, Hannah 124,127; James 11; Mrs.
89
McKENZIE/McKINZEY/McKINSEY, Benjamin
11,31,72,77,78,84,88,149; Reuben 88
McKINDRE, Benjamin 79
McKINLEY, John 106
McMILLEN, David 7
McNUTT, Thomas 86,89,91,98,104,105,116,
117,119,120,144
McPHERSON, Barton 133; Daniel 58; Richard 139
MADDEN, John 53,64,91
MAHAFFE, Hiram 56
MAHAN, David 78,84,88,123; Isaac 20,29,
56,63,70,77,80,85,106,107,114,119,
142,151; John 34,89,98,108,111,115,
117,147
MAJORS, Abner 39,80; Absolom 40,41,49,
50,56,101; Elias 26,27,41,50,72,82,
86,90,91,110,151; John 40,49,56,130,
141; Peter 3,10,16,18,22,76,85,90,
129,135,136; Thomas 140,150
MALONEY, Edward 26
MANES/MANAS/MANIS, George 2,53,61,95
MANOR/MANER, George 73,112,113,115,127,
147
MANLEY, Flemming 67,68,72,79; John 105;

164

RECTOR, Charles 87,148; Cumberland 13,
18,34,42,43,44,56,96,100,101,106,112,
120; Landon 11,14,34,75,86
REDMOND/REDMAN, John 6,7,11,12,13,41,
89,96,98,99,113,135,140; Nancy 135,
140
REDWINE, Willie 91,127
REECE/REESE, James 36,63,122,124; Jesse
1,5,10,16,23,63,71,80,81,86,132,152;
Roger 20,26,29,46,57,69,71,77,79,91,
104,108,132,149; Wm H. 78
RENFRO, Joshua 49; William 122
RENNO, Eli 33,53
REYNOLDS, Henry 140; Jacob 11,96
RHEA/RAY, Aaron 109; Archabald 107,109;
Robert 96,101,102,113; Thomas 147
RICE, Alexander 105,115,117,118,119,
122,132; Benjamin 3,15; Elijah 66,74,
80,82,93; Elijah C. 131; George W.
80; Isaac 15,20,58; James 15; John 1,
2,3,5,7,12,13,14,15,19,22,25,27,31,
33,38,39,40,44,46,47,48,51,52,53,54,
58,60,61,68,66,63,71,75,77,80,81,83,
87,92,94,99,103,104,111; Joseph 33,
71,74,80,82,83,102; Mary 15; Moses
15; William 108,121,127
RICHARDS, Curtis 14; Henry 14; Joshua
113; Richard 128
RICHARDSON, A.D. 44; Isaiah 25; John 63
RICHMOND, John 14; John S. 107,120,147;
Jonathan 104,105; Samuel 147
RIDDLE, Jeremiah 16,17,49; Jerry 10;
Samuel 11,63
RIGGLE, George 148; G.W./George W. 2,3,
6,11,14,22,28,32,55,63,69,96,107,119,
125,136,137; John 10,14,16,63,85,96,
101,102,107,148
RIGGS/RIGG, Addison 56,65,84,85,87,92,
107; Townley 13,52,53,78,84,93,99,
104,108,111,123
RIGHT, David 58
RIGNAY/RIGNEY, Jacob 54; Joab 7,13
RIVERS, William 84
ROARK/RORICK, James 125,126,136,142;
Thomas 14
ROBBINS, Edward 8,9
ROBERTS, Joseph 53; Samuel 93,137,138,
139,145,149,151
ROBINSON/ROBERTSON, Calvin 14,41,87,89,
96,100,144; John 1,5,11,18,19,20,23,
26,30,31,32,34,44,51,54,56,60,61,65,
66,68,69,71,74,75,76,83,86,87,90,93,
98,99,101,104,105,109,111,115; Jona-
than F. 81,92; Mark 18; Robert 35,149
ROBISON, Elender C. 130

ROCKHOLD, Alford 92
RODDY, Isaac 99,101,103,104,112,114,
115,119,121,123,126,134,136,142,143,
144,146; James 10,16,89,98,112,120,
147,148; Jesse 6,58,85,112,120,121,
127,149; John 2,7,11,14,28,31,49,55,
70,71,75,100,107,122,136,142,149;
Lyddia 62,140,143
ROGERS/RODGERS, Benjamin 55; James 5,
6,20,28,34,77,107,108,123,126; John
25,45,54,100,109,140,150,151; John
A. 138,144; William 120,123,124,137;
William M. 113,122,149
ROMINES, Jasper 14,32,85,87,89,90,109;
Samuel 43,44,52,66
RONALDS, Elijah 11
ROPER, David 22,56,62,65,108,113,121,
130; Henry 121; John 92,93,99
ROSEYGRANT, Richard 135
ROSS, Frederick A. 79; John 132; Lewis
132
ROULSTON, Elizabeth 128
ROUSEY(?), John 130
ROWDEN/ROWDON/ROWDAN, Asa 6,62,130;
Samuel 119; Samuel E. 91
RUCKER, James 130
RUE, John 38,141
RUNNELS, Ally 113,121; Elijah 14,28,62,
87,88,96,129; H./Henry 13,114,141;
Jacob 34,42,43,44,47,75,90,96,101;
John 33
RUNYON, John 107,141; West 88; William
70,72,73,80,81,82,86,87,91,92,96,99,
104,152
RUSH, Isaac 14,84,104,108,113,135,136;
Lorenzo 135
RUSSELL, George 63; John 71,78; S.R.
109; William 96,97; William B. 107,
123; William S. 69,101,125,126,137
RUTHERFORD, —— 65
RYAN/RYON/RION, Abner 26; Charles 5,11,
14,31,41,57,75,86,96,101,115,116,139
SAMS, Warren 78,100
SANDERS, Julius 29
SAPP, John 3
SAREW(?), William 129
SCOTT, Charles A. 110,116; Edward 110,
116; Elizabeth 116; Martha Ann 116;
Sarah C. 77; Thomas 77
SCRUGS, Gross 151
SCRUCHFIELD, William 109
SEA, William 25
SEARS/SEERS, William 107,135
SEATON, John 102
SEAY, Thomas 141,147

SEBERS, Philip 147

SEGO, Temperance 60

SELLERS, Isaiah 135; Micah 130; Mike 129

SEVIER, Archibald 60,73; George W. 60; Valentine 28,30

SEYBOLT/SEBOLT, Adam 142; David 84,88

SEYMORE, William 1,11,75,99,117

SHAFFER, Jacob 51; John 50,51; Matthias 141; Nancy 51; Sally 51; Thomas 52, 84,120,147

SHALTEEN, Joseph 2

SHARP, Elisha 13,26,49,147,148,149; Jacob 130

SHAVER, —— 115; Battheas 98,99; Matthias 88,89; Sally 7

SHELTON, Crispien E. 1,7,13,15,18,19, 21,22,25,31,38,39,40,41,44,45,46,54, 57,60,61,63,68,72,74,76,87,92,95,99, 101,104,107,112,119,121,122,123,126, 131,132,133,134,136,138,139,140,142, 143,144,145,146,148,150,151; David 16,18,22,25,29,34,39,40,41,42,46,50, 56,57,59,62,63,71,77,78,86,88,89,95, 96,101,102,110,114,119,121,122,123, 125,135; Palatiah 34,111,132

SILKIRK, John 125

SIMPSON, John 41; John C. 28,34,42,43, 44

SINGLETON, John 10,11,16,17,31,38,55, 75; William 109

SKILLERAN, John 91; William 104

SLOAN, Jacob 49

SLOVER, Jacob 41,49,50,63,72,82,86,90, 98,107,110,111,117,122,130

SMALL, Robert 33,37,53,81,133,137,138, 151

SMILEY, Martin 108,115,117

SMITH, Anderson 3,14,47,48,119,120,127, 139,142; Arthur 111,116; Charles 58; Henry 128; James 18,25,31,34,45,75, 78,85,101,113,134,140,148; John 3,10, 20,29,34,41,50,52,53,68,69,74,75,86; 89,98,106,108,113,115; John A. 20,22, 29,63,67,72,73,80,112,115,116,117, 118; John Y. 28,30; Joseph 109; Milo 115; Mumford 7,11,14,20,42,50,58,90, 103,126,136,137,142; Nathaniel 94, 107,110,111,126,130,146; Randolph 55; Richard 148; Robert 53; Theophelus 13; Thomas 144,145; William 3,4,5,7, 12,14,18,19,20,21,23,25,31,37,38,39, 43,44,45,46,47,48,52,53,54,57,58,59, 60,61,67,69,71,74,75,76,77,78,80,81, 83,87,89,90,95,96,97,99,101,102,103, 105,108,109,111,112,115,116,118,119,

120,121,122,123,124,125,131,139,140, 141,142; William M. 19,22,23,25,31,44, 46,49,56,58,61,65,66,67,68,71,72,74, 80,110; Wright 9,10,13,14,37,40,42,44, 52,63,77,84,100,113,121,122,123,126, 131,142

SNELSON, James 2,13,16,28,34,46,57,58, 61,63,71,72,73,112,147; Samuel 77, 112; William 111,116,147

SPEARS, John 134

SPURGEON, Abraham 152

STACY, Mark 109; Robert 147

STALLONS/STALLIONS, Joseph 144; Matthew 123,131

STANDIFER, James 49

STANLY, Joel 125; Jonathan 70; William 125

STAPLES, David B. 100,124

STARRETT, John 117,119

STEPHENS, George 107; Malcom 106; Thomas 134

STEPHENSON, Matthew 12,13,29

STEWART, Andrew 142; Edward 16,17,28, 29,43,54,108,120,129,142,145,146, 151; James 7,11,12,38,42,52,53,60, 61,66,67,93,95,96,106,107,108,111, 112,114,119,123,124,127,139,151,152; John 11,17,37,42,62,66,95,106,107, 136,151,152; Samuel 88; Samuel P. 25, 54,125,136; William 95

STOCKTON/STOGDEN, Clayton 16,62,84,100; D./Daniel 6,7,11,18,78,114; Daniel D. 110,112,115,116,117,118,122,147; Daniel M. 56,62,78,99,101,103,104,107, 108,112,119,121,122,123,126,135,146, 148; James 39,41,62,70,100,108,115, 121,127,131,132,133; Joseph C. 112, 132

STOKES, Edward 23,75,86,96; George 34; John 34,121

STONER, Michael 5,70,91,121

STORY, John 146

STOUT, Benjamin C. 7,57,71,120,125,142

STREET, Anthony 118,122,143,146

STRICKLAND, Brinkley 49,82,122

STUARD, Edward 10

STULTS, Abner 151

SULLIVAN/SILLIVAN/SULLIVEN, Dempsey 87,109; John 34; William 22,41,50,90

SURCEY, John 21

SWAN, Daniel 53; James 22,25,28,73,74, 89,96,113,120,124,125,134,139,142, 146,148,151; John B. 5,28,29,31,56, 65,66,67; Samuel B. 13; Samuel F. 54; Samuel F.D. 31,62,112; Thomas 5,25; Thomas B. 71,72,87,119,120

166

SWENNEY, William 80
SYKES, Drury 3,10,16,137,142
SYPHERS, George 134
TABOR, Elijah 122
TAFF, John 34,42,43,85
TALLEY, William 101,141
TAYLOR, Archibald 45,46,71,75,107,132;
  Dorcas 38,65,92; James 40,47,49,70,
  80,82,83,95,99,114,125,149; John 18,
  22,23,141,147; Peach 75,76,83,87,90,
  91,92,93,94,95,97,99,101,105,109,111,
  112,119,121,123,134,136,139,146,149;
  Robert 7,14,46,57; Richard 2,122;
  Seaton 107,139
TEMPLETON, Edmund 10; Edward 46,57,61,
  69,75,84,85,86,87,88,106,113,114,119,
  122,126,132,144,145,151
THOMAS, David 14,48; Joseph 128
THOMASON, Arnold 103,134; Elizabeth 103
THOMPSON, Elizabeth 15; George W. 83;
  James 15,44,58,66,68,77; Jane W. 31,
  78; Jesse 1,3,5,7,18,19,22,25,31,39,
  44,46,54,61,65,66,68,69,74,75,76,78,
  82,83,85,86,87,90,95,97,99,101,103,
  104,105,108,112,119,120,121,122,124,
  126,134,135,139,146,143; John 22,34,
  40,41,42,49,56,90,91,102; Joseph 6,
  16,17,38,41,42,56,75,87,130,149;
  Josiah 53,60,67,73; Mary 73; Moses 6,
  18,22,28,34,42,46,53,56,58,60,67,69,
  73,83,86,89,91,96,98,99,100,101,103,
  108,110,115,149; Priscilla/Precilla
  37,78; Thomas 5,18,26,37,78
THRAILKILL, Joseph 45,46; Joseph J. 19;
  Levy 70
TIERNAN, Luke 92,105
TILLERY, Coffield 141,150; Ellen 140;
  Hugh 140,141,150; Jane 140; John 106,
  140,141,142; Margaret 140; Samuel 6,
  46,55,62,105,106,140,141,142,149;
  Thomas 140,141,150; William 45,46,62,
  96,101
TINDLE/TENDAL, Henry 55; John 76; Jos-
  hua 1,6,7,17,31,53,76,84,95,107,129,
  142,143,150,151,152
TODD/TOD, Williamson 14,45,62,63,84
TRIPLET/TRIPLETT, Abner 104,111,112,
  114,120
TUCKER, Thomas T. 56
TURK, Col. 57
TURNEY, Hopkins L. 74,93,133
TYSON, Jesse 149
UNDERWOOD, Alexander 88; John 22,88
URSERY, Robert 130

VAUGHN, William 74
VERNEL, William 22
VERNON, Anderson 87; James 7; James A.
  92; Miles 19,22,31,36,37,38,41,45,46,
  49,50,55,62,63,81,85,88,89,90,91,92,
  93,96,98,107,108,141,149; Obediah 87;
  Solomon 7,100,109,110
WADE/WAADE, John C. 87,92; Tignal 125,
  136,138,139
WAGGONER, Samuel 87
WALDRID, Richard 67
WALDROFT, Richard 142
WALKER, Clarissa 48; Daniel 5,7,13,18,
  19,20,22,25,26,31,32,35,39,41,46,48,
  54,56,61,63,65,66,68,71,74,76,83,85,
  86,87,95,97,98,99,101,105,108,112,119,
  120,121,122,123,124,125,126,134,135,
  136,142,146; David 47,48; Elizabeth 3,
  8,47,48; G./George 32,47,56,68,69,76,
  79,81,129; Hatten 14,141; James 31,45,
  54,69,100,113; Jane 32; Jefferson 47,
  48; John 1,5,41,50,56,60,65,66,67,85,
  108,110,115,117,133,141,149; Jonathan
  48; Mary 24,36,37,48,67,81; Mary Abagail 47,48; Richard 98; R./Robert 18,
  29,63,71,72,73,85,86,93,98,112,120,
  141,147,148; William 3,8,11,14,23,38,
  47,48,56,68,69,72,74,75,76,80,81,83
WALLACE, Henry 3
WALTON, Henry 8,9,10,11,25,33,75,86,
  140; James 11,14,63,70,88,106; William 39,92
WAMMAC, Jacob 84; John 112
WANN, William 5,7,11,13,41,50,56,78,89,
  96,100,109,112
WARD, Duke 49,78
WASHAM, Jeremiah 41,50,85,90,118,122,
  127,136,142
WASSON/WASSEN/WASSUN, Edward 62,107;
  John 2,6,8,10,17,76,85,108,125,136
WASSUM, Jacob 14,89,91,98; Jacob L. 152;
  Jonas 17,30
WATERHOUSE, Blackstone 108,123,128,133,
  146,151; Cyrus 128,133; Darius 128,
  133; Euclid 128,133; Myra 128,133;
  Richard 88,98,106,108,109,112,119,
  120,123,126,128,133,134,135,145,146,
  151; R.G./Richard G. 11,17,42,55,69,
  76,79,87,88,90,98,103,104,105,106,
  108,109,110,112,126,127,128,133,146
WATSON, Obediah 48
WEAKS, George 138,143; William 138,143
WEBB, Allen 144; Gideon 130,131; Julius
  130; William 130
WEEMS, Washington 87

WEESE, John 100,108,134

WEIR, Samuel 129

WELKER, Henry 58,66,82,86; William G. 88; William L. 93,122

WELLS, Andrew 137; George 119

WERE/WARE, Jno/John 79,130

WEST, Isaac 8,34,64,75,81,84,85,86,87, 98,140; Warren 139; William 40,49; William H. 7,22,26,30,38,39,75,98, 99,133

WHALEY, James 79; John 73,85,123,126, 149

WHEELER, Joseph 107

WHERRY, Jackson 58

WHITE, Charles 69; Edward L. 102; Hu A. M. 130; Isaac 44; John 44; William 113

WHITFIELD, Edmund 52; Gaines 52; Needham 52

WHITMORE, Thomas 113,149

WILHELM, Andrew 124

WILKERSON, Lewis 6,16,23,39,49,69,72, 82,102,129

WILLIAMS, David S. 40,53,55; James G. 45,134; John D. 54,87; Joseph 3,11, 18,39,43,85,89,93,98,100,104,108,110, 111,137

WILMOTH/WILLMOTH, William 15,16

WILSON, Betsy S. 148,152; James 6,11, 14,16,18,21,22,23,28,29,32,36,37,41, 42,45,46,48,49,63,68,69,71,74,75,76, 80,81,83,87,88,89,95,97,99,100,101, 102,103,105,107,108,109,112,115,116, 118,119,121,123,126,130,131,132,133, 136,138,142,143,146,148; Nancy 71; Nathaniel 122; Nathaniel W. 104,118, 132,137,141,143,144,148; William 25, 41; William C. 2,7,14,39,41,42,46,49, 54,63,74,75,76,85,97,99,101,121,147, 148,152

WINDLE, Joseph 60

WINTON, Stephen 1,7,13,19,23,25,31,40, 46,49,54,56,57,58,60,61,65,70,74,75, 76,85,97,101,102,105,107,112,115,116, 118,121,123,146,148,149,152

WITT, Abner 34,36,38,40; Charles 36,75, 86,96,101,102,110,115,116,147; Jesse 2,11,21,36,39,40,64,108,141; John 18, 36,38,39,46,65,92,96,101,102,147

WOODS/WOOD, James 130; John 88

WOODSON, Margaret 60,67,73

WOODWARD, Charles 1,6,9,25,30,33,34,42, 43,44,70,80,88,106; Elizabeth 27; Esther 10; James 75,86,94,106,135,

140,150,151; John 1,6,27,30,32,33, 100,106; Susannah 27; Teareasa 27; Thomas 2,8,55,135; William 6,9,11, 33,34,42,43,56,65,66,67,70,85,90, 106,144

WORLEY, Hiram 12,65

WORMACK, Jacob 15; Mary 15

WRIGHT, Abraham 96,101,102; Doctor 32, Jeremiah 130; Matthias 10,16; William 96

WROE/ROE, Thomas C. 109,112,125,133, 134,137,138,139

WYATT/WIATT/WYOTT, Elijah 56,65,70,75, 86,149; Moses 16,70,135

YORK, Josiah 17,38,41,42; Silas 12,13; Thomas 7,29,43,88,98,99; William 12, 13,17

ZEIGLER, William 1,3,7,14

SUBJECTS

AGENCY (Indian) 126

ALABAMA 31,37,67,78

BEATTY'S TURNPIKE 128

BETHEL MEETING HOUSE 141,147,148

BLEDSOE COUNTY, TN 29,106,147

BLUE POND 49,56

BLYTHE'S FERRY ROAD 1,121,125,126

BRAZELTON'S ROAD 11,49

BREEDWELL'S STILL HOUSE 47

BUMBLEBEE FORK (of Piney) 128

BUNKER'S HILL 114,119,125

BURKE'S TURNPIKE GATE 29

CALDWELL COUNTY, KY 81

CALHOUN ROAD 2,70,77,147

CAMP CREEK 129

CAZEY'S MILL 96,99,102,107,109,113

CHEROKEE NATION 114,119

CLEAR CREEK 8,21,114,124,127,134,139, 140,146

COCKE COUNTY, TN 4,95

CONCORD MEETING HOUSE 140

COURTHOUSE (RHEA COUNTY) 135

COVE SPRING 127

COX'S MILL 46,55,68

CRAMER'S COVE 62

CUMBERLAND ROAD 29

DEVIL'S FORK 128

DUSKIN'S FORK 129

ELECTION PRESINCTS 2,3,46,63,90,108

FARMER'S ROAD 11

FEDERAL ROAD 11,13,26,40,41,49,56,100, 112,125,134,135,147

FERRY, Blythe's 1,62,77,126; Braselton's

www.ingramcontent.com/pod-product-compliance
Lightning Source LLC
Chambersburg PA
CBHW080811280326
41926CB00091B/4318